Kathleen Fisher

FRANCES TENENBAUM, Series Editor

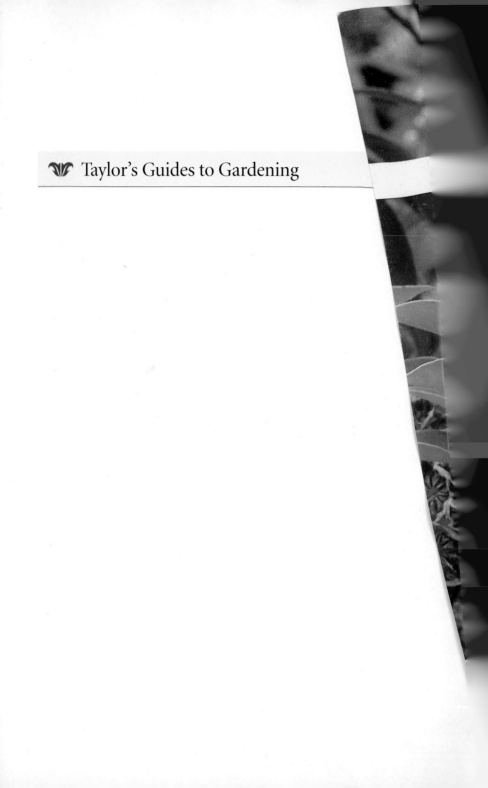

Taylor's Guides to Gardening

❧ Taylor's Guide to

Shrubs

HOW TO SELECT AND GROW MORE THAN
500 ORNAMENTAL AND USEFUL SHRUBS
FOR PRIVACY, GROUND COVERS, AND
SPECIMEN PLANTINGS

HOUGHTON MIFFLIN COMPANY

BOSTON   NEW YORK

Consultants

RICHARD BIR, extension specialist, Nursery Crops, North Carolina State University

BRIAN MAYNARD, associate professor, Department of Plant Sciences, University of Rhode Island

KATHY MUSIAL, curator of living collections, The Huntington, San Marino, California

Copyright © 2000 by Houghton Mifflin Company
Text copyright © 2000 by Kathleen Fisher
Drawings copyright © 2000 by Steve Buchanan

For information about permission to reproduce selections from this book, write to Permissions, Houghton Mifflin Company, 215 Park Avenue South, New York, New York 10003.

Visit our Web site: www.houghtonmifflinbooks.com.

Taylor's Guide is a registered trademark of Houghton Mifflin Company.

Library of Congress Cataloging-in-Publication Data
Fisher, Kathleen, date.
Taylor's guide to shrubs : how to select and grow more than 500 ornamental and useful shrubs for privacy, ground covers, and specimen plantings / [Kathleen Fisher].
    p. cm. — (Taylor's guides to gardening)
    ISBN 0-618-00437-8
    1. Ornamental shrubs. I. Title: Shrubs. II. Series.
SB435 .F558 2001
635.9'76 — dc21   00-036941

Cover photograph by Mark Turner
Drawings by Steve Buchanan
Book design by Anne Chalmers
Typefaces: Minion, News Gothic

Printed in Singapore
TWP 10 9 8 7 6 5 4 3 2

✿ Contents

❧ Introduction

Shrubs are the most versatile plants we can grow in our gardens. Unlike annual flowers or soft-stemmed (herbaceous) perennials that disappear in winter, they remain a presence in the landscape all year. Those we call evergreens even keep their leaves in winter, providing a much appreciated patch of green. The foliage of those we refer to as deciduous may turn rainbow hues, then drop to reveal sinewy branches, perhaps with furrowed bark that will become three-dimensional in the low winter sun. A coating of snow or ice gives them yet another perspective. Still others erupt with colorful berries that we can collect for dried arrangements or leave to attract birds.

While some shrubs can grow 30 feet tall and wide, most are much smaller, so that even the tiniest property can accommodate several. Some are so low growing that they can replace turfgrass as low-maintenance ground covers in such challenging situations as dense shade or steep banks, where they will control erosion as well.

We value some shrubs primarily for their foliage. Medium to small conifers can act as a backdrop for more colorful garden residents, like the black velvet jewelers use to make their diamonds seem to sparkle more. Some have leaves especially amenable to shearing, whether we want a tidy, space-saving hedge or topiary teddy bears. We may plant them simply to serve a utilitarian function, knowing we can count on them to keep stray dogs off the lawn or block the glare of a neighbor's security light, asking in return only a little water in a drought and a light trimming now and then. In some cases the foliage is a thing of beauty in its own right, from the gracefully drooping branches of a false cypress or the variegation on a 'Girard's

Rainbow' leucothoe to the gray spikes of lavender or the herbal fragrance of a bayberry leaf.

We grow many shrubs, of course, just for their flowers. Some of these we value as seasonal symbols. What would early spring be without forsythia, or a sweltering summer without hydrangeas? Some, like rhododendrons and tree peonies, are the Mae Wests of the shrub world, with buxom blooms as big as a baby's head. Many enchant us with their scent. Those of lilacs and mock oranges waft a nostalgic aroma. Some perfumed flowers, like roses, are splendid to look at as well. Others, like daphne, are understated, while those of sweetbox or osmanthus, hidden among the leaves, are for the nose alone.

What's your pleasure? From the purely practical to the sinfully sensuous, you will find it in the world of shrubs.

❦ WHAT IS A SHRUB?

Shrubs are woody plants that differ from trees by being smaller (generally 20 feet or less) and having many primary stems, rather than just one main trunk. There are a few shrubs that grow larger than 30 feet, however, and some trees that grow to only 20 feet, such as many Japanese maples. Some shrubs are pruned to have a single trunk, and some trees, such as birches, can have multiple trunks.

Further confusing the picture are the so-called subshrubs, with initially soft stems that harden and become woody with age. Well-known examples include herbs such as rosemary and lavender.

Other plants are "die-back" shrubs, grown like herbaceous perennials. We may prune them near ground level at the end of each winter to stimulate colorful branches or heavy flowering. Some shrubby plants such as chaste tree (*Vitex* species) are killed to the ground each winter in the northern part of their range, regrowing in spring from the surviving roots.

As a rule, if it has a lot of hard, woody stems and is less than 20 feet tall, it's bound to be a shrub.

❦ ABOUT THIS BOOK

If you are going to choose a shrub for your landscape, there are about half a dozen things it's essential to know, and that's what you'll find in our encyclopedia section. The entries there, as well as in the preceding gallery of photographs, are arranged alphabetically by the genus name—the botanical name for a group of plants with common fundamental traits. Some well-known shrub genera (that's the plural of genus) are *Ilex* (hollies), *Rhododendron,* and *Viburnum.* Some genera contain hundreds of species, which, as the name implies, are set apart by more specific traits and may include trees, vines, and herbaceous species as well as shrubs. Some genera contain only one species. Look in the index if you know only the common name of the plant.

Your first consideration in selecting a shrub will doubtless be, What is its primary attraction? Flowers, foliage, berries, shape, tolerance of drought or pollution, or some combination? You need to know how to take care of it: does it grow easily in any kind of soil and never need pruning, or will you have to create a specially amended planting bed for it and worry about its leaves being marred by disease? What are its best uses in a landscape: will it work well as a sheared formal hedge or survive as a windbreak against salty sea air? You need to know about a shrub's cold hardiness: can you rely on it to survive in your region, or will it need to be brought indoors or protected every winter? Or is it a borderline plant— worth risking in most years but needing protection or special siting in case of an unusual cold snap? Many gardeners will want to know how to propagate their shrubs—creating a new generation from seed or cuttings, either to obtain their own first plants inexpensively, to create more to fill their own landscape, or to share their favorites with friends and neighbors. Each of the entries in our encyclopedia provides this information.

Here in the front of the book, you can find basic guidance on all of these concerns. What are your many options for using shrubs creatively in your landscape? What else do you need to think about when buying shrubs? How do you get them off to the best start when you bring them home, and what care will you need to give them later? We've provided an extensive section on pruning, a topic that even seasoned gardeners find intimidating.

A F E W   B A S I C S

If you have a horticulture degree, or if you enjoy botanizing—tramping around in the wild and identifying plants that you find growing in field and forest—you may need to need to know if a shrub species has its leaves arranged opposite each other, rather than alternately, on the stem. It might also be helpful to know that the leaves are obcordate (shaped like a heart with the stem at the bottom) rather than cuneate (paddle shaped) or hastate (shaped like an arrowhead).

For most home gardeners, these are pretty esoteric descriptions that rarely enter into our decision about purchasing a plant. But there are a few terms that you will find it helpful to know.

Botanical Classifications

All of the entries are arranged by genus, which is a pretty broad category. Yet often an even broader one, the plant family, can be informative. For instance, many plants in the heath family, or Ericaceae, have similar urn-shaped flowers, so it's easy to picture those of *Leucothoe* once you're familiar with those on a blueberry (*Vaccinium* species). Even heath family members with very different flowers, such as azaleas, have similar requirements for healthy growth, such as acidic soil with near perfect drainage.

A step down from genus is the species, which is a group of plants that share many identifying characteristics and interbreed easily. The next division occurring in nature is a variety. Different varieties can occur in different geographical areas and be noted by appearance, such as different flower color, bigger leaves, or smaller stature. Sometimes the variety may be important to you because the plant is more cold hardy or drought tolerant.

A hybrid is a cross between two species. Sometimes hybrids occur naturally, as is the case with many of our native azaleas. But most named hybrids have been developed intentionally by breeders with the goal of combining two desirable characteristics, such as long blooming time and colorful fall foliage.

The word "cultivar" is derived from "cultivated variety." The word "selection" is sometimes used as a synonym. A cultivar name appears in single quotes, and it represents a plant that has been selected by a grower who noticed a valuable trait—anything from heavier flowering to wind resistance—and continued to vegetatively propagate or clone the plant to ensure that subsequent plant generations have the same genes and, thus, the same characteristics. Today some breeders are trademarking their selections, so that plants have both a trademark name (not in quotes) and a cultivar name.

Leaf Characteristics

Shrubs that are evergreen can be either conifers (cone-bearing), with scalelike leaves like those of cypresses or needles like those of pines, or broad-leaved evergreens, such as magnolias. Broad-leaved evergreens are far more common in the South. Some shrubs are semievergreen, losing many but not all of their leaves each fall. Some, such as northern bayberry *(Myrica pensylvanica)*, are evergreen in the southern part of their range, deciduous in the north, and semievergreen in the middle. Deciduous trees, of course, are those that lose all of their leaves every fall. Evergreens shed their leaves as well, but only a small percentage each year.

A few terms that we use for leaf descriptions include "variegated," which means having streaks, blotches, or margins of a second color, usually white or yellow on green. We usually mention if leaves are "toothed," with jagged edges as though trimmed with pinking shears; or lobed, with broad divisions like those of a maple. Compound leaves are composed of smaller leaflets; those described as "pinnately compound" are almost fernlike. Because a great deal of genetic variation can exist in fall coloration of leaves, you will often see phrases such as "*may* develop yellow autumn color."

Flowers

Everyone is aware of the many different shapes of individual flowers. Those of daisies and sunflowers are "composite," with a center of numerous tiny disk flowers surrounded by a wheel of ray flowers. Those of roses get their own shape name, "rosette," while those of a petunia, a tube flaring out in several lobes, are called "salverform."

On many shrubs, the individual flowers are too small to be of much interest. What we admire when we look at a lilac, butterfly bush, rhododendron, clethra, and countless others are the showy flower clusters. Botanists have many names for clusters (which they call an inflorescence): *spike* (flowers attached directly to the stem), *raceme* (flowers attached to the stem with stalks), and *panicle* (a cluster with many branches). They even differentiate between a cluster with outer flowers opening first *(corymb)* and one with outer flowers opening last *(cyme)*. Umbels have an umbrella shape, like those of Queen Anne's lace.

Most of us just want to know if the flowers are in long spiky clusters or wide, fluffy clusters, or if they are borne singly. It does help to know, though, if the flowers are terminal—borne at the end of a branch, where they are quite visible—or if they are borne in the axils. Flowers that bloom in the axil, the angle between stem and leaf, can be harder to see, but they are almost certain to be more numerous. Some shrubs have both terminal and axillary flowers. If flowers are borne terminally, you may want to prune the shrub to produce more terminals, being careful not to prune after the buds have developed.

Flowers can also vary in how their sex organs are distributed. They can have both male and female organs on the same flower, on separate flowers on the same plant, or on separate plants. Plants of the last type are called "dioecious." This is important to know when you are buying plants valued for their berries, like certain hollies. You will need to obtain both male and female plants in order to have their fruits.

Habit

Horticulturists use the word "habit" to refer to the overall shape of a plant. Some of the more common terms to describe the habits of shrubs include "upright" for shrubs with vertical main stems and upward-growing branches, and "loose" or "open" for shrubs that have large gaps between branches, so that you can see between them. Some shrubs are rounded or pyramid shaped, while a few, such as certain conifer selections, form columns. "Suckering" shrubs develop shoots from their roots, so that they form a mass of radiating vertical stems. These suckers may form far from the parent plant, creating huge colonies in the wild. Low-growing shrubs that spread this way are good ground covers. "Prostrate" shrubs sprawl along the ground, not because of suckers, but because their branches grow horizontally. Weeping shrubs, sometimes called "pendulous" or "pendent," have branches that droop.

Hardiness Zones

Most gardeners know about hardiness zones. The cold hardiness map developed by the U.S. Department of Agriculture is now almost universally adopted by reference books and the nursery trade in the United States. That doesn't mean, however, that the hardiness assigned to a plant in this book or any other should be considered gospel.

There are several reasons for this variation. You may have "microclimates" in your landscape where the temperature is warmer or cooler than is typical for your area. Cold air collects at the bottom of hills, for instance, so these places tend to freeze sooner in fall and later in spring. The south side of a fence or building, or the south-facing side of a slope, will be warmer than the north. An eastern exposure brings plants gentle morning sun; plants exposed to the west will get hotter afternoon sun. Wind, drought, and other factors can stress a plant so that it succumbs to cold it might otherwise survive.

Plants may also have subtle variation in their genetic make-up that allows them to tolerate more cold. (And nursery professionals who notice these valuable differences may select, name, and market them as cultivars.) If you plan to grow a shrub that is hardy over a wide range, say USDA Zones 5 to 9, try to buy a plant from a nearby grower. The provenance (origin) of a plant, in regard to both its heredity (where is it native?) and environment (where was it propagated and grown?) can have a lot to do with your eventual success. Buying from zones farther north, rather than south, can increase cold hardiness.

Use hardiness zones as guidelines, and dare to experiment!

❦ INVASIVE PLANTS

Shrubs, like almost everything else, fall in and out of fashion. Sometimes a new disease has made them hard to grow; in other cases, they have simply been overused and we're tired of looking at them.

Today, many plants, including some popular garden shrubs, have fallen out of favor because of their invasive nature. These aren't "weeds" in the old sense of spreading too eagerly in one's own yard. Rather, they invade our dwindling natural spaces and crowd out other plants. Most of these out-of-control plants are nonnative, or alien, species. Catalog descriptions make them sound like ideal, cast-iron garden guests. They lack natural enemies and diseases, are not particular about growing conditions, and propagate easily by seeds, roots, or both. The problem is that they are spread by wind or birds to nature preserves and other uncultivated places, where they outcompete native species that have important roles to play in the local ecology, such as providing food for animals.

Some of these plants are listed in this book for several reasons. Some, like common privet *(Ligustrum vulgare)*, have been widely grown for many years. Maybe you're already growing it, or the local garden center is selling it. If you are aware of its troublesome nature, you can consider replacing it or buying a substitute. Also, a plant that's invasive in one region may be perfectly well behaved somewhere else. Salt cedar *(Tamarix ramosissima)*, which has caused severe problems in the West, appears to grow quite docilely in much of the East. Before you buy any of these plants, you should consult your local Extension Service or a botanical garden about their potential for trouble where you live.

INVASIVES

SPECIES	ORIGIN	PROBLEM AREA	RISK LEVEL
Acer tataricum ginnala (Amur maple)	Asia	central U.S. forests	moderate
Berberis thunbergii (Thunberg barberry)	Asia	New England forest understory	serious
Buddleia davidii (butterfly bush)	China	Mid-Atlantic, Pacific Northwest forest understory	moderate
Cotoneaster (cotoneaster)	Eurasia	West Coast coastal areas and grasslands	moderate
Cytisus scoparius (Scotch broom)	Europe	West Coast woodlands, coastal sage, grasslands	serious
Eleagnus angustifolia (Russian olive)	Europe, Asia	western and northeast U.S., Great Plains wetlands	serious
E. umbellata (autumn olive)	Asia	Midwest, Northeast, Southeast forest understory, old fields	serious
Euonymus alatus (winged euonymus)	Asia	eastern U.S. forest understory	increasing
Ilex aquifolium (English holly)	Europe	northwest U.S. forest understory	moderate
Ligustrum vulgare (common privet)	Europe	eastern U.S. forest understory, old fields	serious
Lonicera maackii (Amur honeysuckle)	Asia	Midwest, midsouth forest understory, old fields	serious
L. morrowii (Morrow's honeysuckle)	Japan	northern U.S. forest understory, old fields	serious
L. tatarica (Tartarian honeysuckle)	Turkey, Russia	northern U.S. forest understory, old fields	serious
Nandina domestica (heavenly bamboo)	Asia	Deep South forest understory	moderate
Rhamnus cathartica (common buckthorn)	Eurasia	northern U.S. forest understory, wetlands	serious
R. fragula (smooth buckthorn)	Eurasia	northern U.S. forest understory, wetlands	serious
Rhodotypos scandens (jetbead)	China, Japan	Midwest, northeast U.S. forest understory	increasing
Rosa multiflora (multiflora rose)	Asia	Midwest, eastern U.S. grasslands, old fields	serious
Schinus terebinthifolius (California pepper tree)	South America	South Florida, southern California, Hawaiian wetlands, forest understory	serious
Sesbania punicea (Scarlet wisteria)	South America	Southeast, California wetlands, old fields	increasing
Spartium junceum (Spanish broom)	Mediterranean	West Coast coastal and wetland areas	serious
Spiraea japonica (Japanese spirea)	Japan	New England, Southeast in any cool, moist habitat	moderate
Tamarix species (tamarix, except *T. aphylla*)	Europe and Asia	western U.S. wetlands	serious

✿ Landscaping with Shrubs

The ways we can use shrubs in the landscape are many, and more often than not, those uses overlap. For example, you might want to plant the viciously thorny trifoliate orange *(Poncirus trifoliata)* under a bedroom window to deter prowlers. Yet come spring, you will enjoy the sweet orange-blossom scent of its flowers, and in fall you can make marmalade from its fruits. So this beautiful beast serves as a barrier plant, a specimen plant, and even an herb!

Take another example. We all know a hedge when we see one: a group of shrubs planted close together in a straight or curving line. But the purpose of the hedge may be to serve as a visual screen, a windbreak, or a backdrop for a perennial border. Or all of the above.

✿ HEDGES

Hedges can be either formal or informal. Most people probably think first of the formal variety, which are sheared into geometric shapes. But not all shrubs, or even most, can tolerate such hard, frequent pruning. The most amenable are small-leaved evergreens such as boxwoods and conifers, like yew. Formal hedges are most appropriate if your house and overall landscape are formal, perhaps a colonial home with square-cornered flower beds and symmetrical walkways. Formal hedges are often the background for a perennial bed or more flamboyant plants.

Choosing to go with an informal hedge greatly expands your options. Ideally, you will be allowing the shrubs to develop their own natural habits with little or no pruning. Therefore, you'll want to select your species or cultivar carefully. Don't buy one that will quickly become too wide for the space you have allotted for it, or one that will develop an open habit if you want it to serve as a privacy screen.

For either hedge type, a mix of shrubs has many advantages. For a formal hedge, shrubs with different foliage colors planted close together can be sheared into what is known as a tapestry hedge, with patches of varying hues blending into their neighbors. An informal mix can provide year-round interest with early and late flowering berries, colorful fall leaves, and possibly even a mix of evergreen and deciduous foliage. A mix of species is also good insurance against plant health problems. Insects and diseases are often specific to particular plants and are less likely to spread among unrelated shrubs. When establishing a hedge, don't be impatient and plant your new shrubs too close to each other. As they grow, they will not only look crushed together, but—especially in humid regions—they may develop disease because they lack good air circulation. To fill in between shrubs as they mature, you can alternate them with ornamental grasses or other tall perennials. Or try staggering a planting of two types of shrubs, with tall conifers in back and shorter deciduous, flowering shrubs in front of and between them.

If you select shrubs that lose their lower branches with maturity, you may want to give them a similar treatment. This is often referred to as underplanting or "facing down" a taller shrub with a smaller one.

❧ SCREENS

Shrubs serve as screens in many ways. They can screen us from the outside world, so that our backyard cookouts and croquet games don't become spectator sports, or screen the outside world from us, so we don't have a constant view of the convenience store across the street. You can use shrubs to hide parts of your own landscape, such as a tool shed, dog run, or compost pile. Shrubs will also help reduce traffic noises and absorb unpleasant odors and pollutants.

A hedge can also act as a windbreak, blocking cold air in winter and hot, drying winds in summer. This not only reduces utility bills and makes your home and yard more pleasant for you but also helps protect more delicate plants you may be trying to grow. Shrubs are actually more effective as windbreaks than solid fences are. Because they are semipermeable, they slow the wind, while wind can go up and over a solid windbreak. A gentle breeze allows air circulation that plants need for good health. But if you want a windbreak, choose your shrubs with care. Some species that are excellent choices for other purposes, such as viburnums, don't tolerate windy situations.

Landscape designers use shrubs to manipulate our perception of the landscape. For example, a garden can seem larger if we can't see all of it at once. Use shrubs to divide your yard into garden "rooms." Plant them alongside a curving path so that a visitor can't quite see what's around the bend, creating a sense of mystery. Shrubs can also be used to frame a view, whether of a special part of your own landscape such as a pond or statuary, or a borrowed view of a distant hillside or church façade.

Most of us learned in elementary drawing classes how to create the illusion of depth, using converging lines for a road disappearing in the distance, or making background objects smaller than those in the fore-ground. By using the same tricks in your landscape, you can create the impression that your garden is larger than it really is. Plant a row of shrubs with those farther from your house planted closer together and pruned lower.

Shrubs can direct not only the eye, but also the feet, telling the mail carrier where to walk and children where to play. Shrubs used in this manner are considered barriers. If you have serious concerns about grown-up trespassers or vandals, you can plant a thorny shrub of barber-ries or roses. To keep out children and animals, a hedge need only be dense enough to impede casual passing and can even be fragrant and inviting. In fact, if you have children, you might consider a kid-friendly hedge such as one with thornless berries that they can eat, or conifers that can be clipped into a secret hideout. (Caution: Yews prune beautifully, but their berries are poisonous.)

Shrubs planted as a hedge can direct the eye and serve as a barrier to animal and human trespassers.

Shrub barriers needn't be tall. Low-growing shrubs such as lavender, germander, and dwarf boxwood have served for centuries to mark the edges of knot gardens and their close relative, the parterre. Shrubs knee-high or lower can visually say, "Don't walk here" or "Stop mowing there" while still allowing an unhampered view of whatever is on the other side.

❧ FOUNDATION PLANTINGS

Several decades ago, when many houses were built on ugly raised cinderblock foundations, Americans decided that the best — or even only — way to use shrubs was to ring them close to the house, like a lace doily around a valentine. To keep these shrubs — usually conifers or privets — from blocking windows and entryways, they had to be severely pruned. Today this style remains a garden cliché, even though house foundations may not be unattractive and our plant choices are so much wider.

By all means, look at the area immediately adjacent to your home as a potential planting bed. But keep in mind that this strip has a number of drawbacks. Overhanging eaves may create a "rainshadow," so that plants here get less moisture than they would on more exposed ground. Concrete and similar building materials may make the soil more alkaline, so that mountain laurels and other heath family members may suffer. Working the soil near the foundation may be frowned upon by the people who protect your home from termites and other pests. And of course, tall shrubs may block views out windows and offer prowlers a place to hide. All of these factors suggest using our foundation beds for a mix of low-maintenance perennials and small shrubs, rather than the demanding — and visually uninteresting — hedges of the past.

❧ MASSING AND GROUND COVERS

"Massing" is a concept usually associated with annuals and perennials, which have been planted close together for a big splash of color. Shrubs can be used in much the same way, but rather than a swath of marigold orange or petunia purple, they bring to an otherwise barren spot a sense of texture, height, and form, as well as green or other foliage color and bloom or berries in season. A single shrub in the middle of a lawn can look lonely. A mass has presence.

You're most apt to see examples of massing in public areas such as traffic islands, the intersection of walkways in parks, or edging the fairway on a golf course. But the same approach can be used to great effect in a private landscape. Pick smaller shrubs, if your space is limited, and fewer of them—but remember that you need at least three to make a mass! Create a mass of drooping leucothoe on a shady slope. Plant a mass of *Zenobia* where your driveway meets the front walk. Situate a mass of fragrant clethra between your picnic table and the neighbors' yard.

Especially effective in masses are shrubs that provide bright fall or winter color, such as the foliage of chokeberry *(Aronia arbutifolia)*, or yellowroot *(Xanthorhiza simplicissima)*, the berries of *Ilex verticillata*, or the stems of *Cornus alba* or *C. stolonifera.*

Ground covers are also masses, just normally lower growing and wider spreading. Goals are often similar: to cover a bare and awkward area, such as a strip between your driveway and the neighbors', or your sidewalk and the street, or a slope that's hard to mow. Shrubs like heaths and heathers, *Gaultheria,* bearberry, or cotoneaster can fill these areas in style, providing more interesting texture than turfgrass along with winter flowers, in the case of heaths and heathers, and berries in the other instances.

Plants in general help reduce wind and water erosion by holding soil with their roots and deflecting heavy rain. But many of the plants categorized as ground covers are especially good at this because they spread by underground roots that knit loose soil into a mat.

🌾 BORDERS AND SPECIMENS

However useful shrubs can be, we grow many not because of any practical value, but because they're beautiful. There are several ways we can highlight these aesthetic qualities. In addition to masses of one species, shrubs can be planted in borders with other shrubs, mingled with herbaceous perennials (resulting in what are called mixed borders) or used alone as specimens.

You can plant a border to bloom in flowers of a single color, to make a big splash of color in a particular season, or for fragrance. Many gardeners take advantage of the wide array of varieties available and attempt to create year-round interest with shape, texture, and color of both foliage and flower.

In a mixed border, shrubs can provide welcome form and substance in the winter when perennials have disappeared underground. A shrub

Shrubs provide year-round form, and some, such as this 'Heatherbun' false cypress (Chamaecyparis thyoides), *offer winter color variation.*

can be planted between bright-colored perennials to keep them from clashing, or to offer afternoon shade to a species that sunburns easily. (If you plant a mixed border in early spring, remember to site sun-loving perennials where they won't be shaded once deciduous shrubs leaf out.)

An all-shrub border lets you create a mass of differing shapes and textures that lasts all year, rather than fading to bare patches as happens in a mixed border. If fragrance is one of your chief thrills in gardening, shrubs can give you pleasure in every season, from lilacs and daphnes in spring, to roses and butterfly bush in summer, and witch hazel and wintersweet in winter. When siting plants for fragrance, think about where you walk or sit most often. And consider your prevailing wind direction at various times of year, so that most of the pleasure doesn't waft into the neighbors' yard instead of yours.

Keep in mind a shrub's appearance when it's not in bloom. Lilacs and mock oranges have little to offer once their sweet-scented flowers are spent, and the foliage of the former can become disfigured by mildew. Situate them toward the back of your border, and give center stage to a 'Carol Mackie' daphne, with its variegated leaves, or a burkwood viburnum that will have bright fruit or foliage in fall.

Remember the changes in seasonal light angles when siting shrubs. In summer, colors that are washed out by harsh midday sun can turn into high drama when sidelit or backlit in the morning or evening. In winter, the sun is at a low angle throughout the day, which will highlight bark, berries, and buds such as the fuzzy gray knobs that form on star magnolias. Include some shiny-leaved shrubs such as hollies, which will make

Variation in leaf size and arrangement on the branch can be as visually arresting as flower color.

your landscape sparkle even without snow. You'll also find that shadows can be an effective garden element, whether cast by shrubs or on them. If you rarely venture into your landscape in winter, be sure to place winter blooms and buds where you can enjoy them from a window, or even along the path to your trash cans!

A specimen is a solitary plant chosen for its showiness or rarity and sometimes also intended to commemorate an event or individual. Site a specimen shrub where it can't be missed — at a fork or at the end of a path, or outside the window of the kitchen or family room. Don't make it compete with similar-sized plants or distracting elements such as a chainlink fence. If it's an evergreen, such as a 'Dragon's Eye' pine, you might give it a background of pale fencing or trellis. A Harry Lauder's walking stick, attractive for contorted deciduous limbs and yellow-brown catkins, could use a dark evergreen background. Planting your specimen on the top of a berm or natural rise in the terrain not only makes it more visible but also will help ensure good drainage.

An "accent" is a plant used in a similar manner, but rather than being planted in a separate bed, it is intended to be an attention grabber amid smaller or contrasting plants.

❧ NATURALIZING

Perhaps because we've lost so much of our wild landscapes, American gardeners today are trying to recreate them at home, with petite prairies in the Plains, desertscapes in the West, and mini-woodlands in the East. We strive to mimic as closely as possible the natural landscape that existed on the site before home construction, so that the plants can be self-sustainable. As a result, we are rediscovering the sometimes understated charm of many of our native shrub species.

Unfortunately, most of us live in highly unnatural environments. Our subdivisions were built by bulldozing all the trees and shrubs and scraping away the topsoil and laying streets and sidewalks that have permanently changed drainage patterns. Thus, we can't just remove our lawns and let native plants return on their own. Such projects take some homework into regional plant communities — species that flourish adjacent to each other in whatever situation we have to offer, whether wet or dry, sunny or shady, sandy or clayey. They require vigilance to prevent alien species from crowding out our native seedlings and transplants.

Nevertheless, gardeners who "naturalize" their properties benefit from increased visits by birds and other wildlife. They enjoy their plants more through the seasons and worry less about maintenance chores.

In a naturalized landscape, rather than relegating the shrubs and other plantings to narrow beds on the edges of lawns, the situation is reversed, with paths winding through wide swaths of grasses, perennials, and shrubs. The shrubs often grow in clumps. One designer suggests digging a hole the size of a bathtub for every three shrubs to achieve this natural effect.

In naturalizing, even more than in other types of landscaping, it's important to not get carried away with collecting endless numbers of species. In nature, plants are a lot like housemates: only so many can get along harmoniously in a limited space on limited resources. The resources you save will include your own time and energy.

❧ Buying, Planting, and Caring for Shrubs

So you've done your homework and decided on shrubs that a) will be the perfect size for that hedge you need, b) will bloom in spring with lilacs just like Grandma's, or c) bring birds flocking to your backyard. Now where do you find them?

Don't limit your explorations to the garden center of the nearest home improvement store. Because of Americans' burgeoning interest in gardening, some of these outlets have excellent plant selections. But even if they have the species you want, the staff may be untrained in horticulture, and the plants may not always receive the best care. Seek advice about sources from neighbors, the staff of the closest botanical garden, or the garden columnist for your local newspaper. Often, an absolute gem of a nursery is just a pleasant spring (or autumn) morning's drive away. You may not have heard of them because they're putting all their capital into plants, rather than advertising.

Mail-order nurseries are a favorite resource for avid gardeners seeking unusual plants. Some of these nurseries specialize in natives, some in exotics just discovered abroad. Some handle what nursery professionals call "liners"—small shrubs that will need to be grown bigger in your home nursery bed before being transplanted to the landscape. Others routinely ship shrubs and trees 6 feet tall or more.

Although gardeners are understandably impatient to have their landscapes look mature with full-sized plants, there are advantages to choosing smaller shrubs. You will usually succeed at getting a larger proportion of the root mass in the ground undamaged, so that growth takes off faster than it would with a bigger shrub.

Obviously, when you buy by mail you can't inspect your purchase to make sure that it's healthy and well shaped. Plants are bound to endure some stress during the shipping process, and some nurseries are much better than others about packing their plants carefully. Shipping costs add to the price of the plant. Nor do you always get what you pay for. Some fairly pricey plants can be disappointing. Don't be swayed by gorgeous color photographs. If you don't know anyone who has used the nursery, buy just one or two plants to test their quality.

❦ PLANTING TIME

Spring is the traditional planting time, when local nurseries have their most tempting displays of blooming annuals and emerging perennials. But it isn't necessarily the best time to plant shrubs. In milder areas, say, USDA Zone 7 and south, fall planting may give shrubs their best start. The ground remains warm so that roots continue to grow and become established without expending energy on new shoots, leaves, and flowers. Planting shrubs after they have broken dormancy in early spring can expose them to damage from late frosts, while planting in late spring can expose them to drought stress.

Some specialty nurseries will ship plants only at the time they are most likely to survive. Rose growers ship in late winter, while some suppliers of tree peonies may ship only in fall. Local experts can give you the best advice.

Whether you plant in spring or fall, wait until the soil is neither too wet nor too dry. Soil should form a ball when you squeeze it in your hand, then fall apart when you release it. In regions of heavy spring rains, this is another reason why spring may not be the ideal planting time. If the soil is too wet, you can only wait. If the ground is dry, you can water it the night before planting in the morning.

❦ YOUR NEW SHRUBS' ROOTS

The shrubs you buy through mail order will either be in containers or bare-root. Except for roses, those at local nurseries will be in containers or balled-and-burlapped. Each of these has its own quirks at planting time.

Bare-root plants usually arrive in shreds of cellulose or other material intended to keep the roots damp. They are shipped when dormant, in spring or fall, but still mustn't be allowed to dry out. Sellers usually recommend soaking the roots for about 24 hours before planting. If conditions aren't ideal for planting—too muddy, for instance—either pot the plant in a container temporarily, or "heel it in" (covering the roots loosely with soil) in a nursery bed.

Container plants that have been grown correctly are easy to work with. Just turn the container upside down, holding the stem between your fingers, and rap it against a fence or other immovable object to release it for planting. If the shrub doesn't come out of the container easily, it may be root-bound, meaning the roots have grown to the edge of the pot and back, forming a tangled ball. You may need to cut the pot away with a knife or scissors. Then use your fingers to tease loose as many of the roots as possible. Cut apart any roots that are hopelessly tangled, but keep such cuts to a minimum.

The largest shrubs and trees, of the size installed by professional landscapers, come balled-and-burlapped. They have been field grown, then dug up and their roots and surrounding soil wrapped in real or plastic burlap. Real burlap will degrade in the soil. Today, much of the burlap is synthetic and leaving it on is tantamount to leaving a container plant in its pot. (One slightly risky test some people use is to hold a lit match to a piece of the material. Real burlap will burn, while the synthetic version melts.)

If you have any doubts, remove the burlap. To prevent the soil from falling away with its wrapping, it's best to maneuver the shrub into the hole, then slide the burlap out from under it. If the shrub is too heavy to lift, cut away all of the burlap except for what remains directly underneath it.

☙ IMPROVING YOUR SOIL

We used to hear that a planting hole should be dug deep and amended heavily, under the impression that shrubs and trees had long roots like carrots. Now we know that most roots grow in the top 1 or 2 feet of soil but often spread widely. Amending only the soil immediately adjacent to the shrub is like coddling a child: the roots are less prepared to cope when they hit the real world of clay or rock.

Instead, amend a shallow area to the width you might expect your shrub to grow in the next few years. Rather than digging a hole in which to do all this, try creating a raised bed by mounding soil amendments higher than the surrounding terrain. This is not only easier on your back but also helps ensure good drainage. The vast majority of shrubs—

whether they prefer sun or shade, acid or alkaline conditions—need soil that is moisture retentive but well drained, that is, "well aerated."

This might sound like an oxymoron, but soil that contains a high percentage of organic matter—well-rotted compost, leafmold, or pine bark—will both retain moisture and provide enough air space for water to drain quickly away from roots. These amendments also add nutrients to the soil.

Don't add hardwood chips or bark, which in breaking down rapidly use nitrogen and make it unavailable to your plants. People with clay soils often hear that they should add sand for better drainage. Don't do this either, since clay and sand can combine to form a substance the consistency of cement. Peat moss is an alternative amendment, but not an environmentally friendly one, since most of it has to be bagged and shipped all the way from Canada, where it is mined from wetlands.

Pile your compost or other amendments, plus topsoil from anywhere in your yard where drainage isn't so important, several inches high over the area where you will be planting your shrubs, then work it in with a spading fork. If you will be planting a hedge, amend the whole row. Remember, your goal is to improve drainage for the entire planting area, not just your planting hole. If you can't improve your drainage, you should seek shrubs that tolerate wet soil, such as silky dogwood or buttonbush.

The advice is similar for changing the pH of your soil, which you can certainly do by regularly adding lime to acid soil or sulfur to alkaline soil. The happiest solution for both gardener and plant is to seek shrubs that do well in the conditions that already exist in the garden.

❦ PLANTING SHRUBS

Generally, a planting hole need be only a couple of inches deeper than the rootball (so you can make sure it isn't on top of a rock or hardpan—soil so compacted that it is impervious to water). If you have recently amended the bed, the planting hole can be only a little wider than the rootball. Otherwise, it needs to be two or three times as wide so that the soil is adequately loosened.

Handle all of your plants by the rootball, not the stem. This may be difficult in the case of a heavy balled-and-burlapped shrub. Try to bring it home on a slick drop cloth, which you can then use to lift it and slide it to your planting hole.

For bare-root plants, such as roses, see if you can determine from looking at the plant how deep it was planted previously. You may be able to see a slight difference in color on the stem. Otherwise, make sure the hole will be deep enough to cover the roots. A knot or bump between roots and stem is a graft union, common on roses and cultivars of many other woody plants. The union should be about an inch below the soil surface. Build up a mound in the bottom of the hole and drape the roots over it. Then backfill with the soil you removed from the hole, watering occasionally to settle the soil around the roots.

Container plants are the most straightforward to plant. Remove them from the container and position them in the planting hole slightly higher than they were previously growing, since you can count on the loose backfill settling. Remember, refill your hole with the soil you removed from it, not special amendments.

If you have a big balled-and-burlapped plant, you may want to check the depth of your hole with a measuring device before you roll the shrub into the hole. Otherwise, if you find that your shrub is sitting below the surrounding soil, you will have to rock it back and forth as you pitch soil underneath it. (You'll probably have to do some of this anyway, since it's almost impossible to get a hole perfectly level.) Leave the burlap on until you have the shrub well positioned, then loosen it and slip it out from under the shrub before backfilling.

It's a good idea to backfill the hole about halfway, then water the soil to help it settle before filling the rest of the hole. This will increase contact between roots and soil. Use any leftover soil to make a rim around your planting hole, then slowly but thoroughly fill this "saucer" with water. Never step on the soil to firm it, which could damage roots. Unlike trees, shrubs rarely need staking unless they will be exposed to strong winds.

Once the soil is thoroughly damp, mulch the area around the shrub. Mulch will suppress weeds, help the soil retain moisture, and modify temperature extremes. If weeds tend to be a big problem for you, you may want to first put down a layer of landscape fabric, which will smother weeds that sprout from seeds still in the soil. Most people just put down a layer of organic mulch, such as bark, pine needles, or leaves. A layer 4 inches deep should be plenty; you'll need to replenish it as it decomposes, but as it does so, it is enriching your soil. Keep the mulch pulled away from the stem of the shrub to prevent rot and deter pests.

🌾 SHRUBS IN CONTAINERS

Gardeners who grow plants in containers usually have strong feelings about the type of soil they use. Many champion soilless mixtures, similar to the type used for starting seeds. They are easy to buy already mixed and are disease-free and lightweight.

The downside to these soilless mixes is that they contain no nutrients, so that you will have to fertilize frequently. To reduce the need for fertilizer, many gardeners like to add some compost or rich garden loam to a soilless mix. Before adding these ingredients, it's a good idea to kill potential disease organisms by heating the soil to 180°F for about 30 minutes in an oven or microwave. If you don't like the idea of soil in your oven (or the odors it may emit), you can heat it over an outdoor grill.

Containers allow temperate-climate gardeners to expand their choices to include tender species such as this glory bush.

If your shrub is somewhat top-heavy, adding soil or compost to your mix may also make it more stable in high winds. An alternative is to add a couple of inches of sand to the bottom of the container before planting.

Shrubs in containers lack access to ground water and will have to be watered much more frequently, perhaps daily in hot, dry weather. Soil in terra cotta pots dries out faster than soil in plastic pots. Water the pot until water runs out the holes in the bottom. Use your finger to make sure the rootball is getting wet; soil can pull away from the sides of a pot that becomes too dry, so that water runs down the sides without benefiting the plant's roots.

Fertilize once or twice a month with a balanced fertilizer from spring to midsummer.

❧ WATERING

Once established, shrubs rarely need watering. Their roots go farther and deeper than those of herbaceous plants. But they will need supplemental watering during their first year and any time during a drought. Give them a long slow soak, not a quick sprinkle.

Avoid wetting the leaves of your shrubs, unless you're directing a stream of water at them to dislodge insect pests. Leaves that are wet overnight can develop fungal diseases. Water at the root zone in the morning or evening, when less water will be lost to evaporation. Drip irrigation, or leaky hoses, are an efficient way to water. If you're watering by hand, fill up the basin around the shrub completely. If your soil is sandy, you may want to fill the basin twice. Learn how long it takes to saturate the rootball of your soil with a hose turned on low. (Check with your finger to make sure the area is moist.) Then you can leave the hose while you go about other chores. Set a timer if you think you might forget.

If you have a shrub in a location where a hose won't reach, you can water with a recycled 2½-gallon water jug—the type that has a spigot. Cut a hole in the top for filling it and just barely open the spigot.

❧ FERTILIZING

To grow well, plants need nitrogen, phosphorus, potassium, and traces of about a dozen other elements such as calcium, magnesium, and sulfur. In

the short run, it doesn't matter whether the source is organic or nonor-
ganic. In the long run, the difference is a little like deciding to spend your
money on a trip around the world or on a mutual fund: regularly adding
an organic amendment like compost to your soil is an investment that
pays off in the overall health of your garden. Organic amendments work
more slowly than inorganic fertilizers, though, so you can't wait to use
them when your plants are in crisis.

Compost is a balanced fertilizer as well. Before you apply other types
of fertilizer, you should have your soil tested to find out if it is deficient in
any or all of the three so-called macro-elements.

Organic sources of nitrogen (which helps "green up" leaves and produces rapid vegetative growth, so should be applied early in the season)
include alfalfa, blood meal, cottonseed meal, fish emulsion, and com-
posted manures. Cow manure is the lowest in nutrients. Apply high-
nitrogen manures sparingly, since too much can burn a plant, and never
use fresh manure.

Organic sources of phosphorus (which stimulates root growth and
should be added to the hole when you plant your shrubs) include bone
meal and colloidal phosphate.

Organic sources of potassium (which promotes flowering and fruiting) include alfalfa, fish emulsion, and kelp. It can be added in early
spring or early fall.

Never fertilize in late fall, which can stimulate tender new growth
that can be damaged by frost. Water plants well before and after fertilizing.

❦ PESTS AND DISEASES

The best way to deal with insects and other pests and diseases that can
disfigure or kill your shrubs is to prevent them.

Don't buy shrubs that are known to be magnets for pests that are
prevalent in your area. Where Japanese beetles are common, for example,
gardeners can pretty well count on members of the rose family being
chewed to bits in midseason. In the humid South, lilacs and many other
plants are invariably disfigured by blights and mildew. If you buy these
susceptible plants anyway, gird yourself to handpick the insects or tolerate the discolored leaves, rather than blasting away with chemicals.

A healthy plant, like a healthy person, can better fend off disease,
while a plant weakened by drought or poor nutrition, like an injured ani-

mal, attracts predators. Keep your plants healthy with regular watering, well-amended soil, ample air circulation, and good garden sanitation. Remove damaged or diseased leaves and shoots and put them in the trash, not the compost. Clean pruners and other tools after using them on diseased plants, and keep them sharp so that they won't tear bark. Pick up old leaves, shred them, and compost them. Keep your garden well weeded. Avoid causing physical damage with mowers and other power tools.

Many insect problems can be prevented by spraying shrubs in winter with a dormant oil, which smothers overwintering eggs. In spring and summer, spraying foliage with neem, a chemical derived from an East Indian tree, will kill any insect that feeds on it.

Encourage birds, which eat many insects. Avoid using strong chemicals, which will kill natural predators.

Don't replant where shrubs have died of disease. Companion planting of strong-smelling plants such as mint, alliums, and marigolds often deters insects, and the alliums may also help prevent fungal diseases by adding sulfur to the soil.

Pests

These are some of the insects that most often munch or suck on shrubs. Learn to recognize them and use safe, appropriate measures to combat them.

APHIDS. Distorted or stunted leaves or flowers may indicate the presence of these soft-bodied insects, which you can often see in clusters on stems or under the leaves. They suck the juice from the plant, causing blisters, and often spread viruses. They also leave a sticky "dew" that can feed sooty mold. Smother their eggs with dormant oil spray in winter, or go after the adults with insecticidal soap. If you take no action, damage may be controlled by natural predators such as ladybugs and lacewings.

JAPANESE BEETLES. These metallic green beetles, most prevalent in the East, eat flowers and leaves. Handpick adults and drown them in soapy water. Spray with insecticidal soaps. Larvae, which overwinter underground, can be treated with milky spore, a form of Bt (*Bacillus thuringiensis,* a bacterium). Pheromone traps may attract as many beetles as they kill, so keep them far away from any favorite plants.

LACE BUGS. Pale mottling on the leaves of broad-leaved evergreens such as azaleas and mountain laurel may be a sign of these nymphs. In winter, spray twigs and the underside of leaves with dormant oil, and use insecticidal soap when eggs hatch in spring and throughout the summer. There may be several generations in a single season.

LEAF-CUTTING BEES. Round holes at the edge of rose, bougainvillea, or other leaves are a sign of this half-inch bee. Like most bees, they are otherwise beneficial to the garden and should be tolerated unless they threaten the health of the plant.

LEAFHOPPERS. If pale spots appear in a coarse pattern on the tops of leaves, look for these jumping insects. Because they are so hard to hit with a kill-on-contact spray, try a neem product.

LEAF MINERS. Leaves will show a pattern of white or brown lines, which mark the path of fly larvae, moths, or beetles. If you catch the symptoms early, remove and destroy the affected leaves.

LEAF ROLLERS. Leaves appear folded over or one leaf may be attached to another with a fine thread, and the leaf has dried-out brown patches. The culprit is a small green or yellow moth caterpillar. You can squish it between your fingers or pull off the leaf and drop it in soapy water.

SCALE. Related to aphids, these sucking insects can also stunt plant growth. They are flat and round and become immobile when mature. You can usually find them on a leaf's lower surface. You can scrub them off with a toothbrush dipped in rubbing alcohol.

SLUGS AND SNAILS. A silvery trail near your plants is a sign of these mollusks, which can eat holes in leaves or devour seedlings. Slugs like damp, dark places (they're active at night) and may be more numerous in areas that are heavily mulched. You can trap them in shallow containers of beer or under citrus rinds, or repel them with a ring of copper sheeting or diatomaceous earth.

SOWBUGS, PILLBUGS. These "roly-poly" bugs are generally beneficial, since they eat decaying matter and help break down your compost. But they will nibble on seedlings and other tender growth, so discourage them by keeping old plant material away from young plants.

SPIDER MITES. Leaves turn dull and develop a fine mottling. You'll need a hand lens to see these eight-legged pests, which are reddish or yellow. Spray undersides of leaves with water or insecticidal soap, or invest in a predator mite, *Metaseiulus occidentalis,* as a biological control.

TENT CATERPILLARS. These caterpillars form silky nests and can defoliate shrubs, although they are more common on trees. Pull off the nests and caterpillars and destroy them.

Diseases

ANTHRACNOSE. This name covers a number of fungal diseases that cause brown spots that enlarge into circular patches and may distort shoots. There is no reliable cure, but good care will reduce susceptibility.

BLACKSPOT. This is the most common disease of roses. Prevent it with good garden hygiene. Treat by spraying with a tablespoon each of baking soda and dishwashing soap in a gallon of water.

CANKER. This swelling of the stem is caused by several bacteria and fungi. Prune off affected shoots.

CHLOROSIS. When leaves yellow between veins it usually signals a soil deficiency, most commonly of nitrogen or iron. Have your soil tested before treating.

FIREBLIGHT. A bacteria that causes leaves and stems to look as

though they have been burned.
Rose family members are especially
susceptible. Remove diseased parts.
There is no treatment.

LEAF SCORCH. The edges of leaves
turn brown and then yellow, usually as the result
of drying conditions. Prevent by adequate watering
and protection from winds.

LEAFSPOTS. Spotted leaves can result from infection
by viruses, bacteria, and fungi. Some of these infections can be prevented by not splashing leaves. Remove spotted leaves,
and if the problem persists, try spraying with
Bordeaux mix.

POWDERY MILDEW.
This fungus usually appears
as a white powder on the upper
side of leaves. Prevent it by watering at the roots,
mulching to avoid splashing, and not buying
susceptible plants.

ROOT ROT. This condition, marked by
declining vigor and the death of a plant, is usually
the result of poor drainage, especially on plants like rhododendrons with fine, shallow roots. Plant in raised beds. Avoid excessive
mulching. There is no cure.

SOOTY MOLD. This black sooty deposit on the top of leaves is
caused by fungi, often spread by aphids and their kin. Wash leaves off
with water.

Pruning

Pruning may be the most intimidating activity that a gardener can contemplate. All of us have seen thoughtless butcher jobs of trees and shrubs and may have become absolutely convinced that one snip, poorly placed or timed, will maim or kill a plant.

The good news is that most shrubs require little or no pruning. A cut or two at an early age may keep some species behaving beautifully for a lifetime, like a well-trained puppy. Others are friskier, requiring regular exercise on your part to keep them healthy, handsome, or within bounds of a small property. Learning which is which isn't difficult. Spend some time observing the growth habits of those that interest you, in public gardens or in the gardens of friends and neighbors.

WHY WE PRUNE

Knowing why you are pruning will go a long way toward keeping you from pruning too much or at the wrong time. The reasons fall into three main categories: good health, improved appearance, and controlled growth.

The most obvious reason to prune any shrub is to remove branches that are broken or diseased. Branches that rub against each other can be an entry point for disease. Pruning will also prevent disease by stimulating healthy new growth, allowing better air circulation between branches, and reducing density so that shrubs are more resistant to damage from ice, snow, and wind.

Pruning improves the appearance of shrubs by removing branches that spoil symmetry and shape. It encourages flowers and fruits or colorful new shoots, as with red-twigged dogwoods and many willows.

While most people think of pruning as limiting growth, you can see from some of these examples that pruning can actually jump-start new growth. This is particularly true in spring, when shoot growth is most rapid. Pruning side growth can make a shrub taller, while shearing the top will make it bushier. Knowing the growth habits of shrubs, and a few terms relating to that growth, will give you a confidence boost when you head out with your pruners and loppers.

TIP BUD. This is the fat bud at the end of a shoot, sometimes called a leader bud or an apical bud. Like other types of leaders, it calls the shots, in this case using hormones to tell other buds along the stem to remain dormant. This is especially true for shoots growing vertically. On shoots growing horizontally, "lower" buds will remain active and grow vertically. The key to much of pruning involves controlling these buds: removing the tip bud to trigger growth in the dormant buds, or pruning to a point above a particular dormant bud to stimulate growth at that point.

SHOOTS. This is a term that usually refers to unbranched growth less than a year old. It's fairly easy to discern this new growth, since it's usually shinier and of a slightly different color — perhaps greener, yellower, or redder, depending on the variety — than older branches. Because it's also more supple, it prunes off easily, but pruning this vigorous wood will also stimulate more growth than will pruning into older wood.

SUCKERS. Many shrubs are described as "suckering." A sucker is a vertical branch that forms from the roots of a shrub. Some shrubs sucker only moderately, while others sucker vigorously to form huge colonies. Suckering can be advantageous if you want a large mass for a ground cover or naturalizing, or if you want shrubs to grow together quickly to form a hedge or control erosion. Suckers are also an easy way to propagate new plants for elsewhere in your yard or to share with friends. If these aren't among your goals, however, you will want to keep suckers pruned off.

Some shrubs, such as roses, some rhododendrons, and witch hazel cultivars, are grown as grafts. This involves coaxing a cutting of one plant to grow on the rootstock of a more vigorous and more common species. These rootstocks often put up suckers, which should be removed as soon as you notice them, since they will overwhelm the less vigorous but more desirable plant that has been grafted onto them.

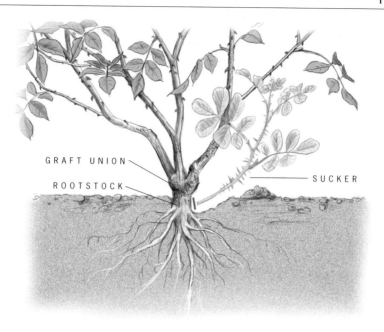

GRAFT UNION

ROOTSTOCK

SUCKER

You should remove suckers that sprout from the rootstock of a grafted plant.

W A T E R S P R O U T S . These are vigorous, whiplike shoots that grow vertically from older limbs, usually as the result of damage to that limb or poor pruning. On a very young tree, they can mature into healthy, flowering or fruiting branches. But usually they are too spindly and too much smaller than the parent limb to be attractive. They can be rubbed off with a finger if you notice them soon enough. Otherwise, remove them completely with pruners and rub off any regrowth.

🎋 T O O L S

Less can be more when it comes to buying garden tools. Purchase high-quality tools and take care of them, rather than collecting new gadgets to gather dust in the shed.

Top-of-the-line cutting tools come with replaceable parts. For pruning shrubs, you'll need a pair of hand pruners or clippers, a pair of loppers, and a pruning saw. You can buy excellent tools through the mail.

But before you buy, try to visit a good garden supply store where you can actually hold tools to test the comfort of their grip and their weight in your hand. Well-designed tools combine lightweight handles, curved for a firm grip that won't strain your hand, and well-forged steel blades that hold their edge without constant sharpening. Good cutting tools come with a rubber "shock absorber" to reduce fatigue from the motion of the blades closing on a branch.

LOPPERS . For branches larger than ¾ inch and smaller than 2 inches, you'll need one of these tools, which range anywhere from about 15 inches to more than 30 inches long. Longer handles would seem to be advantageous, since they will allow you to reach more out-of-the-way branches, but in practice, you'll usually find that trying to reach through a lot of other branches just reduces your leverage and your aim. The long handles tend to get in the way. Especially with shrubs, shorter handles give you more control. In the past, wooden handles were recommended because of their lighter weight, but today's fiberglass and metal alloy handles are more ergonomically designed.

PRUNERS . These are used to cut branches ¾ inch in diameter or less. So-called anvil-type pruners crush branches, possibly paving the way for disease. Instead, choose bypass pruners. These have two sharp blades that overlap similar to scissors, making a cleaner cut. Good ones have a sap groove to keep the blades from getting gummed up. You can pay a few dollars more for a rotating handle that allows more natural wrist motion and lessens the chance of blistering during prolonged pruning sessions.

PRUNING SAW . These saws have straight or curved blades 7 to 12 inches long. Some blades are fixed, while others fold back into the handle. Most gardeners prefer the latter type, since it can be carried in a tool pouch or a deep pocket. Test the locking mechanism on these saws to make sure that they snap open securely and easily. Good blades are made of high-carbon steel with chrome plating to prevent binding and clogging. Large teeth make rougher cuts but work faster, reducing wear and tear on the gardener. Keep in mind that these saws work only on the pull stroke, so you don't waste energy bearing down on the push stroke.

SHEARS . These have a long cutting blade, compared to the loppers' short blade. As the name implies, they are designed for shearing back formal hedges, as they cut many branch tips in a single swipe. Hedge shearing is hard work, so it's important to look for a tool that is lightweight and well balanced. Make sure that the blades don't overbalance the handle, or vice versa. Some people find curved handles easier on their joints. Shears must be kept razor sharp to avoid "chewing" the foliage of your hedge and crushing stems. Some have a single notch in one blade, or serrated edges, which helps them grasp stems.

You can buy gas or electric shears if you have a huge hedge to cut. Keep in mind that the latter needs an extension cord that you'll need to avoid cutting into, and both add to your neighborhood's noise pollution.

❦ WHEN TO PRUNE

If your shrub's chief attraction is flowers, and they bloom for a relatively limited period, the general rule is a simple one: prune after flowering. Shrubs that bloom in the spring are *generally* blooming on the previous year's shoots. Pruning soon after flowering will encourage a summer of vigorous growth and the development of the next year's flower buds. Shrubs that bloom late in the season — mid- to late summer or fall — are *generally* blooming on the current season's growth. Prune them just before growth commences in the spring, to stimulate vigorous growth as early as possible.

Unless you live in a frost-free area, avoid pruning before the last frost in spring, as well as too late in summer. Pruning stimulates tender new growth that can be damaged by a hard freeze.

If you are willing to sacrifice some flowers, or even a whole season of bloom, there are some arguments for breaking the prune-after-bloom rule. Pruning deciduous shrubs before they have leafed out in spring gives you a clear view of their "bones," so you can closely inspect dormant buds and clearly observe any branches that are damaged or awkwardly angled. Pruning in summer will give you a better sense of your finished product: how open it will be and the effect on the mass of foliage and any shadows that it casts. Summer is also a good time to remove suckers and water sprouts. Regrowth is less vigorous in summer, especially where summer drought is common, so summer is a good time to prune if you want to limit growth.

Conifers are usually pruned in late spring or early summer to remove or reduce the light green new growth on their tips, called their "candles." Depending on how much you need to control their size, you may need to lightly trim back a second flush of candles later in the season. Arborvitae will even put out three flushes of growth.

Some trees "bleed" sap when pruned too early in spring. These include some that are listed in this book as shrubs because of their size and growth habit, such as maples and dogwood species.

Exceptions to these rules are addressed under "Types of Pruning," below.

❦ WHERE TO PRUNE

As long as you remember that new growth will develop from buds, it is easy to find the correct place to cut. If shrubs have opposite branches, cut straight across a pair of healthy buds or shoots. If branches are alternate, cut above an outward-facing bud or shoot. The cut should leave no more than ¼ inch of stem above the bud and should be made at a 45-degree angle to the stem, roughly parallel to the bud.

If you are removing an entire branch or shoot, don't cut it flush with the parent branch. Leave the very slight swelling between the two, called a branch collar, that will help the cut area heal and prevent disease.

If you are thinning a shrub with strongly vertical stems, you can remove one-fifth to one-third of the stems clear to the ground.

❦ TYPES OF PRUNING

MANICURING. Remove dead, diseased, or damaged limbs as soon as you notice them on any shrubs. During dormancy, look for any branches that cross and remove one of them to prevent rubbing, which can be an entry point for disease. This is also the time to remove branches that are spoiling the shape or symmetry of your shrub.

DEADHEADING. This is the process of removing spent blooms, either by hand, with pruners, or with shears. Fastidious flower gardeners religiously remove the spent blossoms on daylilies and other perennials, to keep them looking neat and also to redirect energy that would otherwise go into forming fruits and seeds back into roots and shoots. On shrubs, deadheading is done most often on large flowers that turn brown and don't fall, such as gardenias and rhododendrons, or to stimulate rebloom on flowers such as butterfly bush and roses. Obviously, this type of pruning is done immediately after flowering.

PINCHING. Pinching is an easy way to prune the soft growth of plants, using only your fingernails. Experienced flower gardeners are probably familiar with pinching back chrysanthemums through mid-summer, to develop bushy plants with heavy bloom. You can pinch off the tip bud of shrubs for similar results. Rhododendrons are commonly pruned this way, as is rosemary, after flowering.

HEADING BACK. Heading cuts remove part of a branch with the goal of improving form or limiting size. Depending on when and where you cut, and the type of shrub you're working with, you may stimulate a dense "brush" of short new shoots. This may help fill in a bare place in the center of a shrub, but on outside shoots it can be unattractive if the new growth is at an awkward, narrow angle.

This is more likely to happen if you prune in spring, if you prune above a dormant bud, or if you prune a vertical rather than a horizontal shoot. You can prevent this by heading back to an existing shoot or branch, rather than a dormant bud, or correct it by thinning out some of the brushy shoots later in the season.

THINNING. A thinning cut removes an entire branch back to where it attaches to an older branch, or even back to the ground. A thinning cut is used to control vertical growth as well as to open up a too-dense shrub to allow more sun to reach interior branches. Thinning will stimulate

Thinning cuts allow more light to reach the interior of a plant and stimulate growth.

interior growth on a mature plant whose foliage has become limited to the tips of branches.

Some vigorously growing shrubs, such as butterfly bush *(Buddleia)* and blue-mist shrub *(Caryopteris),* are routinely pruned to within a few inches of the ground each spring. On other shrubs, a portion of the oldest stems — usually one-third to one-fifth — is removed to the ground to maintain younger and more vigorous branches. These are usually strongly vertical growers, such as abelia, kerria, lilac, mock orange, mophead hydrangea, and weigela.

LIMBING UP. This term usually refers to trees, on which lower and drooping branches are removed to reveal the trunk. Some shrubs, such as silverbell *(Halesia)* or seven-son flower *(Heptacodium),* are frequently pruned to a tree form by removing side branches. Others, such as pieris, develop thin lower branches with age, and these can be removed to show handsome bark as well as to bring more light into the garden.

REJUVENATION/ SHEARING. In the section on tools, we mentioned that shearing is normally reserved for formal hedges. However, some other shrubs can be sheared to renovate them if they have been neglected and growth has become restricted to the ends of branches.

When pruning hedges, remember to keep the bottom of the plants wider than the top so that sun reaches all of the leaves. Tapering the plants in this manner also ensures that snow will fall off, rather than weighing down and possibly breaking limbs, and helps deflect wind. If your hedge is new, concentrate on pruning side branches until it reaches

Shearing is a severe form of pruning that is generally reserved for formal hedges.

*Some shrubs are pruned to the ground each spring.
Others should have a portion of the old stems removed.*

the desired height. When shearing conifers, always avoid cutting into bare wood. Avoid using shears on broad-leaved evergreens.

If your shrubs need rejuvenation because they have become thin in the center, don't shear off all the leaves at once! You can stimulate growth in the center with what is sometimes called pluck pruning—cutting out a hole or holes that will bring sun into the center of the shrub. Or if you don't mind the shrub looking awkward for a couple of seasons, you can shear one side back severely, and then the other.

☙ SPECIAL PRUNING PROJECTS

Espalier

Training a fruiting shrub or tree into the formal, two-dimensional shape known an espalier is an exacting art, since most espalier techniques require encouraging strong tip leaders that signal lower branches *not* to fruit. A more informal espalier with a shrub valued for foliage, or one that produces terminal flowers, is considerably easier. In addition to the artistic impression of the espalier when trained against a wall, trellis, or strong wires, it saves a great deal of space. Espaliering a shrub against a south-facing wall can allow you to grow a shrub that is borderline hardy in your area.

Some of the common formal espalier shapes include the vertical cordon (with almost no horizontal growth), double cordon (a row of U-shaped shrubs), the palmette verrier (candelabra), palmette oblique (with branches at 45-degree angles), and the Belgian fence (a row of Y-shaped shrubs with branches overlapping). But shrubs can also be trained to informal fan or ladder shapes. In most cases you should head back vertical growth, encouraging and tying down several strong horizontal branches, and removing all growth toward or away from you.

Topiary and Standards

Topiary is the art of training certain plants—primarily shrubs of some type—into geometric or sculptural shapes. Some of the shrubs best suited to this purpose are boxwoods, holly, bay, cotoneaster, and ligustrum. Some formal gardens, such as Ladew in Monkton, Maryland, specialize in hedges and displays entirely of topiary. For most home gardens, a single topiary makes a strong focal point. Simple shapes such as cones can be clipped using guide wires or stakes. Those that are more complex usually require chicken wire forms that are left in place for several years.

A standard might be considered a very simple topiary, shaped like a lollipop with a length of bare stem below a ball of branches. Popular plants for standards include roses and oleanders, as well as herbs such as rosemary, lemon verbena, and sweet bay.

Gallery
of Plants

▲*Abelia* × *grandiflora*

Glossy Abelia

SIZE: To 6 feet

Full sun to part shade

Moisture-retentive acid soil

Late summer pinkish white flowers with
persistent sepals

Hedging, masses

Semievergreen; Zones 6 to 10

P. 231

▼*Abeliophyllum distichum*

White Forsythia

SIZE: To 5 feet

Full sun

Fertile, well-drained soil

White spring flowers, arching branches

Masses, shrub borders

Deciduous; Zones 5 to 9

P. 232

Abutilon × hybridum
'Souvenir Le Bonn'
Chinese Lantern

SIZE: To 10 feet
Full sun
Fertile, well-drained soil
Bell-shaped flowers, variegated maplelike leaves
Wall training, containers
Evergreen; Zones 9 to 10
P. 233

Abutilon megapotamicum
'Super'
Trailing Abutilon

SIZE: To 8 feet
Full sun
Fertile, well-drained soil
Yellow flowers with red calyces
Wall training, containers
Evergreen, semievergreen; Zones 8 to 10
P. 233

▲*Acacia cultriformis*
Knife Acacia
SIZE: To 12 feet
Full sun
Heat and drought tolerant
Yellow spring flowers
Screen or windbreak
Evergreen; Zones 9 to 11
P. 234

▼*Acca sellowiana*
Pineapple Guava
SIZE: To 10 feet
Full sun; part shade if fruit isn't expected
Light loamy soil, tolerates sand and salt
Spring flowers white outside, red inside
Hedge, specimen
Evergreen; Zones 8 to 10
P. 235

Acer palmatum var. *dissectum*
Japanese Maple
SIZE: Varies with cultivar
Dappled shade
Moist, well-drained soil
Delicate dissected leaves, often red or
    variegated
Mixed borders, specimen
Deciduous; Zones 6 to 8
P. 236

Acer tataricum ssp.*ginnala*
Amur Maple
SIZE: To 20 feet
Sun or shade
Tolerates wind, drought
Colorful fall foliage
Naturalizing; can be invasive
Deciduous; Zones 3 to 7
P. 237 `

Aesculus parviflora
Bottlebrush Buckeye
SIZE: To 12 feet
Sun to part shade
Acidic, well-drained organic soil
White bottlebrush late-summer flowers, yellow
  fall foliage
Shrub borders, specimen
Deciduous; Zones 5 to 8
P. 237

Aesculus pavia
Red Buckeye
SIZE: To 15 feet
Sun to part shade
Acidic, well-drained soil rich in organic matter
Red tubular early-summer flowers
Shrub borders, attracting hummingbirds
Deciduous; Zones 5 to 8
P. 238

Aloysia citriodora
Lemon Verbena
SIZE: To 8 feet
Full sun
Fertile soil kept moderately moist
Lemon-scented foliage used in tea, cooking,
    potpourri
Often containerized to overwinter indoors
Deciduous; Zones 8 to 11
P. 238

Amelanchier alnifolia
(flowers)
Alder-leaved Serviceberry
SIZE: Averages 12 feet
Sun or part shade
Moist, fast-draining acid soil
White spring flowers, edible berries
Woodland edge, attracting birds
Deciduous; Zones 4 to 5
P. 239

Amelanchier alnifolia (berries)
Alder-leaved Serviceberry
SIZE: Averages 12 feet
Sun or part shade
Moist, fast-draining acid soil
White spring flowers, edible berries
Woodland edge, attracting birds
Deciduous; Zones 4 to 5

P. 239

Andromeda polifolia
Bog Rosemary
SIZE: To 12 inches
Shade
Moist, acidic soil
White or pale pink flowers spring to early
    summer
Rock garden, bog, front of border
Evergreen; Zones 2 to 6

P. 240

Aralia elata 'Variegata'
Variegated Japanese Angelica Tree
SIZE: To 20 feet
Sun or shade
Fertile, humusy, well-draining soil, out of wind
Large umbels of white flowers in midsummer
Accent, mixed borders
Deciduous; Zones 4 to 9
P. 241

Aralia spinosa (flowers)
Devil's Walking Stick
SIZE: To 15 feet
Sun or shade
Fertile, organic, well-aerated soil
Large clusters of white flowers in summer
Accent, security
Deciduous; Zones 4 to 9
P. 241

Aralia spinosa (habit)
Devil's Walking Stick
SIZE: To 15 feet
Sun or shade
Fertile, organic, well-aerated soil
Large clusters of white flowers in summer
Accent, security
Deciduous; Zones 4 to 9
P. 241

Arbutus unedo
Strawberry Tree
SIZE: To 20 feet
Prefers sun
Humusy soil at first, then drought tolerant
White autumn flowers, yellow to red fruit
Shrub border
Evergreen; Zones 7 to 10
P. 242

Arctostaphylos patula
Green Manzanita

SIZE: To 6 feet

Sun or shade

Tolerates poor soil, salt, wind

Pink or white flowers in spring or early
  summer

Slopes, coastal sites

Evergreen; Zones 7 to 9

P. 243

Arctostaphylos uva-ursi (flowers)
Common Bearberry, Kinnikinick

SIZE: To 1 foot

Sun or shade

Tolerates most soil conditions, wind

Pink-tinged white spring flowers

Ground cover

Evergreen; Zones 2 to 6

P. 243

Arctostaphylos uva-ursi (berries)
Common Bearberry, Kinnikinick
SIZE: To 1 foot
Sun or shade
Tolerates most soil conditions, wind
Bright red berries
Ground cover
Evergreen; Zones 2 to 6
P. 243

Ardisia japonica
Marlberry
SIZE: To 18 inches, indefinite spread
Shade
Moist, well-drained acid soil out of wind
White or pale pink summer flowers, red berries
Ground cover
Evergreen; Zones 7 to 9
P. 244

Aronia arbutifolia
'Brilliantissima' (flowers)
Red Chokeberry cultivar

SIZE: To 8 feet tall, 5 feet wide
Full sun for heavy fruiting
Moist or dry soil, neutral to acid
White spring flowers, red fall foliage
Masses, naturalizing, wildlife
Deciduous; Zones 4 to 9
P. 244

Aronia arbutifolia
'Brilliantissima' (berries)
Red Chokeberry cultivar

SIZE: To 8 feet tall, 5 feet wide
Full sun for heavy fruiting
Moist or dry soil, neutral to acid
Red berries, red fall foliage
Masses, naturalizing, wildlife
Deciduous; Zones 4 to 9
P. 244

Aronia melanocarpa
Black Chokeberry
SIZE: To 5 feet
Fruits best in full sun
Moist or dry soil, neutral to acid
White spring flowers, dark purple fruits,
    purple-red fall foliage
Massing, naturalizing
Deciduous; Zones 3 to 8
P. 244

Asimina triloba (habit)
Pawpaw
SIZE: To 20 feet
Full sun for best fruit
Rich, moist, well-drained neutral to acid soil
Exotic-looking leaves, edible fruits
"Edible" gardens; tropical effect
Deciduous; Zones 5 to 8
P. 245

Asimina triloba (flower)
Pawpaw
SIZE: To 20 feet
Full sun for best fruit
Rich, moist, well-drained neutral to acid soil
Dark red flowers, large edible fruits
"Edible" gardens; tropical effect
Deciduous; Zones 5 to 8
P. 245

Atriplex canescens
Four-wing Saltbush
SIZE: To 6 feet tall, 8 feet wide
Full sun
Moderately fertile, dry soil
Unusual four-winged fruits
Coastal or desert gardens
Evergreen; Zones 7 to 9
P. 246

Aucuba japonica 'Variegata'
Gold Dust Japanese Aucuba
SIZE: To 10 feet
Part to full shade
Tolerates most soils, but not wind
Glossy, variegated leaves
Hedges, shady corners
Evergreen; Zones 7 to 10
P. 247

Baccharis halimifolia
Groundsel Bush
SIZE: To 10 feet
Full sun
Moderate to poor, sandy or salty soil
Silky white seed heads in autumn
Coastal gardens, naturalizing
Semievergreen or deciduous; Zones 5 to 9
P. 248

▲*Berberis darwinii*
Darwin Barberry
SIZE: To 10 feet
Full sun
Well-drained soil
Gold or orange spring flowers, blue berries
Hedges, borders
Evergreen; Zones 7 to 9
P. 249

▼*Berberis julianae*
Wintergreen Barberry
SIZE: To 10 feet
Full sun
Well-drained soil
Yellow late-spring flowers, blue-black berries
Hedges, borders
Evergreen; Zones 6 to 9
P. 249

Berberis verruculosa
Warty Barberry
SIZE: To 5 feet
Full sun
Well-drained soil
Yellow spring flowers, blue-black berries
Low hedge, borders
Evergreen; Zones 6 to 9
P. 250

Brugmansia × *candida*
Brugmansia
SIZE: To 15 feet
Full sun
Fertile, moist, well-drained soil
Fragrant white long-blooming flowers
Specimens, containers
Evergreen; Zones 10 to 11
P. 250

▲*Brunfelsia pauciflora*
Yesterday, Today, and Tomorrow
SIZE: From 3 to 10 feet

Dappled or part shade

Rich, moist soil, excellent drainage

Pansy-shaped flowers open purple, turn lavender, then white

Borders, containers

Evergreen; Zones 9 to 11

P. 251

▼*Buddleia alternifolia* 'Argentea'
Fountain Buddleia cultivar
SIZE: To 12 feet

Full sun

Moisture-retentive soil, well drained

Lilac purple midsummer flowers, gray willow-like leaves

Borders, butterfly gardens

Deciduous; Zones 5 to 9

P. 252

Buddleia davidii 'Black Knight'

Butterfly Bush cultivar

SIZE: To 10 feet
Full sun
Moist, well-drained soil
Fragrant dark purple summer flowers
Borders, butterfly gardens
Deciduous; Zones 6 to 9
P. 252

Buddleia davidii 'Dartmoor'

Butterfly Bush cultivar

SIZE: To 10 feet
Full sun
Moist, well-draining, moderately fertile soil
Many branches, deep lilac-colored flowers
Butterfly gardens, borders
Deciduous; Zones 6 to 9
P. 252

▲*Buddleia* 'Lochinch' (habit)
Butterfly Bush hybrid
SIZE: To 10 feet
Full sun
Relatively fertile, moisture-retentive soil
Cones of lavender-blue flowers
Mixed borders, butterfly gardens
Deciduous; Zones 6 to 9
P. 252

▼*Buddleia* 'Lochinch' (flowers)
Butterfly Bush hybrid
SIZE: To 10 feet
Full sun
Relatively fertile, moisture-retentive soil
Cones of lavender-blue flowers
Mixed borders, butterfly gardens
Deciduous; Zones 6 to 9
P. 252

▲ *Buxus microphylla*
'Compacta'

Kingsville Dwarf Boxwood

SIZE: To 1 foot
Best in part shade
Neutral, organic, well-drained soil
Dense mound of small leaves
Edging, low hedge
Evergreen; Zones 6 to 9
P. 253

◄ *Buxus sempervirens*
'Graham Blandy'

Edging Boxwood cultivar

SIZE: To 9 feet
Best in part shade
Neutral, organic, well-drained soil
Narrow shape
Accent, hedge, borders
Evergreen; Zones 6 to 8
P. 254

Buxus sempervirens 'Suffruticosa'

Edging or Dwarf Boxwood

SIZE: To 5 feet
Best in part shade
Neutral, organic, well-drained soil
Dense mound, small leaves
Edging, low hedge
Evergreen; Zones 6 to 8
P. 254

Callicarpa bodinieri var. *giraldii*

Chinese Beautyberry

SIZE: To 10 feet
Full sun or dappled shade
Well-drained soil, moderately fertile
Heavy clusters of purple-pink berries
Open woods, borders
Deciduous; Zones 5 to 9
P. 254

Callicarpa dichotoma
Purple Beautyberry
SIZE: To 5 feet
Full sun or dappled shade
Moderately fertile, well-drained soil
Purple berries along branches
Open woods, borders
Deciduous; Zones 6 to 9
P. 255

Callistemon citrinus
Common Bottlebrush
SIZE: To 15 feet
Full sun
Neutral to acid, moderately fertile soil
Red bottlebrush flowers spring and summer
Hedge, espalier, specimen, attracting hum-
　　mingbirds
Evergreen; Zones 8 to 11
P. 255

Callistemon 'Little John'
Common Bottlebrush cultivar
SIZE: To 3 feet
Full sun
Neutral to acid, moderately fertile soil
Red bottlebrush flowers all year
Borders, containers
Evergreen; Zones 8 to 11
P. 255

Calluna vulgaris 'Gold Haze'
Scotch Heather cultivar
SIZE: To 12 inches
Part shade
Poor acid soil, perfect drainage
Golden foliage, white flowers
Underplanting other acid-lovers
Evergreen; Zones 4 to 7
P. 256

Calluna vulgaris 'Kinlochruel'
Scotch Heather cultivar

SIZE: To 10 inches
Part shade
Poor acid soil, perfect drainage
Double white flowers
Seaside gardens in mild climates
Evergreen; Zones 4 to 7
P. 256

Calycanthus floridus
Carolina Allspice

SIZE: To 8 feet tall, 10 feet wide
Full sun to part shade
Fertile, organically rich, moist soil
Fragrant foliage, fruit-scented straplike dark
red flowers in late spring
Fragrance gardens, naturalizing
Deciduous; Zones 5 to 9
P. 257

Camellia japonica 'Kumasaka'
Japanese Camellia cultivar

SIZE: To 15 feet
Part shade
Deep, rich, acid soil
Rosy pink double or peony-form flowers winter
    to early spring
Hedges, borders, specimens
Evergreen; Zones 7 to 10
P. 258

Camellia japonica 'Wilmetta'
Japanese Camellia cultivar

SIZE: To 15 feet
Part shade
Deep, rich, acid soil
Single white flowers winter to early spring
Hedges, borders, specimens
Evergreen; Zones 7 to 10
P. 258

Carissa macrocarpa
Natal Plum

SIZE: From 8 to 18 feet
Full sun for best fruiting
Tolerates wet or dry soil, sand, salt
Fragrant white flowers year-round
Security hedge, espalier
Evergreen; Zone 10
P. 259

Carpenteria californica
Bush Anemone

SIZE: To 6 feet
Sun or light shade
Most soils; tolerates salt, drought
Fragrant white flowers, mid- to late summer
Hedge, borders
Evergreen; Zones 8 to 10
P. 260

Caryopteris × clandonensis 'Blue Mist'

Blue-mist Shrub

SIZE: To 3 feet
Full sun or part shade
Loose, moderately fertile, well-drained soil
Blue fringe flowers in late summer
Mixed bed or border, low hedge
Deciduous; Zones 5 to 9
P. 260

Cassia bicapsularis

Cassia

SIZE: To 10 feet
Full sun
Tolerates dry, infertile soil
Yellow flowers from late fall to winter
Borders, specimen
Evergreen; Zone 10
P. 261

Ceanothus americanus
New Jersey Tea
SIZE: To 4 feet
Best in full sun
Excellent drainage
Small white midsummer flowers
Difficult conditions
Deciduous; Zones 4 to 8
P. 262

Ceanothus 'Concha'
Ceanothus cultivar
SIZE: To 7 feet
Best in full sun
Excellent drainage
Dark blue flowers
Specimen, slopes, coastal or other dry sites
Evergreen; Zones 8 to 10
P. 262

▲*Cephalanthus occidentalis*
Buttonbush
SIZE: To 6 feet tall, 8 feet wide
Full sun
Rich, moisture-retentive soil
White ball flowers from late summer to fall
Natural pondsides, wildlife gardens
Deciduous; Zones 5 to 11
P. 264

▼*Cephalotaxus harringtonia*
Japanese Plum Yew
SIZE: From 10 to 20 feet
Part shade
Richly organic, moisture-retentive, neutral soil
Linear leaves in spirals, oval fruits
Specimen, shrub border
Evergreen; Zones 5 to 9
P. 264

Cercis chinensis
Chinese Redbud
SIZE: To 10 feet
Full sun or part shade
Deep, rich, moisture-retentive soil
Rosy purple flowers in early spring
Specimen, borders
Deciduous; Zones 6 to 9
P. 265

Cestrum nocturnum
Night Jessamine
SIZE: To 12 feet
Sun to part shade
Fertile soil
Fragrant pale green or ivory flowers, late summer
Ccontainerize to winter indoors
Evergreen; Zones 10 to 11
P. 266

Chaenomeles speciosa 'Hollandia'

Flowering Quince cultivar

SIZE: To 10 feet
Best in full sun
Moderately fertile soil
Large red flowers, reblooms
Mixed beds and borders; forcing, arrangements
Deciduous; Zones 5 to 8
P. 266

Chaenomeles × superba 'Cameo'

Flowering Quince cultivar

SIZE: To 5 feet
Best in full sun
Moderately fertile soil
Double apricot flowers
Mixed beds and borders; forcing, arrangements
Deciduous; Zones 5 to 9
P. 267

▲*Chamaecyparis obtusa* 'Nana Lutea'

Hinoki False Cypress cultivar

SIZE: To 5 feet
Full sun
Moist, well-drained, acid to neutral soil
Irregular pyramid
Specimen, shrub or mixed border
Evergreen; Zones 5 to 8
P. 267

▼*Chamaecyparis pisifera* 'Filifera Aurea Nana'

Hinoki False Cypress cultivar

SIZE: To 3 feet
Full sun
Moist, well-drained, acid to neutral soil
Pendulous, velvety, dark gold foliage
Specimen or borders
Evergreen; Zones 4 to 8
P. 268

Chimonanthus praecox (flowers)

Wintersweet

SIZE: To 12 feet tall and 10 feet wide
Full sun to part shade
Loamy, well-drained, moist soil
Fragrant yellow flowers in winter
Site for winter interest
Deciduous; Zones 7 to 9
P. 268

Chimonanthus praecox (habit)

Wintersweet

SIZE: To 12 feet tall and 10 feet wide
Full sun to part shade
Loamy, well-drained, moist soil
Fragrant yellow flowers in winter
Site for winter interest
Deciduous; Zones 7 to 9
P. 268

Chionanthus retusus (habit)
Chinese Fringetree

SIZE: To 25 feet

Full sun to part shade

Deep, rich, moist, well-drained soil, acid to
    neutral; prefers hot summers

White flowers in late spring

Specimen

Deciduous; Zones 6 to 8

P. 269

Chionanthus retusus (flowers)
Chinese Fringetree

SIZE: To 25 feet

Full sun to part shade

Deep, rich, moist, well-drained soil, acid to
    neutral; prefers hot summers

White flowers in late spring

Specimen

Deciduous; Zones 6 to 8

P. 269

Chionanthus virginicus
Fringetree

SIZE: From 12 to 20 feet

Full sun to part shade

Deep, fertile, moist, well-drained soil, acid to
  neutral; does best with long hot summers

White fringe flowers in late spring

Specimen

Deciduous; Zones 5 to 9

P. 269

Choisya ternata
Mexican Orange Blossom

SIZE: To 9 feet

Full sun or light shade

Light, fertile, well-drained soil

White flowers throughout spring

Screen, informal hedge, espalier

Evergreen; Zones 8 to 10

P. 270

Cistus × corbariensis
White Rock Rose
SIZE: To 4 feet
Full sun
Light, fertile, well-drained acid soil
White flowers from red buds, late spring
Slopes, fire-prone regions
Evergreen; Zones 8 to 10
P. 271

Cistus × purpureus
Orchid Rock Rose
SIZE: To 3 feet
Full sun
Light, fertile, well-drained acid soil
Dark pink summer flowers with maroon base
Slopes, fire-prone regions
Evergreen; Zones 8 to 10
P. 271

Clerodendrum trichotomum
Harlequin Glory Bower
SIZE: To 15 feet
Full sun to part shade
Rich, loamy, moisture-retentive soil
White flowers, red calyxes, blue-green fruit
Specimen, shrub border
Evergreen; Zones 7 to 10
P. 272

Clethra alnifolia 'Rosea'
Summersweet cultivar
SIZE: To 8 feet
Sun or shade
All nonalkaline soils
Scented pale pink flowers in late summer
Woodlands, masses, mixed borders
Deciduous; Zones 4 to 9
P. 273

Clethra barbinervis
Japanese Clethra
SIZE: To 20 feet
Sun or shade
All soils except alkaline
Dangling flowers in late summer, colorful fall foliage
Deciduous; Zones 6 to 8
P. 273

Comptonia peregrina
Sweet Fern
SIZE: From 2 to 4 feet, twice as wide
Full sun to part shade
Tolerates poor, sandy soils
Glossy fernlike foliage, fragrant when crushed
Naturalizing, holding slopes
Deciduous; Zones 2 to 6
P. 274

Convolvulus cneorum
Silverbush
SIZE: From 2 to 4 feet
Full sun
Light, dry soil
White saucer flowers, silvery foliage
Rock garden, evening garden
Evergreen; Zones 8 to 10
P. 274

Coprosma repens
'Pink Splendor'
Mirror Plant cultivar
SIZE: To 10 feet tall, 6 feet wide
Full sun or part shade
Neutral to acid, moderately fertile soil
Shiny variegated leaves
Evergreen; Zones 8 to 10
P. 275

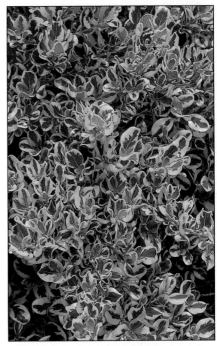

Cornus alba (berries)
Tartarian Dogwood
SIZE: To 10 feet
Full sun to part shade
Moist, well-aerated, organically rich soil
White flowers and berries
Naturalizing, masses, borders
Deciduous; Zones 2 to 8
P. 276

Cornus alba (twigs)
Tartarian Dogwood
SIZE: To 10 feet
Full sun to part shade
Moist, well-aerated, organically rich soil
Red stems
Naturalizing, masses, borders
Deciduous; Zones 2 to 8
P. 276

▲*Cornus alba*
'Elegantissima Variegata'

Tartarian Dogwood cultivar

SIZE: To 10 feet
Full sun to part shade
Moist, well-aerated, organically rich soil
Leaves have white margins
Masses, borders
Deciduous; Zones 2 to 8

P. 276

▼*Cornus alternifolia* (flowers)
Pagoda Dogwood

SIZE: To 20 feet
Full sun to part shade
Well-drained, organically rich, moist soil
Fragrant yellow-white flowers in late spring
Specimen, borders
Deciduous; Zones 3 to 7

P. 276

Cornus alternifolia (fall foliage)
Pagoda Dogwood
SIZE: To 20 feet
Full sun to part shade
Well-drained, organically rich, moist soil
Horizontal habit, purple-red fall foliage
Specimen, borders
Deciduous; Zones 3 to 7
P. 276

Cornus mas (flowers)
Cornelian Cherry
SIZE: To 20 feet
Full sun to part shade
Moist, well-drained soil with organic
    amendments
Profuse small yellow flowers in late winter
Woodland edges, naturalizing
Deciduous; Zones 4 to 8
P. 276

▲*Cornus mas* (berries)

Cornelian Cherry

SIZE: To 20 feet

Full sun to part shade

Moist, well-drained soil with organic amendments

Edible red fruit

"Edible" gardens, naturalizing

Deciduous; Zones 4 to 8

P. 276

▼*Corylopsis glabrescens*

Fragrant Winter Hazel

SIZE: Averages 10 feet

Part shade

Fertile, moist, well-drained acid soil

Yellow midspring flowers

Borders, specimens

Deciduous; Zones 5 to 8

P. 278

Corylopsis pauciflora
(fall foliage)
Buttercup Winter Hazel
SIZE: To 6 feet
Part shade
Acidic, fertile, moist but well-draining soil
Yellow fall foliage
Borders, specimens
Deciduous; Zones 6 to 8
P. 278

Corylopsis pauciflora
(flowers)
Buttercup Winter Hazel
SIZE: To 6 feet
Part shade
Acidic, fertile, moist but well-draining soil
Pale yellow flowers in midspring
Borders, specimens
Deciduous; Zones 6 to 8
P. 278

Corylopsis spicata (habit)
Spike Winter Hazel
SIZE: To 6 feet
Part shade
Fertile, moist, well-aerated acid soil
Yellow flowers with pink stamens
Borders, specimens
Deciduous; Zones 5 to 8
P. 278

Corylopsis spicata (flowers)
Spike Winter Hazel
SIZE: To 6 feet
Part shade
Fertile, moist, well-aerated acid soil
Yellow flowers with pink stamens
Borders, specimens
Deciduous; Zones 5 to 8
P. 278

Corylus avellana 'Contorta'
European Filbert cultivar

Harry Lauder's Walking Stick

SIZE: To 20 feet
Full sun to part shade
Tolerates alkaline soil
Dangling catkins, twisted branches
Specimen, accent, dried arrangemets
Deciduous; Zones 3 to 8
P. 279

Cotinus coggygria
Smoke Tree

SIZE: To 15 feet
Full sun to part shade
Moderately fertile soil
Fluffy fruiting panicles, gray or pink; colorful
  fall foliage
Specimen
Deciduous; Zones 5 to 8
P. 280

Cotoneaster apiculatus
Cranberry Cotoneaster

SIZE: To 18 inches tall, 6 feet wide

Full sun

Moderately fertile soil

White flowers, red berries, red or bronze fall
leaves

Ground cover, rock gardens

Deciduous; Zones 4 to 7

P. 281

Cotoneaster horizontalis
Rockspray Cotoneaster

SIZE: To 3 feet tall, 6 feet wide

Full sun

Average soil

Pink-tinged flowers, red fruit

Wall-training, specimen

Deciduous; Zones 5 to 7

P. 281

Cotoneaster horizontalis 'Variegatus'
Rockspray Cotoneaster cultivar
SIZE: To 3 feet tall, 6 feet wide
Full sun
Average soil
Pink-tinged flowers, red fruit
Wall-training, specimen
Deciduous; Zones 5 to 7
P. 281

Cotoneaster salicifolius
Willow-leaved Cotoneaster
SIZE: To 15 feet tall
Full sun
Moderately fertile soil
Woolly white flowers, red berries
Hedge, shrub border
Evergreen; Zones 6 to 8
P. 282

Cryptomeria japonica
'Globosa Nana'

Japanese Cryptomeria cultivar

SIZE: To 5 feet
Full sun or light shade
Deep, fertile, humusy, moist soil
Dome or pyramid shape
Borders, accent
Evergreen; Zones 5 to 8
P. 282

Cryptomeria japonica
'Vilmoriniana'

Japanese Cryptomeria cultivar

SIZE: To 2 feet
Full sun or light shade
Loose, rich, moisture-retentive soil
Gray-green foliage bronzes in fall
Rock gardens, mixed borders
Evergreen; Zones 5 to 8
P. 282

Cyrilla racemiflora
Leatherwood
SIZE: From 3 to 10 feet
Full sun to part shade
Rich, moisture-retentive, acid soil
Fragrant white flowers in late summer; colorful
  fall foliage
Shrub border, naturalizing, pondside
Deciduous; Zones 6 to 10
P. 283

Cytisus × *praecox*
Warminster Broom
SIZE: To 4 feet
Full sun
Poor to average, neutral to acid soil
Yellow spring flowers
Mixed or shrub border; invasive in West
Deciduous; Zones 6 to 9
P. 284

Daboecia cantabrica
Irish Heath, Connemara, St. Dabeoc's Heath

SIZE: From 12 to 20 inches tall, twice as wide
Full sun
Rich acid soil
Rosy purple flowers summer to fall
Masses, heath gardens
Evergreen; Zones 7 to 8
P. 284

Daphne × burkwoodii 'Carol Mackie'
Burkwood Daphne cultivar

SIZE: To 4 feet
Full sun to part shade
Fertile, organic, moist soil
Variegated leaves, fragrant pale pink flowers
Borders, accent
Semievergreen; Zones 4 to 7
P. 285

Daphne caucasica
Caucasian Daphne
SIZE: To 5 feet
Full sun to part shade
Rich, moisture-retentive, mulched soil
Fragrant white reblooming flowers, red or black
    berries
Shrub border, fragrance garden
Deciduous; Zones 5 to 7
P. 285

Daphne cneorum
Rose Daphne, Garland Flower
SIZE: To 8 inches
Full sun or part shade
Well-amended, moist soil
Fragrant white or rosy flowers
Rock gardens
Evergreen; Zones 4 to 7
P. 285

Daphne genkwa (habit)
Lilac Daphne
SIZE: To 4 feet
Full sun or part shade
Deep, fertile, moist soil
Lilac-colored spring flowers
Borders
Deciduous; Zones 6 to 8
P. 286

Daphne genkwa (flowers)
Lilac Daphne
SIZE: To 4 feet
Full sun or part shade
Deep, fertile, moist soil
Lilac-colored spring flowers
Borders
Deciduous; Zones 6 to 8
P. 286

Daphne odora 'Aureo-Marginata'

Winter Daphne cultivar

SIZE: To 6 feet

Full sun to part shade

Loose, well-amended, moist soil

Fragrant white or lavender flowers in late winter

Accent, borders

Evergreen; Zones 7 to 9

P. 286

Decaisnea fargesii

Blue-bean

SIZE: To 15 feet

Full sun or partial shade

Fertile soil, out of wind

Yellow-green flowers, blue seedpods

Specimen

Deciduous; Zones 7 to 9

P. 286

Deutzia crenata 'Nikko'
Nikko Deutzia

SIZE: To 2 feet tall, 4 feet wide

Full sun or light shade

Moderately fertile soil

Small white flowers in late spring, burgundy fall
  foliage

Front of border

Deciduous; Zones 5 to 8

P. 287

Diervilla sessilifolia 'Butterfly'
Southern Bush Honeysuckle cultivar

SIZE: To 5 feet

Best in full sun

Wide range of soils

Tubular yellow summer flowers

Masses, naturalizing; hilly, windy sites

Deciduous; Zones 4 to 8

P. 288

Disanthus cercidifolius
Disanthus
SIZE: To 10 feet
Light shade
Rich, moisture-retentive, slightly acid soil
Purple-red flowers in fall with colorful foliage
Specimen; shrub border
Deciduous; Zones 5 to 8
P. 289

Edgeworthia paperifera
Edgeworthia
SIZE: To 5 feet
Full sun or dappled shade
Moist, rich soil
White tubular late-winter flowers with yellow "mouths"
Shrub border, specimen
Deciduous; Zones 8 to 10
P. 289

Elaeagnus × ebbingei 'Gilt Edge'

Variegated Eleagnus hybrid

SIZE: From 6 to 12 feet

Sun or shade

Tolerates poor, dry, salty soil

Creamy fall flowers, yellow-gold leaf margins

Naturalizing, attracting birds

Deciduous; Zones 7 to 9

P. 290

Eleutherococcus sieboldianus 'Variegatus'

Five-leaf Aralia cultivar

SIZE: To 8 feet

Sun or shade

Tolerates poor, dry soil

Greenish flowers in late spring, black fruits

Accent

Deciduous; Zones 4 to 8

P. 290

Embothrium coccineum
Chilean Firebush
SIZE: From 10 to 30 feet tall, 15 feet wide
Full sun to part shade
Acidic, moisture-retentive soil
Orange-red flowers in late spring
Specimen, shrub border
Evergreen; Zones 8 to 10
P. 291

Enkianthus campanulatus
Redvein Enkianthus
SIZE: From 8 to 15 feet
Sun to part shade
Humusy, neutral to acid soil
Red-veined spring flowers, colorful fall foliage
Shrub border
Deciduous; Zones 5 to 8
P. 291

▲*Enkianthus perulatus*
White Enkianthus
SIZE: To 6 feet
Sun to part shade
Neutral to acid humus-rich soil
White spring flowers, scarlet fall foliage
Deciduous; Zones 5 to 8
P. 292

▼*Erica arborea*
Tree Heath
SIZE: To 12 feet
Full sun
Sandy soil amended with peat
Honey-scented white spring flowers
Mixed or shrub borders
Evergreen; Zones 7 to 10
P. 292

Erica carnea 'Pirbright Rose'

Winter Heath cultivar

SIZE: To 6 inches
Full sun
Sandy, peaty soil
Bright pink flowers
Ground cover
Evergreen; Zones 5 to 7
P. 293

Escallonia × *exoniensis* 'Frades'

Escallonia cultivar

SIZE: To 12 feet
Full sun
Neutral to acid soil, mild climate
Rosy flowers for many months
Espalier
Evergreen; Zones 8 to 9
P. 293

Escallonia × langleyensis 'Apple Blossom'

Pink Escallonia cultivar

SIZE: To 5 feet
Full sun
Neutral to acid soil, mild climate
Pale pink flowers from spring through fall
Borders
Evergreen; Zones 8 to 9

P. 294

Euonymus alatus

Winged Euonymus

SIZE: From 10 to 15 feet
Full sun
Moisture-retentive soil
Fuchsia-red fall foliage
Shrub borders, masses; invasive in East, upper Midwest
Deciduous; Zones 4 to 8

P. 294

Euonymus americanus
Strawberry Bush
SIZE: To 6 feet
Full sun
Moisture-retentive soil
Unusual red and orange seedpods
Woodland gardens
Deciduous; Zones 6 to 9
P. 295

Euonymus europaeus
European Spindle Tree
SIZE: To 25 feet
Full sun
Moisture-retentive soil
Unusual seedpods
Shrub border; invasive in East and upper Midwest
Deciduous; Zones 4 to 7
P. 295

Euonymus japonicus 'Silver King'

Japanese Spindle Tree cultivar

SIZE: To 6 feet tall, 3 feet wide
Full sun
Tolerates poor soil, heat
Variegated foliage
Hedge or screen
Evergreen; Zones 6 to 9
P. 295

Exochorda × macrantha 'The Bride'

Pearlbush hybrid

SIZE: From 4 to 6 feet
Full sun or part shade
Best in acidic loam
White flowers in early spring
Mixed or shrub borders
Deciduous; Zones 4 to 8
P. 296

Fallugia paradoxa
Apache Plume
SIZE: From 5 to 8 feet
Full sun
Dry soil, hot dry summers
Long-lasting white flowers, feathery seed heads
Desert gardens
Deciduous; Zones 6 to 10
P. 296

× *Fatshedera lizei*
Fatshedera
SIZE: To 5 feet tall, 10 feet wide
Full sun to moderate shade
Moderately fertile soil
Bold lobed leaves, greenish white fall flowers
Can be espaliered or containerized
Evergreen; Zones 8 to 10
P. 297

Fatsia japonica 'Variegata'
Fatsia cultivar
SIZE: From 6 to 10 feet
Dappled shade
Fertile, moisture-retentive soil
Clusters of white flowers in fall, black berries
Accent, coastal gardens
Evergreen; Zones 8 to 10
P. 297

Forsythia suspensa var. *sieboldii*
Weeping Forsythia
SIZE: To 10 feet
Full sun or dappled shade
Average soil
Yellow flowers on arching branches
Slopes, espalier
Deciduous; Zones 6 to 8
P. 298

Forsythia viridissima 'Bronxensis'
Green-stem Forsythia cultivar
SIZE: To 1 foot tall, 3 feet wide
Full sun or dappled shade
Average soil
Yellow spring flowers
Ground cover, slopes, banks
Deciduous; Zones 6 to 8
P. 298

Fothergilla major (habit)
Large Fothergilla
SIZE: To 10 feet
Best bloom and fall color in full sun
Rich, moisture-retentive, acid soil
Colorful fall foliage
Masses, shrub or mixed border
Deciduous; Zones 4 to 8
P. 299

Fothergilla major (flowers)
Large Fothergilla
SIZE: To 10 feet
Best bloom and fall color in full sun
Rich, moisture-retentive, acid soil
Cylindrical white flowers in midspring
Masses, shrub or mixed border
Deciduous; Zones 4 to 8
P. 299

Fouquieria splendens (habit)
Ocotillo
SIZE: From 10 to 25 feet
Full sun
Poor to average sandy soil
Bright red flowers, dramatic form
Desert garden accent, attracting hummingbirds
Deciduous; Zones 8 to 11
P. 300

Fouquieria splendens (detail)
Ocotillo
SIZE: From 10 to 25 feet
Full sun
Poor to average sandy soil
Dramatic thorny branches
Desert garden accent, attracting hummingbirds
Deciduous; Zones 8 to 11
P. 300

Fremontodendron californicum
Common Flannel Bush
SIZE: To 20 feet
Full sun
Poor to average, well-drained soil, out of wind
Lemon yellow midspring flowers
Can be wall trained
Evergreen; Zones 8 to 10
P. 301

Gardenia augusta
Gardenia

SIZE: Usually 5 to 6 feet (varies by cultivar)
Dappled to part shade
Rich, humusy, neutral to acid soil
Thick-petaled white flowers late spring to mid-summer
Use as hedge, containerize to bring indoors
Evergreen; Zones 8 to 11
P. 301

Garrya × issaquahensis
Silk-Tassel Tree

SIZE: To 12 feet
Full sun to part shade
Well-drained soil out of wind
Yellowish purple winter catkins
Specimen, informal hedge or screen
Evergreen; Zones 8 to 10
P. 302

Gaultheria procumbens
Checkerberry
SIZE: To 6 inches
Full sun to part shade
Peaty, acid, moist soil
White flowers, red berries, fragrant foliage
Ground cover
Evergreen; Zones 3 to 6
P. 303

Gaultheria shallon
Salal
SIZE: To 5 feet
Full sun to part shade
Acid soil, peat enriched and moist
Pink-tinged early-summer flowers, purple-
black berries
Naturalizing, attracting birds
Evergreen; Zones 6 to 8
P. 303

Gaultheria × wisleyensis 'Wisley Pearl'

Gaultheria hybrid cultivar

SIZE: To 4 feet

Full sun to part shade

Acidic, peaty, moisture-retentive soil

White spring to early-summer flowers, dark red fruits

Borders, naturalizing

Evergreen; Zones 7 to 9

P. 303

Genista lydia

Broom

SIZE: To 2 feet

Full sun

Poor, sandy, dry soil

Yellow flowers in early summer

Rock gardens, front of border

Deciduous; Zones 6 to 8

P. 304

▲*Grevillea rosmarinifolia*
Grevillea
SIZE: To 6 feet

Full sun

Moderately fertile, neutral to acid soil; tolerates
   drought

Red flowers (sometimes pink or white) autumn
   to spring

Specimen, wall-training, borders

Evergreen; Zones 9 to 11

P. 305

▼*Grewia occidentalis*
Lavender Starflower
SIZE: Usually 10 feet

Full sun to part shade

Fertile, moisture-retentive soil

Pink and purple flowers in summer

Bank cover, topiary, espalier

Evergreen; Zones 8 to 11

P. 305

Hamamelis × intermedia 'Arnold Promise'

Witch Hazel hybrid cultivar

SIZE: To 20 feet
Full sun or part shade
Moist, moderately fertile, acid soil
Large bright yellow winter flowers
Site for winter interest
Deciduous; Zones 5 to 9
P. 306

Hamamelis × intermedia 'Diane'

Witch Hazel hybrid cultivar

SIZE: To 20 feet
Full sun or part shade
Moist, moderately fertile, acid soil
Straplike, red winter flowers
Winter or woodland garden
Deciduous; Zones 5 to 9
P. 306

▲*Hamamelis × mollis*
Chinese Witch Hazel
SIZE: To 15 feet
Sun or part shade
Moist, acid, moderately fertile soil
Fragrant yellow flowers with red calyxes, late
   winter
Mixed borders
Deciduous; Zones 5 to 9
P. 307

▼*Hamamelis virginiana*
Common Witch Hazel
SIZE: To 20 feet
Sun or part shade
Moist, acidic, moderately fertile soil
Fragrant yellow late-fall flowers
Naturalizing
Deciduous; Zones 3 to 8
P. 307

Hebe 'Autumn Glory'
Hebe cultivar
SIZE: To 2½ feet
Full sun to part shade
Poor to average, neutral to alkaline soil
Purple flowers midsummer to winter
Low hedge, mixed borders
Evergreen; Zones 9 to 10
P. 308

Helichrysum petiolare
Licorice Plant
SIZE: Stems trail to 4 feet
Full sun
Well-drained, poor to moderate soil
Woolly gray leaves
Hanging baskets
Evergreen; Zones 10 to 11
P. 309

Heptacodium miconioides
Seven-son Flower of Zhejiang
SIZE: To 20 feet
Full sun; dappled shade in South
Fragrant white flowers; fruit capsules with reddish purple sepals
Specimen, shrub border
Deciduous; Zones 5 to 9
P. 309

Heteromeles arbutifolia
Christmas Berry
SIZE: Usually 10 feet
Full sun to part shade
Well-drained soil; tolerates wind, drought
Small white flowers in summer; red berries in winter
Screen, attracting birds
Evergreen; Zones 8 to 10
P. 310

Hibiscus rosa-sinensis 'Cooperii'

Chinese Hibiscus cultivar

SIZE: To 8 feet
Full sun
Organic, neutral to alkaline soil
Red flowers, variegated foliage
Container, hedge, screen, borders
Evergreen; Zones 9 to 11
P. 311

Hibiscus rosa-sinensis 'Hula Girl'

Chinese Hibiscus cultivar

SIZE: To 8 feet
Full sun
Organic, neutral to alkaline soil
Yellow flowers with red throats, long blooming
Container, hedge, screen, borders
Evergreen; Zones 9 to 11
P. 311

▲*Hibiscus syriacus* 'Diana'
Rose-of-Sharon cultivar
SIZE: To 10 feet
Full sun
Organic, neutral to alkaline soil
Pure white summer flowers
Hedge, mass, borders
Deciduous; Zones 5 to 9
P. 311

▼*Hippophae rhamnoides*
Sea Buckthorn
SIZE: To 20 feet
Full sun
Poor sandy soil with some organic amendments
Silvery leaves, orange berries
Coastal gardens, holding slopes
Deciduous; Zones 3 to 8
P. 312

▲ *Holodiscus discolor*

Ocean Spray

SIZE : From 3 to 20 feet

Full sun to part shade

Rich, fertile, moist soil

Clusters of white flowers, late spring to early summer

Naturalizing, attracting birds

Deciduous; Zones 6 to 9

P. 312

▼ *Hydrangea arborescens* 'Annabelle'

Smooth Hydrangea cultivar

SIZE : To 5 feet

Needs shade in hot summers

Fertile, moisture-retentive soil

White "snowball" summer flowers

Mixed borders, specimen

Deciduous; Zones 4 to 9

P. 313

Hydrangea macrophylla
Big-leaf Hydrangea, mophead form
SIZE: Averages 6 feet
Full sun to part shade
Tolerates wind, salt, but not drought
Blue flowers in acid soil, pink in alkaline
Specimen, borders, coastal sites
Deciduous; Zones 6 to 9
P. 313

Hydrangea macrophylla 'Blue Wave'
Big-leaf Hydrangea, lacecap cultivar
SIZE: To 6 feet
Best in light shade
Moisture-retentive soil
Blue flowers in acid soil, pink in alkaline
Coastal gardens, borders, masses
Deciduous; Zones 6 to 9
P. 313

Hydrangea paniculata 'Grandiflora'

PeeGee Hydrangea

SIZE: From 10 to 20 feet
Full sun to part shade
Organic, moisture-retentive, well-drained soil
Flower cones first white, then pink, then brown
Specimen, borders
Deciduous; Zones 4 to 8
P. 314

Hydrangea paniculata 'Tardiva'

Panicle Hydrangea cultivar

SIZE: To 15 feet
Full sun to part shade
Well-amended, moist soil
Late-summer, early-fall flowers
Specimen, borders
Deciduous; Zones 4 to 8
P. 314

Hydrangea quercifolia
Oakleaf Hydrangea
SIZE: To 8 feet
Best with light shade
Moist, organically rich soil
Late-spring white flowers, red fall foliage
Naturalizing, borders
Deciduous; Zones 5 to 9
P. 314

Hypericum 'Hidcote'
St. Johnswort hybrid
SIZE: To 5 feet
Full sun
Well-drained soil, mild climates
Golden yellow flowers from summer to fall
Hedge, borders, masses
Evergreen; Zones 6 to 9
P. 315

Ilex cornuta 'Burfordii'
Burford Holly

SIZE: To 15 feet

Full sun to part shade

Best in moderately fertile, moisture-retentive soil

Spiny leaves, red berries

Hedge, screen, shrub border

Evergreen; Zones 7 to 10

P. 316

Ilex crenata 'Dwarf Pagoda'
Japanese Holly cultivar

SIZE: Slow growing to 30 inches

Sun or shade

Moist, relatively fertile soil

Small dense leaves and irregular form

Specimen or accent

Evergreen; Zones 5 to 9

P. 316

Ilex decidua
Possumhaw
SIZE: To 18 feet
Sun or shade
Tolerates moist or dry soil, some alkalinity
Persistent orange-red berries
Naturalizing
Deciduous; Zones 4 to 9
P. 316

Ilex 'Sparkleberry'
Holly Hybrid cultivar
SIZE: To 10 feet
Sun or shade
Prefers moist, acid soils
Persistent red fruits
Massing, naturalizing
Deciduous; Zones 3 to 9
P. 318

Illicium anisatum
Star Anise
SIZE: To 12 feet
Shade or part shade
Moist, rich, acid soil out of wind
Fragrant white spring flowers
Screening, masses
Evergreen; Zones 7 to 9
P. 319

Itea virginica
Virginia Sweetspire
SIZE: To 5 feet, suckering
Best in full sun
Moist fertile soil, but adaptable
Tassels of white summer flowers
Naturalizing, mixed or shrub borders
Deciduous; Zones 6 to 9
P. 320

Itea virginica 'Henry's Garnet'

Virginia Sweetspire cultivar

SIZE: To 5 feet, suckering
Best in full sun
Moist fertile soil, but adaptable
Colorful fall foliage
Naturalizing, mixed or shrub borders
Deciduous; Zones 6 to 9
P. 320

Jasminum humile 'Revolutum'

Italian Yellow Jasmine cultivar

SIZE: To 6 feet
Full sun or part shade
Fertile, well-drained soil
Yellow flowers, late spring to early summer
Wall-training, borders
Evergreen; Zones 8 to 10
P. 321

Jasminum nudiflorum
Winter Jasmine
SIZE: To 6 feet
Full sun to part shade
Well-drained soil
Yellow flowers in late winter
Wall-training, mixed borders
Deciduous; Zones 6 to 9
P. 321

Juniperus sabina 'Broadmoor'
Savin Juniper cultivar
SIZE: To 3 feet tall and 10 feet wide
Full sun
Any well-drained soil
Gray-green foliage
Tall ground cover
Evergreen; Zones 4 to 7
P. 322

▲ *Juniperus squamata* 'Blue Star'

Blue Star Juniper
SIZE: To 3 feet
Full sun
Any well-drained soil
Silver-blue foliage
Accent, rock garden, borders
Evergreen; Zones 4 to 7
P. 323

▼ *Juniperus virginiana* 'Grey Owl'

Eastern Red Cedar cultivar
SIZE: To 6 feet
Full sun
Any well-drained soil
Silver-gray foliage
Informal hedge, shrub border
Evergreen; Zones 4 to 9
P. 323

Kalmia angustifolia
Sheep Laurel

SIZE: To 2 feet high, 10 feet wide

Part shade

Rich, acid, moist but well-drained soil

Early-summer flowers of lavender-pink to dark red

Naturalizing

Evergreen; Zones 2 to 7

P. 323

Kalmia latifolia 'Carousel'
Mountain Laurel cultivar

SIZE: To 10 feet

Part shade

Acid soil, rich, moist, well drained

Starry, calico flowers

Woodland gardens, borders, informal hedge

Evergreen; Zones 4 to 9

P. 324

Kalmia latifolia 'Olympic Fire'

Mountain Laurel cultivar

SIZE: To 10 feet
Part shade
Fertile, rich, acid soil with excellent drainage
Red buds open to pink flowers
Slopes, borders, woodland gardens
Evergreen; Zones 4 to 9
P. 324

Kerria japonica 'Pleniflora'

Japanese Kerria, double form

SIZE: To 6 feet
Full sun to part shade
Moderately fertile soil
Golden pompon flowers in spring, sporadically
    through season
Mixed borders
Deciduous; Zones 4 to 9
P. 324

Kolkwitzia amabilis
Beautybush
SIZE: From 6 to 10 feet
Full sun
Fertile, loamy, well-drained soil
Pink flowers in midspring
Shrub border
Deciduous; Zones 4 to 8
P. 325

Lagerstroemia 'Tonto'
Crape Myrtle cultivar
SIZE: To 12 feet
Full sun
Fertile, moist, well-aerated soil
Fuchsia-colored summer flowers
Masses, hedges, screens, specimens
Deciduous; Zones 7 to 9
P. 326

Laurus nobilis
Sweet Bay
SIZE: Usually 5 to 10 feet
Full sun
Moisture-retentive, well-drained soil
Fragrant foliage used in cooking
Containers, train as topiary
Evergreen; Zones 9 to 11
P. 326

Lavandula angustifolia 'White Dwarf'
English Lavender cultivar
SIZE: To 3 feet
Full sun
Poor to average, well-drained alkaline soil
Fragrant white late-summer flowers
Low hedge, herb garden, mixed border
Evergreen; Zones 5 to 8
P. 327

Lavandula × intermedia 'Grosso'

Lavender hybrid cultivar

SIZE: Less than 2 feet

Full sun

Well-drained alkaline soil, low to moderate fertility

Strongly scented lavender flowers

Mixed border, containers

Evergreen; Zones 5 to 8

P. 327

Lavandula stoechas

French Lavender

SIZE: To 2 feet

Full sun

Well-drained alkaline soil, low to moderately fertile

Dark purple flowers with fuchsia bracts

Mixed border, containers

Evergreen; Zones 8 to 9

P. 328

Lavatera maritima
Tree Mallow
SIZE: To 6 feet
Full sun
Loose, well-drained, moderately fertile soil
Pale pink summer flowers
Screen, borders, specimens
Evergreen; Zones 8 to 10
P. 328

Ledum glandulosum
Trapper's Tea
SIZE: To 5 feet
Full sun or part shade
Rich, acid, moist soil
White flowers in late spring
Rock gardens or heather companions
Evergreen; Zones 2 to 6
P. 329

Leiophyllum buxifolium
Box Sand Myrtle
SIZE: Variable; average 18 inches, suckering
Full sun to part shade
Moisture-retentive, well-drained acid soil
White flowers with pink edge, late spring
Rock or rhododendron garden
Evergreen; Zones 5 to 8
P. 330

Leptospermum scoparium
'Pink Pearl'
New Zealand Tea Tree *cultivar*
SIZE: To 10 feet
Full sun or part shade
Fertile, acid, moisture-retentive soil; best in
  mild, dry climates
Pink buds open to double white or pink flowers
Hedge or screen
Evergreen; Zones 9 to 10
P. 331

Leptospermum scoparium 'Ruby Glow'

New Zealand Tea Tree cultivar

S I Z E : To 10 feet

Full sun or part shade

Fertile, acid, moisture-retentive soil; best in
    mild, dry climates

Pink buds open to double white or pink flowers

Hedge or screen

Evergreen; Zones 9 to 10

P. 331

Lespedeza thunbergii

Thunberg Lespedeza

S I Z E : To 8 feet

Full sun

Tolerates sandy, infertile soil

Rosy purple flowers in late summer

Mixed border

Deciduous; Zones 5 to 8

P. 332

Leucophyllum frutescens
Texas Sage
S I Z E :   To 8 feet
Full sun
Slightly acid soil with excellent drainage
Silvery foliage, magenta flowers
Hedge, specimen
Evergreen; Zones 8 to 10
P. 332

Leucothoe fontanesiana
Drooping Leucothoe
S I Z E :   To 6 feet
Full to part shade
Rich, organic, moisture-retentive acid soil
Drooping white midspring flowers
Edging, rock garden, slopes, rhododendron
  garden
Evergreen; Zones 5 to 8
P. 333

Leycesteria formosa
Pheasant-eye
SIZE: To 6 feet, suckering
Full sun
Rich, organic, moist soil
White flowers with red bracts; red berries
Shrub border, wildlife garden
Deciduous; Zones 7 to 10
P. 335

Ligustrum obtusifolium
Border Privet
SIZE: To 12 feet
Full sun or part shade
Any well-drained soil
White summer flowers
Hedge, screen
Deciduous; Zones 4 to 7
P. 336

Ligustrum vicaryi
Golden Privet
SIZE: To 15 feet
Full sun or part shade
Tolerates all conditions but poor drainage
White flowers in late spring, dark berries
Hedge, screen
Semievergreen; Zones 5 to 8
P. 336

Lindera obtusiloba
Japanese Spicebush
SIZE: Rarely to 20 feet
Full sun in North, part shade in South
Organic, acid, moist, well-aerated soil
Yellow spring flowers, red then black fall berries
Attracting birds, woodlands
Deciduous; Zones 6 to 8
P. 337

Lithodora diffusa
'Grace Ward'
Lithodora cultivar

SIZE: To 6 inches tall, 2 feet wide
Full sun
Neutral to alkaline soil with excellent drainage
Blue flowers in late spring, summer
Ground cover
Evergreen; Zones 6 to 8
P. 338

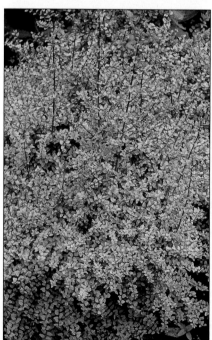

Lonicera nitida
'Baggesen's Gold'
Boxleaf Honeysuckle cultivar

SIZE: To 3 feet
Sun or shade
Moist, well-drained soil
Golden foliage
Low hedges, borders, massed plantings
Evergreen; Zones 7 to 9
P. 338

▲ *Lonicera pileata*
Privet Honeysuckle
SIZE: To 3 feet tall, 6 feet wide
Best in full sun
Moisture-retentive, well-aerated soil
White spring flowers, dark purple berries
Tall ground cover, massing
Semievergreen; Zones 6 to 8
P. 339

▼ *Loropetalum chinense* 'Burgundy'
Chinese Fringe-flower cultivar
SIZE: From 6 to 10 feet
Full sun to part shade
Rich, moist, well-drained acid soil
Spidery magenta flowers in early spring
Specimen, shrub border
Evergreen; Zones 8 to 9
P. 339

Magnolia liliiflora × *stellata* 'Randy'

Little Girl hybrid magnolia

SIZE: To 10 feet
Part shade
Rich, moist, well-drained soil
Flowers purple outside, white inside
Border or specimen
Deciduous; Zones 4 to 7
P. 340

Magnolia sieboldii

Oyama Magnolia

SIZE: To 12 feet
Part shade
Rich, moist, well-drained soil
Fragrant white flowers with red stamens
Border or specimen
Deciduous; Zones 6 to 8
P. 341

Magnolia stellata 'Centennial'
Star Magnolia cultivar
SIZE: Rarely to 20 feet
Part shade
Rich, moist, well-drained soil
White flowers with numerous narrow petals
Border or specimen
Deciduous; Zones 4 to 10
P. 341

Mahonia aquifolium 'Smaragd' (Emerald)
Oregon Grape-holly cultivar
SIZE: To 6 feet
Full to part shade
Acidic, organic, well-aerated moist soil
Yellow spring flowers, blue berries
Shady borders, woodlands
Evergreen; Zones 5 to 8
P. 342

Mahonia bealei
Leatherleaf Mahonia
SIZE: To 12 feet
Full to part shade
Organic, well-draining, acid soil
Fragrant yellow flowers, bright blue berries
Borders, attracting birds
Evergreen; Zones 7 to 9
P. 342

Mahonia repens
Creeping Mahonia
SIZE: Under 1 foot
Full to part shade
Well-amended, sharply draining, moist soil
Midspring yellow flowers, blue-black berries
Ground cover
Evergreen; Zones 4 to 7
P. 343

Michelia figo
Banana Shrub
SIZE: To 2 feet
Best in part shade
Rich, moisture retentive, acidic sandy loam
Fruit-scented yellow-green midspring flowers
Site to enjoy fragrance; can be espaliered
Evergreen; Zones 8 to 10
P. 343

Microbiota decussata
Russian Arborvitae
SIZE: To 1 foot tall, 15 feet wide
Full sun to part shade
Moist, well-drained soil; best in cool climates
Flat sprays of foliage, tiny cones
Ground cover or front of border
Evergreen; Zones 3 to 7
P. 344

▲*Myrica pensylvanica* (habit)
Bayberry
SIZE: Averages 9 feet
Full sun to part shade
Tolerates a wide range of soils, neutral to acid
Leathery leaves, blue-gray berries
Naturalizing, seaside gardens
Deciduous in North, evergreen in South;
    Zones 3 to 6
P. 345

▼*Myrica pensylvanica*
(berries)
Bayberry
SIZE: Averages 9 feet
Full sun to part shade
Tolerates a wide range of soils, neutral to acid
Leathery leaves, blue-gray berries
Naturalizing, seaside gardens
Deciduous in North, evergreen in South;
    Zones 3 to 6
P. 345

▲*Myrtus communis*
Common Myrtle
SIZE: Usually 10 to 12 feet
Full sun to light shade
Needs excellent drainage
Fragrant leaves, white late-summer flowers,
    blue-black berries
Espalier, topiary, containers
Evergreen; Zones 8 to 11
P. 346

▼*Nandina domestica*
Heavenly Bamboo
SIZE: To 6 feet, clump-forming
Berries best in full sun
Any relatively moist soil
White flowers in late spring, red berries from
    fall to winter
Masses, borders, small spaces
Evergreen; Zones 7 to 10
P. 347

▲*Nerium oleander* 'Tangier'

Oleander cultivar

SIZE: To 6 feet
Full sun to light shade
Tolerates salty, dry, or waterlogged soil
Single pink flowers
Screen, border, container
Evergreen; Zones 8 (south) to 11
P. 348

▼*Neviusia alabamensis*

Alabama Snow-wreath

SIZE: To 6 feet, suckering
Sun to part shade
Best in moisture-retentive, well-drained loam
White midspring flowers of feathery stamens
Specimen, shrub border
Deciduous; Zones 4 to 8
P. 348

Oemleria cerasiformis
Oso Berry
SIZE: To 8 feet tall, 12 feet wide
Full sun to part shade
Well-drained, moderately moist, fertile soil
Clusters of white flowers in late winter
Shrub border, naturalizing
Deciduous; Zones 6 to 10
P. 349

Osmanthus delavayi
Delavay Osmanthus
SIZE: Usually to 10 feet
Best in part shade, out of winter sun
Acidic, fertile, moist but well-drained soil
Fragrant white midspring flowers
Screen, hedges, massing
Evergreen; Zones 7 to 9
P. 350

Osmanthus heterophyllus 'Variegatus'
Variegated False Holly
SIZE: Usually to 10 feet
Best in part shade, out of winter sun
Acidic, fertile, moist but well-drained soil
Fragrant midautumn flowers, shiny toothed
    foliage
Screen, hedges, massing
Evergreen; Zones 6 to 9
P. 350

Paeonia 'Gauguin'
Tree Peony hybrid
SIZE: To 6 feet
High shade
Deep organic soil, neutral to slightly acid
Orange flowers streaked with gold
Specimen, borders
Deciduous; Zones 4 to 8
P. 352

▲*Paeonia* 'Joseph Rock' (*P. suffruticosa* var. *rockii*)

Joseph Rock Tree Peony

SIZE: To 6 feet

High shade

Neutral to slightly acid, deep organic soil

White flowers with maroon centers

Specimen, borders

Deciduous; Zones 4 to 8

P. 351

▼*Paxistima canbyi*

Cliff-green

SIZE: To 1 foot tall, 5 feet wide

Full sun to part shade

Poor alkaline soil with organic amendments

Greenish white summer flowers

Ground cover, rock garden

Evergreen; Zones 3 to 7

P. 352

Philadelphus 'Natchez'
Natchez Mock Orange
SIZE: To 10 feet
Full sun for best flowering
Does best in organic, moist soil
Heavy production of white flowers
Shrub border
Deciduous; Zones 5 to 8
P. 354

Philadelphus virginalis
Double Mock Orange
SIZE: To 10 feet
Full sun for best flowering
Does best in organic, moist soil
White flowers in late spring
Shrub border
Deciduous; Zones 5 to 8
P. 354

Phlomis fruticosa
Jerusalem Sage
SIZE: To 4 feet
Full sun
Tolerates poor soil if drainage is good
Balls of golden yellow midsummer flowers
Masses, borders, rock gardens
Evergreen; Zones 7 to 10
P. 355

Photinia × fraseri
Photinia
SIZE: To 15 feet
Full sun to part shade
Fertile, well-drained soil
Colorful foliage, white flowers
Hedge or screen
Evergreen; Zones 7 to 10
P. 355

Photinia serrulata
Chinese Photinia
SIZE: To 25 feet
Full sun to part shade
Fertile, well-drained soil
Bronzy white flowers, red berries
Hedge or screen
Evergreen; Zones 6 to 9
P. 356

Phygelius aequalis
Phygelius
SIZE: To 3 feet
Full sun in in North, part shade in South
Loose, well-amended soil
Rosy flowers from late summer to fall
Mixed border; often grown as dieback shrub
Evergreen; Zones 8 to 10
P. 356

Physocarpus opulifolius 'Luteus'

Ninebark cultivar

SIZE: From 6 to 10 feet
Full sun to part shade
Adapts to most soils
White late-spring flowers, red seed capsules
Naturalizing, informal hedges
Deciduous; Zones 2 to 7
P. 357

Picea abies 'Repens'

Norway Spruce cultivar

SIZE: To 3 feet
Full sun
Neutral, moist, well-drained soil
Spreading form, mounded in center
Borders, accent, rock garden
Evergreen; Zones 3 to 7
P. 358

Picea omorika 'Nana'

Serbian Spruce cultivar

SIZE: To 8 feet
Full sun
Moist, well-draining, neutral soil
Drooping branches
Specimen, shrub border, background
Evergreen; Zones 4 to 7

P. 359

Picea pungens 'Montgomery'

Colorado Spruce cultivar

SIZE: To 8 feet
Full sun
Moist, well-aerated, neutral soil
Silvery blue foliage
Specimen, shrub border, background
Evergreen; Zones 3 to 7

P. 359

Pieris floribunda
Mountain Pieris

SIZE: From 2 to 6 feet

Full sun in North, part shade in South; doesn't
like humidity

Organic, moist, well-draining acid soil

Upright clusters of white flowers in midspring

Borders, masses, along walks or walls

Evergreen; Zones 4 to 6

P. 360

Pieris 'Forest Flame'
Pieris hybrid

SIZE: To 4 feet

Full sun in North, part shade in South

Organic, moist, well-aerated soil

Bright red new growth, heavy flowering

Specimen, masses, shrub border, low hedge

Evergreen; Zones 7 to 8

P. 360

▲*Pieris japonica*
'Mountain Fire'
Japanese Pieris cultivar
SIZE: To 12 feet
Full sun in North, part shade in South
Well-drained organic, acidic soil
Early red foliage
Hedge, screen, specimen
Evergreen; Zones 5 to 7
P. 360

▼*Pinus mugo* 'Gnom'
Swiss Mountain Pine cultivar
SIZE: To 15 inches
Full sun
Any well-drained soil; best in mild climates
Wide mound shape
Rock gardens, mixed border
Evergreen; Zones 3 to 7
P. 361

Pinus strobus 'Nana'
Eastern White Pine cultivar
SIZE : To 3 feet
Full sun
Any well-drained soil; best in mild climates
Usually globe shaped
Borders, accent
Evergreen; Zones 3 to 7
P. 361

Pinus sylvestris 'Beuvonensis'
Scotch Pine cultivar
SIZE : To 3 feet
Full sun
Well-drained soil; mild climate
Irregular dome shape
Borders, accent
Evergreen; Zones 3 to 7
P. 362

Pittosporum tobira
Japanese Mock Orange

SIZE: From 6 to 15 feet
Sun or shade
Adaptable; tolerates drought, wind
Fragrant, creamy, early-spring flowers; unusual
    seedpods
Seaside plants, hedge, container
Evergreen; Zones 9 to 10
P. 362

Polygala × dalmaisiana
Polygala hybrid

SIZE: To 5 feet
Best in full sun
Moist, well-draining, acid soil
Magenta flowers from midsummer to fall
Mixed or shrub border
Evergreen; Zones 9 to 11
P. 363

Poncirus trifoliata
Trifoliate Orange
SIZE: From 8 to 20 feet
Full sun
Well-drained acid soil
White midspring flowers, yellow fruits
Hedge, border, wall-training
Deciduous; Zones 6 to 9
P. 364

Potentilla fruticosa
'Tangerine'
Potentilla cultivar
SIZE: To 2 feet
Part shade to retain color
Alkaline to slightly acid soil, well drained
Yellow-copper to orange-red flowers
Mixed border
Deciduous; Zones 2 to 6
P. 364

▲*Prostanthera rotundifolia*
Round-leaved Mint Bush
SIZE: To 6 feet

Full sun

Slightly acid, well-drained soil; tolerates sand, drought

Lavender spring flowers, scented foliage

Masses, border, specimen

Evergreen; Zones 9 to 10

P. 365

▼*Prunus americana*
Wild Plum
SIZE: To 20 feet, suckering

Full sun

Any well-drained soil

Fragrant white spring flowers, edible fruit

Screen, naturalizing

Deciduous; Zones 3 to 8

P. 366

Prunus besseyi
Western Sand Cherry
SIZE: To 5 feet, suckering
Full sun
Any well-drained soil
White midspring flowers, edible blue-black
    fruits
Naturalizing, attracting birds
Deciduous; Zones 3 to 6
P. 366

Prunus glandulosa
Dwarf Flowering Almond
SIZE: To 5 feet
Full sun
Well-drained soil, with some organic amend-
    ments
White or pink spring flowers
Specimen, shrub border
Deciduous; Zones 4 to 8
P. 367

Prunus 'Hally Jolivette'

Dwarf Flowering Cherry hybrid

SIZE: To 15 feet
Full sun
Amended, well-drained soil
Double white flowers from pink buds, mid-spring
Specimen
Deciduous; Zones 5 to 7
P. 367

Prunus laurocerasus 'Otto Luyken'

Otto Luyken Cherry Laurel

SIZE: To 4 feet tall, 8 feet wide
Shade to part shade
Excellent drainage; best in mild climates
Clusters of fragrant white flowers with showy stamens
Masses, shrub border
Evergreen; Zones 6 to 8
P. 367

Punica granatum (fruit)
Pomegranate
SIZE: Usually 10 feet
Best in full sun
Fertile, moist soil with good drainage
Edible fruit, colorful foliage
Shrub border, mass, container
Deciduous; Zones 8 to 10
P. 368

Punica granatum 'Wonderful'
Pomegranate cultivar
SIZE: Usually 10 feet
Best in full sun
Fertile, moist soil with good drainage
Fountainlike habit, orange-red flowers
Shrub border, mass, container
Deciduous; Zones 8 to 10
P. 368

Pyracantha coccinea 'Mohave'
Scarlet Firethorn cultivar
SIZE: From 6 to 10 feet
Full sun
Neutral to acid soil; tolerates heat, drought
Abundant white flowers, orange-red berries
Espalier, specimen, shrub border, security
    hedge
Evergreen; Zones 6 to 9
P. 369

Pyracantha 'Watereri'
Firethorn hybrid
SIZE: To 8 feet
Best in full sun
Neutral to slightly acid soil; best in hot, dry
    climates
Few thorns, many dark red berries
Specimen, shrub border, espalier
Evergreen; Zones 7 to 10
P. 369

Rhaphiolepis 'Ballerina'
Indian Hawthorn cultivar

SIZE: Under 2 feet
Best in full sun
Neutral to slightly acid soil, tolerates some
  drought
Rosy pink flowers
Container, front of border, walkway
Evergreen; Zones 8 to 10
P. 370

Rhaphiolepis umbellata
Yeddo Hawthorn

SIZE: To 6 feet
Flowers best in full sun
Moist, well-drained, neutral to slightly acid soil
White midspring flowers
Hedge, screen
Evergreen; Zones 8 to 10
P. 370

Rhododendron arborescens
Sweet Azalea
SIZE: From 10 to 20 feet
Dappled shade
Organic, well-drained acid soil
Fragrant white flowers with pink stamens
Woodland gardens, borders
Deciduous; Zones 5 to 8
P. 372

Rhododendron atlanticum
Coastal Azalea
SIZE: Rarely to 3 feet
High shade
Moist, well-drained, acid soil
Sweet-scented white to pink flowers, showy sta-
mens
Front of azalea bed, edge of woods
Deciduous; Zones 6 to 8
P. 372

▲*Rhododendron austrinum*
Florida Flame Azalea
SIZE: To 10 feet
Dappled shade
Moist, well-aerated, acid soil
Yellow-orange fruit-scented spring flowers
Open woods, naturalizing
Deciduous; Zones 7 to 9
P. 372

▼*Rhododendron calendulaceum*
Flame Azalea
SIZE: From 6 to 12 feet
Dappled shade
Organically amended acid soil
Late-spring yellow-orange flowers
Open woods, borders
Deciduous; Zones 6 to 7
P. 372

▲*Rhododrendron canescens*
Piedmont Azalea
SIZE: To 12 feet or more
High shade
Moist, well-aerated, acid soil
Sweet-scented light pink flowers
Open woods, fragrance garden
Deciduous; Zones 6 to 8
P. 372

▼*Rhododendron catawbiense*
Catawba Rhododendron
SIZE: To 10 feet
High shade
Acidic, moist, well-drained soil
Large trusses of rosy purple spring flowers
Hedge, shrub border, naturalizing
Evergreen; Zones 5 to 8
P. 372

▲*Rhododendron vaseyi*
Pinkshell Azalea
SIZE: Usually to 6 feet
High shade
Acid soil, tolerates some drought
Clusters of pink flowers, burgundy fall foliage
Woodland gardens, shady borders
Deciduous; Zones 5 to 7
P. 375

▼*Rhododendron yakushimanum*
Rhododendron species
SIZE: To 3 feet
Dappled shade
Acidic, moist, well-aerated soil
Pink buds open to white flowers
Woodland garden, shady border
Evergreen; Zones 5 to 8
P. 375

Rhodotypos scandens
Jetbead
SIZE: From 3 to 6 feet tall, 8 feet wide
Sun or shade
Adapts to most soils
White flowers in late spring, black fruits
Borders, masses
Deciduous; Zones 5 to 8
P. 376

Rhus chinensis
Chinese Sumac
SIZE: To 20 feet
Best color in full sun
Neutral to acid, well-drained soil
Cream-colored late-summer flowers,
    orange-red fruits
Shrub border, naturalizing
Deciduous; Zones 5 to 7
P. 377

Rhus copallina
Flameleaf Sumac
S I Z E : To 25 feet
Full sun
Dry, rocky, windy sites
Picturesque branches, red fall berries
Naturalizing coastal or mountain gardens
Deciduous; Zones 4 to 9
P. 377

Rhus glabra
Smooth Sumac
S I Z E : To 15 feet
Best in full sun
Well-drained, neutral to acid soil
Conical flowers, fruit clusters, colorful fall
    foliage
Shrub border, naturalizing
Deciduous; Zones 3 to 9
P. 377

Rhus trilobata
Skunkbush Sumac
SIZE: To 6 feet, suckering
Full sun
Tolerates alkaline soil, well drained
Colorful fall foliage, red fruits on females
Nauturalizing, informal hedge or border
Deciduous; Zones 4 to 6
P. 378

Rhus typhina 'Laciniata' (habit)
Cutleaf Staghorn Sumac
SIZE: To 20 feet
Best color in full sun
Excellent drainage, neutral to acid soil
Yellow-green flowers, red fruits and fall foliage
Naturalizing, shrub borders
Deciduous; Zones 4 to 8
P. 378

Rhus typhina 'Laciniata' (fruit)
Cutleaf Staghorn Sumac
SIZE: To 20 feet
Best color in full sun
Excellent drainage, neutral to acid soil
Yellow-green flowers, red fruits and fall foliage
Naturalizing, shrub borders
Deciduous; Zones 4 to 8
P. 378

Ribes aureum
Golden Currant
SIZE: From 3 to 9 feet
Best in sun, tolerates shade
Average soil
Fragrant yellow spring flowers
Massing, informal borders
Deciduous; Zones 2 to 7
P. 379

▲*Ribes odoratum*
Clove Currant
SIZE : To 7 feet, suckering
Best in sun
Average soil
Scented yellow spring flowers, burgundy fall
  leaves, edible berries
"Edible" gardens, difficult sites
Deciduous; Zones 4 to 6
P. 379

▼*Ribes sanguineum*
Winter Currant
SIZE : From 4 to 12 feet
Full sun for best fruit and berries
Ordinary soil
Pink or red spring flowers
Massing, difficult sites
Deciduous; Zones 5 to 7
P. 379

▲*Ribes speciosum*
Fuchsia-flowered Gooseberry
SIZE: To 6 feet
Needs some shade in dry climates
Moist, well-draining soil
Red, fuchsialike flowers from winter to spring
Often grown against walls for effect, protection
Semievergreen; Zones 8 to 10
P. 379

▼*Robinia hispida* 'Rosea'
Rose Acacia cultivar
SIZE: To 8 feet
Full sun
Tolerates poor, dry soil
Light pink to deep rosy lavender late-spring
    flowers
Stabilizing sandy slopes
Deciduous; Zones 5 to 8
P. 380

▲*Rosa* 'Graham Thomas'

Austin Rose cultivar

SIZE: To 4 feet

Full sun

Rich, well-drained, organic soil

Fragrant golden yellow, reblooming

Specimen, borders

Deciduous; Zones 5 to 9

P. 381

▼*Rosa* 'Perdita'

Austin Rose cultivar

SIZE: To 4 feet

Full sun

Well-amended, organic soil

Fragrant, double, reblooming apricot flowers

Rose garden, specimen

Deciduous; Zones 5 to 9

P. 381

▲*Rosa* Bonica ('Meidomonac')

Rose cultivar

SIZE: To 5 feet

Full sun

Fertile, well-amended soil

Double light pink flowers from spring to fall

Hedge, borders

Deciduous; Zones 4 to 10

P. 381

▼*Rosa* Carefree Beauty ('Beubi')

Rose cultivar

SIZE: To 4 feet

Full sun

Organic, well-drained soil

Long-blooming fragrant, semidouble pink
  flowers; orange hips

Low hedge, borders

Deciduous; Zones 4 to 9

P. 381

Rosa 'The Fairy'
Rose cultivar
SIZE: To 3 feet
Tolerates part shade
Fertile, well-drained soil
Small double pink flowers from summer to fall
Tall ground cover, low hedge
Deciduous; Zones 5 to 10
P. 381

Rosa foetida 'Bicolor'
Austrian Copper Rose
SIZE: To 5 feet
Full sun
Well-amended, moist soil with good drainage
Single copper-red flowers backed with yellow
Specimen, borders
Deciduous; Zones 4 to 8
P. 381

Rosa gallica var. *officinalis*
Apothecary's Rose
SIZE: To 3 feet
Full sun
Well-amended soil with good drainage
Late-spring semidouble pink flowers, orange-
 red hips
Herb gardens, mixed borders
Deciduous; Zones 4 to 8
P. 382

Rosa glauca
Redleaf Rose
SIZE: To 6 feet
Afternoon shade in South
Fertile, moist, well-drained soil
Deep pink spring flowers, orange-red hips,
 gray-purple foliage
Masses, herb gardens, borders
Deciduous; Zones 2 to 8
P. 382

Rosa × *harisonii*
Harison's Yellow Rose
SIZE: To 5 feet
Full sun
Well-amended soil
Semidouble or double bright yellow spring
  flowers
Mixed borders
Deciduous; Zones 3 to 8
P. 382

Rosa Meidiland Alba
SIZE: To 2½ feet
Full sun
Well-amended soil
Double white reblooming flowers
Low hedge, borders
Deciduous; Zones 5 to 9
P. 382

Rosa rugosa 'Fru Dagmar Hastrup'
Rugosa Rose cultivar

SIZE: To 4 feet

Full sun

Amended soil, moist and well draining

Pale pink flowers, dark red hips

Mixed borders, herb gardens, banks, coastal gardens

Deciduous; Zones 2 to 9

P. 382

Rosa rugosa 'Hansa'
Rugosa Rose cultivar

SIZE: To 6 feet

Full sun

Moist, well-aerated, fertile soil

Red-purple semidouble flowers, abundant hips

Coastal gardens, erosion control, herb gardens

Deciduous; Zones 2 to 9

P. 383

▲*Rosa rugosa*
'Rosearie de l'Hay'

Rugosa Rose cultivar

SIZE: To 8 feet

Full sun

Organic, well-drained soil

Crimson-purple flowers

Specimen, borders, banks, seaside gardens

Deciduous; Zones 2 to 9

P. 382

▼*Rosmarinus officinalis*

Rosemary

SIZE: From 2 to 6 feet

Full sun

Well-drained soil of moderate fertility

Blue flowers in late spring, scented foliage

Container, low hedge, border, herb garden

Evergreen, Zones 8 to 10

P. 384

▲*Rosmarinus officinalis* 'Prostratus'

Rosemary cultivar

SIZE: To 2 feet high, 4 to 8 feet wide
Full sun
Well-drained soil of moderate fertility
Blue flowers, weeping habit
Container, edge of wall
Evergreen; Zones 8 to 10

P. 384

▼*Rubus odoratus*

Flowering Raspberry

SIZE: To 6 feet, suckering
Full sun
Average, well-drained soil
Fragrant mauve summer flowers, red fall foliage
Naturalizing, difficult situations
Deciduous; Zones 5 to 8

P. 385

Rubus spectabilis
Salmonberry
SIZE: To 6 feet, forming thickets
Full sun
Ordinary, well-drained soil
Purple-pink spring flowers, pink or red fruits
Naturalizing, site for winter interest
Deciduous; Zones 5 to 8
P. 385

Ruta graveolens
Rue
SIZE: To 3 feet
Full sun
Well-drained, neutral to acid soil
Yellow-green flowers midsummer
Low hedge, herb garden, mixed border
Evergreen; Zones 4 to 9
P. 386

Salix chaenomyloides
Japanese Pussy Willow
SIZE : To 15 feet tall
Full sun
Fertile clay loam; tolerates wet conditions
Long catkins tinged with pink and gold
Wet soil, pondside
Deciduous; Zones 6 to 8
P. 387

Salix hastata 'Wehrhahnii'
Willow cultivar
SIZE : To 4 feet
Full sun
Moderately fertile clay or loam
Silvery catkins in early spring
Hedge, screen, specimen, border
Deciduous; Zones 5 to 8
P. 387

▲*Sambucus canadensis*
American Elder
SIZE: To 12 feet
Best in full sun
Moist, well-drained soil
White, flat-topped summer flowers, edible purple-black berries
Naturalizing, attracting birds, herb garden
Deciduous; Zones 3 to 9
P. 388

▼*Sambucus racemosa* 'Plumosa Aurea'
European Red Elder cultivar
SIZE: To 12 feet
Dappled shade
Moisture-retentive, well-drained soil
Chartreuse foliage, yellow spring flowers, red berries
Shrub or mixed border
Deciduous; Zones 5 to 7
P. 389

Santolina chamaecyparissus
Lavender Cotton

SIZE: To 2 feet

Full sun

Well-drained average soil

Delicate, pale gray foliage; gold button summer
 flowers

Herb gardens, edging, front of border

Evergreen; Zones 6 to 9

P. 389

Santolina rosmarinifolia
Green Santolina

SIZE: To 2 feet

Full sun

Average soil, excellent drainage

Gold button flowers in summer, pungent
 foliage

Rock gardens, herb gardens, low hedge, edging

Evergreen; Zones 7 to 10

P. 389

Sarcococca hookeriana var. *humilis*

Sweetbox variety

SIZE: To 18 inches, suckering

Best in partial shade

Moisture retentive, well-aerated, organic acid soil

Fragrant white flowers in early spring, blue-black fruits

Low hedge, edging, ground cover

Evergreen; Zones 5 to 10

P. 390

Shepherdia canadensis

Russet Buffalo Berry

SIZE: From 6 to 10 feet

Full sun

Dry, alkaline soil

Silvery leaves, small yellow-white flowers, edible yellow-red berries on females

Attracting birds, naturalizing, hedges

Deciduous; Zones 2 to 6

P. 391

Skimmia japonica (flowers)
Japanese Skimmia
SIZE: To 4 feet
Part to full shade
Moist, well-draining, organic soil
White, fragrant spring flowers, red berries
Woodland gardens, shrub borders
Evergreen; Zones 7 to 8
P. 391

Skimmia japonica (berries)
Japanese Skimmia
SIZE: To 4 feet
Part to full shade
Moist, well-draining, organic soil
White, fragrant spring flowers, red berries
Woodland gardens, shrub borders
Evergreen; Zones 7 to 8
P. 391

Sorbus reducta
Dwarf Mountain Ash
SIZE: To 3 feet
Full sun or high shade
Relatively fertile, well-drained slightly acid loam
White spring flowers, pink berries, colorful fall foliage
Low hedge
Deciduous; Zones 5 to 8
P. 392

Spartium junceum
Spanish Broom
SIZE: From 6 to 10 feet
Full sun
Poor, dry, rocky or sandy soil
Yellow flowers in early summer
Stabilizing banks; invasive in West
Deciduous; Zones 8 to 10
P. 393

Spiraea × bumalda 'Anthony Waterer'

Bumald Spirea cultivar

SIZE: To 4 feet
Full sun
Well-drained soil
Rosy pink summer flowers
Massing, shrub borders
Deciduous; Zones 4 to 8
P. 394

Spiraea × bumalda 'Goldflame'

Bumald Spirea cultivar

SIZE: To 4 feet
Full sun
Well-drained soil
Pink summer flowers, yellow new foliage
Massing, low hedge, shrub borders
Deciduous; Zones 4 to 8
P. 394

▲*Spiraea nipponica* 'Snowmound'

Snowmound Nippon Spirea

SIZE: To 5 feet

Full sun

Well-drained soil

Blue-green foliage, abundant white flowers in late spring

Masses, low hedge

Deciduous; Zones 4 to 8

P. 394

▼*Spiraea prunifolia*

Bridalwreath Spirea

SIZE: From 6 to 9 feet

Full sun

Well-drained soil

Double white flowers in midspring

Specimen, hedge, shrub border

Deciduous; Zones 4 to 8

P. 394

Spiraea thunbergii
Thunberg Spirea
SIZE: To 6 feet
Full sun
Well-drained soil
White spring flowers on arching branches
Specimen, hedge
Deciduous; Zones 4 to 8
P. 395

Stachyurus praecox
Early Spiketail
SIZE: From 6 to 10 feet
Part or high shade
Moist, well-draining, organic acid soil
Tassels of buds open to yellow-green flowers
Specimen, woodland edge
Deciduous; Zones 6 to 8
P. 395

Staphylea colchica
Colchis Bladdernut
SIZE: To 10 feet, suckering
Full sun to part shade
Moist, well-drained soil
Panicles of white spring flowers
Naturalizing, shrub border, woodland edge
Deciduous; Zones 6 to 7
P. 396

Stephanandra incisa
Cutleaf Stephanandra
SIZE: To 7 feet
Full sun to part shade
Moist, well-aerated, organic acid soil
Greenish white spring flowers, colorful fall
   foliage
Hedges, massing
Deciduous; Zones 5 to 8
P. 397

Styrax americanus
American Snowbell
SIZE: To 10 feet
Part shade
Moist to wet peaty soil
Fragrant white spring flowers
Specimen, woodland edge
Deciduous; Zones 6 to 8
P. 398

Styrax obassia
Fragrant Snowbell
SIZE: To 20 feet or more
Part shade
Moist, well-drained, acid soil
Fragrant white flowers in spring
Specimen, rhododendron companion
Deciduous; Zones 5 to 8
P. 398

▲*Symphoricarpos albus*
Common Snowberry
SIZE: From 3 to 6 feet
Sun or shade
Wide range of soils
Persistent white berries
Naturalizing, erosion control
Deciduous; Zones 3 to 7
P. 398

▼*Symplocos paniculata*
Sapphireberry
SIZE: From 10 to 20 feet
Full sun to light shade
Moist, well-aerated, fertile, neutral to acid soil
White flowers in late spring, turquoise berries
   in fall
Informal hedge or screen
Deciduous; Zones 4 to 8
P. 399

Syringa × chinensis
Chinese Lilac
SIZE: From 8 to 15 feet
Full sun
Neutral to alkaline, well-amended soil
Delicate habit, fragrant lavender flowers
Specimen, masses, foundations, borders
Deciduous; Zones 3 to 7
P. 400

Syringa × hyacinthiflora
'Excel'
Lilac hybrid cultivar
SIZE: To 12 feet
Full sun
Neutral to alkaline, moist, well-drained soil
Fragrant soft pink to lilac flowers in spring
Borders, foundations, masses
Deciduous; Zones 3 to 7
P. 400

Syringa meyeri 'Palibin'
Meyer Lilac cultivar
SIZE: To 5 feet
Full sun
Well-amended, neutral to acid soil
Reddish purple buds open pink-white or pink-lavender
Specimen, borders, masses
Deciduous; Zones 4 to 7
P. 401

Syringa patula 'Miss Kim'
Manchurian Lilac cultivar
SIZE: To 8 feet
Full sun
Neutral to acid, well-draining moist soil
Pale lilac flowers in upright clusters
Specimen, borders, masses
Deciduous; Zones 4 to 7
P. 401

Syringa persica
Persian Lilac
SIZE: From 4 to 8 feet
Full sun
Well-drained soil, neutral to acid
Fragrant pale lilac flowers
Borders, foundations
Deciduous; Zones 3 to 7
P. 401

Syringa reticulata
Japanese Tree Lilac
SIZE: To 30 feet
Full sun
Neutral to acid soil, generously amended
White flowers from spring to late summer
Specimen
Deciduous; Zones 4 to 7
P. 402

▲ *Tamarix ramosissima*
Salt Cedar
SIZE: To 15 feet
Full sun
Adapts to most soils
Rosy pink flowers in late spring
Shrub border; invasive in West
Deciduous; Zones 3 to 8
P. 402

▼ *Taxus baccata* 'Repandens'
English Yew cultivar
SIZE: From 2 to 4 feet
Sun or shade
Average soil; tolerates pollution and drought
Sickle-shaped leaves, drooping branch tips
Specimen, accent
Evergreen; Zones 5 to 7
P. 403

▲ *Taxus cuspidata* 'Nana'
Dwarf Japanese Yew
SIZE: Over many years, to 10 or 20 feet
Sun or shade
Any well-drained soil, out of wind
Wide-spreading, produces red fruits
Specimen, accent
Evergreen; Zones 4 to 7
P. 403

▼ *Taxus cuspidata* 'Green Wave'
Yew cultivar
SIZE: To 4 feet tall, 8 feet wide
Full sun to dense shade
Adapts to any well-drained soil
Graceful spreading branches
Hedge, screen, accent
Evergreen; Zones 4 to 7
P. 403

Tecoma stans

Yellow Bells, Trumpet Bush

SIZE: To 20 feet

Full sun

Deep, fertile, moist, well-drained soil

Bright yellow flowers from early summer to winter

Shrub border, screening

Evergreen; Zone 10

P. 404

Ternstroemia gymnanthera 'Burnished Gold'

Ternstroemia cultivar

SIZE: Usually 4 feet

Part shade

Moisture-retentive, well-aerated, organic acid soil

Fragrant creamy flowers in late spring; yellow-bronze foliage

Specimen, hedge, screen

Evergreen; Zones 7 to 9

P. 404

▲ *Tetrapanax papyrifer*
Rice-paper Plant
SIZE: To 15 feet, suckering
Full sun
Average, well-drained soil
Creamy panicles in fall, orange-red berries
Shrub border
Evergreen; Zones 7 to 10
P. 405

▼ *Teucrium chamaedrys*
Wall Germander
SIZE: To 18 inches
Full sun
Poor, sandy, neutral to alkaline soil
Rosy pink flowers, summer to fall
Edging, container, topiary
Evergreen to Zone 7; Zones 5 to 10
P. 406

Teucrium fruticans 'Azureum'

Shrubby Germander cultivar

SIZE: To 3 feet
Full sun
Poor to average, neutral to alkaline soil
Edging, container, mixed border
Silvery green leaves, pale blue summer flowers
Evergreen; Zones 8 to 10
P. 406

Thuja occidentalis 'Hetz Midget'

American Arborvitae cultivar

SIZE: To 4 feet
Full sun or light shade
Moist, well-draining, fertile soil
Globe shape
Accent, mixed borders
Evergreen; Zones 3 to 7
P. 406

Thuja occidentalis 'Rheingold'
American Arborvitae cultivar

SIZE: To 4 feet
Full sun or light shade
Moist, well-aerated, fertile soil
Globe shape, dark gold foliage
Mixed or shrub border, accent
Evergreen; Zones 3 to 7
P. 406

Thuja occidentalis 'Smaragd' (Emerald)
American Arborvitae cultivar

SIZE: To 15 feet tall, 4 feet wide
Full sun to light shade
Fertile, well-aerated soil; tolerates some drought
Narrow pyramid habit
Accent, screen
Evergreen; Zones 3 to 7
P. 406

Thujopsis dolobrata 'Nana'
Hiba Arborvitae cultivar
SIZE: To 3 feet
Sun in North, part shade in South
Organic, moist, acid soil
Graceful mounded habit
Mixed or shrub border, edging
Evergreen; Zones 5 to 7
P. 407

Tibouchina urvilleana
Glory Bush
SIZE: To 15 feet
Full sun
Fertile, moist, acid soil
Satiny, deep purple flowers summer through
    fall
Shrub border
Evergreen; Zone 10
P. 408

Tsuga canadensis 'Jeddeloh'
Canadian Hemlock cultivar
SIZE: To 4 feet tall, 6 feet wide
Part shade
Moist, well-drained soil, preferably acid
Hemispherical habit
Borders, accent
Evergreen; Zones 3 to 7
P. 409

Tsuga canadensis 'Jervis'
Canadian Hemlock cultivar
SIZE: To 2 feet
Part shade
Best in acid soil, moist and well drained
Dense and irregular habit
Accent, borders
Evergreen; Zones 3 to 7
P. 409

Tsuga canadensis 'Pendula'

Canadian Hemlock cultivar

SIZE: To 12 feet
Part shade
Moist, well-drained soil, preferably acidic
Broadly spreading and weeping habit
Specimen
Evergreen; Zones 3 to 7
P. 409

Vaccinium corymbosum (fall foliage)

Highbush Blueberry

SIZE: From 6 to 12 feet
Full sun to part shade
Acidic, moisture-retentive, well-drained soil
Colorful fall foliage
Hedge, mixed or shrub borders
Deciduous; Zones 3 to 7
P. 409

Vaccinium corymbosum 'Sunshine Blue' (flowers)

Highbush Blueberry cultivar

SIZE: From 6 to 12 feet
Full sun to part shade
Acidic, moisture-retentive, well-drained soil
White midspring flowers, edible berries
Hedge, mixed or shrub borders
Deciduous; Zones 3 to 7
P. 409

Viburnum acerifolium

Mapleleaf Viburnum

SIZE: To 6 feet
Sun or shade
Acid, well-drained soil; tolerates drought
Creamy flat-topped spring flowers, black fruits
Naturalizing, masses
Deciduous; Zones 4 to 8
P. 410

Viburnum alnifolium

Hobblebush

SIZE: Usually to 6 feet

Full sun to part shade

Moist, well-drained, acid soil

Lacy white flowers, red fruits turning purple-
black

Naturalizing

Deciduous; Zones 4 to 7

P. 410

Viburnum × burkwoodii 'Mohawk'

Burkwood Viburnum cultivar

SIZE: To 7 feet

Full sun to part shade

Moist, well-aerated acid soil

Intensely fragrant white spring flowers open
from red buds

Specimen, borders

Deciduous to semievergreen; Zones 5 to 8

P. 410

Viburnum carlesii
Korean Spice Viburnum
SIZE: To 6 feet
Full sun to part shade
Moist, well-drained, acid soil
Fragrance garden, borders, informal hedge
Deciduous; Zones 5 to 8
P. 411

Viburnum cassinoides
Witherod Viburnum
SIZE: Usually to 6 feet
Full sun to part shade
Moist, organically enriched acid soil
White midsummer flowers; berries green, pink, red, blue, black
Naturalizing, shrub border
Deciduous; Zones 3 to 8
P. 411

Viburnum 'Cayuga'
Viburnum hybrid
SIZE: To 5 feet
Sun to part shade
Acid soil, well amended
Pink flower buds open to white in spring
Borders, masses
Deciduous; Zones 5 to 8
P. 411

Viburnum dentatum
Arrowwood Viburnum
SIZE: To 10 feet
Full sun to part shade
Moist, well-draining, acid soil
Flat-topped clusters of white spring flowers;
    blue-black fruits
Attracting birds, naturalizing, informal hedge
    or screen
Deciduous; Zones 3 to 8
P. 411

▲ *Viburnum dilatatum*
'Erie' (flowers)
Linden Viburnum cultivar
SIZE: To 9 feet
Full sun to part shade
Moist, well-draining, acid soil
Flat clusters of white spring flowers
Informal hedge or screen, shrub border
Deciduous; Zones 5 to 7
P. 411

▼ *Viburnum dilatatum* (fruit)
Linden Viburnum
SIZE: To 9 feet
Full sun to part shade
Moist, well-draining, acid soil
Red berries, colorful fall foliage
Informal hedge or screen, shrub border
Deciduous; Zones 5 to 7
P. 411

Viburnum 'Eskimo'
Viburnum hybrid
SIZE: To 5 feet
Full sun or part shade
Moist, well-aerated, acid soil
White snowball spring flowers, red fruits turn black
Shrub border, massing
Semievergreen; Zones 6 to 8
P. 412

Viburnum lantana 'Mohican'
Wayfaring Tree cultivar
SIZE: To 7 feet
Full sun to part shade
Acid to slightly alkaline soil, tolerates some drought
Flat-topped cream flowers; yellow berries turn red, black
Hedge, screen, shrub border
Deciduous; Zones 4 to 7
P. 412

▲ *Viburnum opulus* (fruit)
Cranberrybush Viburnum
SIZE: From 8 to 12 feet
Full sun to part shade
Moist, acid soil
Lacecap white flowers, yellow berries turn red
Attracting birds, screen, shrub border
Deciduous; Zones 3 to 8
P. 413

▼ *Viburnum opulus* 'Roseum' (flowers)
Snowball Bush
SIZE: From 8 to 12 feet
Full sun to part shade
Moist, acid soil
White snowball flowers
Specimen, screen, shrub border
Deciduous; Zones 3 to 8
P. 413

Viburnum plicatum var. *tomentosum* (flowers)
Doublefile Viburnum
SIZE : To 6 feet tall, 12 feet wide
Full sun to part shade
Moist, well-aerated, acid soil
White lacecap flowers in double rows
Specimen, shrub border
Deciduous; Zones 5 to 8
P. 413

Viburnum plicatum var. *tomentosum* (fruit)
Doublefile Viburnum
SIZE : To 6 feet tall, 12 feet wide
Full sun to part shade
Moist, well-aerated, acid soil
Red berries turn black
Specimen, shrub border
Deciduous; Zones 5 to 8
P. 413

Viburnum trilobum
American Cranberrybush Viburnum
SIZE: From 8 to 12 feet
Full sun to part shade
Moist, acid soil
White lacecap flowers, red fruits, colorful fall foliage
Shrub border, hedge, screen
Deciduous; Zones 2 to 7
P. 414

Vitex agnus-castus
Chaste Tree
SIZE: Usually 10 feet
Full sun
Any well-drained soil
Lavender summer flowers, fragrant foliage
Hedge, specimen, shrub border
Deciduous; Zones 7 to 10
P. 415

Weigela florida 'Red Prince'
Weigela cultivar
SIZE: To 5 feet
Full sun
Adapts to most soils
Long-blooming rich red flowers
Shrub border
Deciduous; Zones 5 to 8
P. 415

Weigela florida 'Variegata'
Weigela cultivar
SIZE: To 6 feet
Full sun
Adapts to most soils
Light pink flowers, variegated foliage
Shrub border
Deciduous; Zones 5 to 8
P. 415

Wisteria macrostachys 'Clara Mack'

White Kentucky Wisteria

SIZE: Variable when trained as shrub
Full sun
Adapts to wide range of soils
Lightly scented white flowers
Train as specimen shrub or against wall
Deciduous; Zones 4 to 8

P. 417

Xanthoriza simplicissima

Yellowroot

SIZE: To 3 feet, suckering
Full sun to part shade
Moist soil
Colorful fall foliage
Ground cover
Deciduous; Zones 3 to 9

P. 418

Yucca aloifolia
Dagger Plant
SIZE: Usually to 10 feet
Full sun
Any well-drained soil
White summer flowers, pointed leaves
Accent, container
Evergreen; Zones 7 to 10
P. 418

Yucca filamentosa
'Golden Sword'
Adam's Needle cultivar
SIZE: To 2½ feet tall, 5 feet wide
Full sun
Any well-aerated soil
Off-white summer flowers, variegated foliage
Accent, container
Evergreen; Zones 4 to 9
P. 418

Zenobia pulverulenta
Dusty Zenobia

SIZE: From 2 to 6 feet tall, 6 feet wide

Full sun or part shade

Moist, acid soil

White summer flowers, blue-green foliage that turns yellow-orange or burgundy

Massing, pondsides

Deciduous or semievergreen; Zones 6 to 9

P. 419

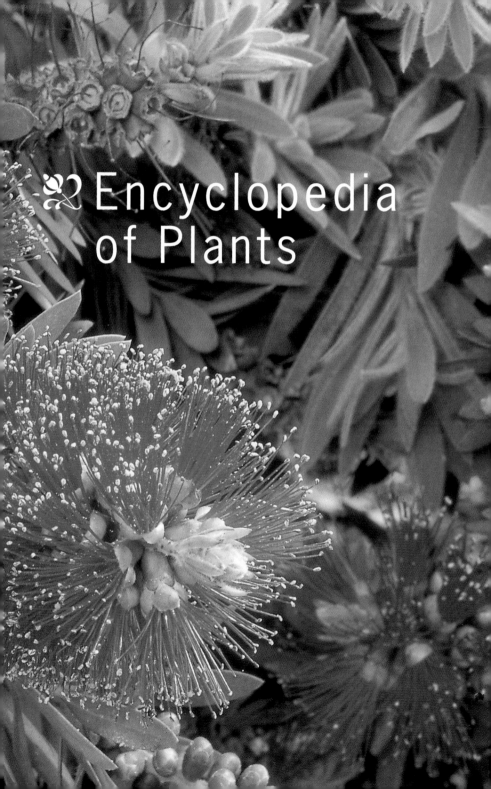
Encyclopedia of Plants

❧ Encyclopedia of Plants

❦ *Abelia*

uh-BEEL-yuh. Honeysuckle family, Caprifoliaceae

This genus encompasses up to 30 species of evergreen and deciduous shrubs found on hills and in open woods in Mexico, the Himalayas, and East Asia. Gardeners grow a handful of species and, particularly, the following two hybrids, for their glossy green leaves and arching branches. Small pink to white funnel-shaped flowers bloom in mid- to late season, and when they drop, lobed calyces often remain to extend the season of interest.

HOW TO GROW

Give abelias sun or part shade and moisture-retentive acid soil. They are popular for hedges and work well on banks or in masses. They require minimal pruning but can be pruned hard in spring if they outgrow their space. You can propagate them easily from cuttings or seeds sown as soon as they are collected.

A. × *grandiflora*   P. 40

a. × grand-ih-FLOR-uh. Glossy Abelia. This rounded, many-branched semievergreen shrub grows 6 feet tall and wide, sometimes larger in the South. Flowering begins from midspring to midsummer, depending on the region, and lasts into fall. The lightly scented pink-tinged white flowers appear on the ends of the arching branches. Rosy sepals with two to five lobes can persist for months after flowers fall. In the South, so do the lustrous oval leaves, often tinged bronzy purple through winter. Variegated cultivars include the trademarked Confetti and 'Sunrise'. Zones 6 to 10.

A. 'Edward Goucher'. A slightly smaller hybrid, about 5 feet tall and wide, with bumpy-surfaced leaves emerging bronze. The trumpet-shaped flowers are lavender pink, blooming heavily from early summer until frost, and the sepals are usually two-lobed. Zones 6 to 10.

❧ *Abeliophyllum*

uh-beel-ee-oh-FY-lum. Olive family, Oleaceae.

A single species of deciduous shrub from the hills of Korea, related to forsythia and grown for its fragrant early-spring flowers.

HOW TO GROW
White forsythia needs full sun to flower best, as well as fertile, well-drained soil. After blooming, cut back all stems to strong buds near the ground to encourage a denser, fountainlike shape. Use it in masses, or in a shrub border. Propagate with softwood cuttings or layering. Buds are less likely to be killed by late frosts than those of true forsythia. Zones 5 to 9.

A. distichum   P. 40
a. DISS-tih-kum. White Forsythia. An open, spreading shrub 5 feet tall and wide with arching branches. In late winter or early spring, cross-shaped fragrant white flowers bloom in axillary racemes before the leaves appear. The bare stems and the base of the flower may have a purplish tinge. 'Roseum' has pink flowers. Zones 5 to 9.

❧ *Abutilon*

uh-BEW-tih-lon. Mallow family, Malvaceae.

This genus of some 150 species of perennials, annuals, and deciduous and evergreen shrubs and small trees is native to warm climates throughout the world, although the most popular species hail from South America. Their leaves, often lobed, have earned them the common names of flowering maple and parlor maple, but they are valued by gardeners primarily for their bell-shaped or occasionally saucer-shaped pendent flowers, sometimes with calyces and stamens in contrasting colors.

HOW TO GROW
Flowering maple needs full sun and moderately fertile, well-drained soil. Some species develop an almost vinelike habit, which makes them ideal

for training against a sunny wall, especially where they are borderline hardy. Where they are not cold hardy they are grown in containers for overwintering indoors, but there they can be susceptible to whitefly and scale. Blooming on new growth, they can be pruned anytime by pinching or, if heavier pruning is needed (up to one-third or even one-half of branch length), in late winter or very early spring. Propagate from seeds, softwood cuttings in spring, or semihard cuttings in summer.

A. × hybridum   P. 41
a. × hy-BRID-um. Chinese Lantern. This popular evergreen hybrid grows to 10 feet tall and wide with arching branches and maplelike leaves, often variegated. The common name was inspired by the bell-shaped flowers, which bloom on their long stalks from mid- to late spring, some almost continuously. Appearing singly in the leaf axil, they can be red, orange, peach, yellow, white, pink, or purple. Zones 9 to 10.

A. megapotamicum   P. 41
a. meg-uh-poh-TAM-ih-kum. Trailing Abutilon. This evergreen or semievergreen shrub grows quickly to an average of 8 feet tall and wide. The slender, arching shoots are interesting against a wall or pruned hard for a hanging basket. Leaves up to 3 inches long are shaped like arrowheads. From late spring until fall, yellow flowers with purple stamens jut out of bright red dangling calyces. Zones 8 to 10.

A. pictum
a. PIK-tum. An evergreen shrub sometimes reaching 15 feet tall and eventually as wide, this native of Brazil has lobed leaves and orange bell-shaped flowers with red veins. They bloom from late spring until fall on long stalks. 'Thomsonii' has yellow-variegated leaves and slightly paler flowers. Zones 8 to 10.

A. vitifolium
a. vy-tih-FOL-lee-um. This deciduous shrub from Chile grows quickly up to 15 feet tall and about half as wide. The leaves, which can be 6 inches long, are shaped like grape leaves, so the species gets its name from that genus, *Vitis*. Both leaves and stems are covered with gray down. The five-petaled, saucer-shaped summer flowers can be either white or lavender blue and droop from long stalks. Zones 8 to 9.

☙ *Acacia*

uh-KAY-shuh. Pea family, Fabaceae.

Sometimes called wattle or mimosa, this is a huge genus of evergreen or deciduous shrubs, trees, and vines hailing from the tropics or warm temperate areas of Australia, Africa, and the Americas. About 30 species are available as seeds or plants. In many species, ferny leaves on young plants give way to flattened leafstalks called phyllodes. The balls or spikes of flowers, always yellow and often fragrant, are sometimes followed by ornamental seedpods.

HOW TO GROW

Acacias like full sun but tolerate poor soil, heat, drought, and wind. If they receive adequate water when planted, they can form deep roots that will help anchor banks and slopes. They can be trained when young as shrubs (by removing the central leader) or trees (by limbing up) and make good screens or windbreaks. The pods attract birds. Propagate from seeds soaked overnight.

A. cultriformis
P. 42

a. kul-trih-FOR-miss. Knife Acacia. An evergreen averaging about 12 feet tall and wide, this shrub earns its common name from 1-inch silvery green phyllodes that are asymmetrical, like a paring knife. The flowers bloom early to midspring. Zones 9 to 11.

A. decora

a. deh-KOR-uh. Graceful Wattle. A rounded evergreen 6 to 8 feet tall and wide with 2-inch, lance-shaped phyllodes and profuse, bright yellow, fragrant spring flowers. It takes to shearing for a hedge. Zone 10.

A. greggii

a. GREG-ee-eye. Catclaw Acacia. This deciduous native of the southwestern United States and northern Mexico grows 6 to 8 feet tall as a shrub and 10 feet when pruned as a tree. Its finely divided leaves are feathery. The common name comes from curved thorns that cover the branches. Late-spring bloom sometimes repeats in fall. Needs some extra pruning to reshape the natural form, which is a dense, spreading tangle. Zones 9 to 10.

A. redolens

a. REH-doh-lenz. This dense evergreen can grow more than 20 feet tall, with gray-green phyllodes and yellow puffball flowers in spring. Better known than the species may be its sideways-growing cultivar, 'Prostrata', which stays about 2 feet tall but can spread to 15 feet wide. A useful ground cover in poor soil, it is sometimes sold as 'Ongerup'. Zone 10.

A. verticillata

a. ver-tiss-il-AY-tuh. Prickly Moses. Growing 15 feet tall and wide, this evergreen species is distinguished by dark green ¾-inch needlelike phyllodes, sometimes in whorls. It has a bushy habit if pruned, but its natural habit is open with twisted branches. Inch-long spikes of yellow flowers bloom in midspring. Zones 9 to 10.

❦ Acca (syn. Feijoa)

AK-uh. Myrtle family, Myrtaceae.

This genus contains two or three species of evergreen shrubs from dry habitats in South American subtropics. Only one is commonly grown, for its showy midsummer flowers and, in the southern part of its range, edible fruits.

HOW TO GROW

Acca prefers a light, loamy soil in full sun, but can tolerate shade where fruiting isn't an issue. (Fruit needs temperatures that stay above 40°F.) Sometimes used as a hedge, it tolerates dry, sandy soil and salt spray but not cold wind. Prune lightly after flowering if grown only as an ornamental. Propagate by seeds or semiripe cuttings.

A. sellowiana P. 42

a. sel-oh-wee-AY-nuh. Pineapple Guava. This native of Brazil and Uruguay grows 8 to 10 feet tall and wide with opposite, oval leaves that are a lustrous, powdery blue-green and up to 1½ inches long. The late-spring flowers, 1½ inches across, are four thick, cupped petals, white on the back and red inside, with a starburst of showy stamens. The 2-inch egg-shaped fruits are green with a red tinge, maturing to yellow in late summer and early fall. Zones 8 to 10.

❦ Acer

AY-sur. Maple family, Aceraceae.

Most of the 150 maple species are evergreen or deciduous trees—from North and Central America, Europe, Asia, and North Africa—but a few are small or slow growing enough to qualify as shrubs. Palmately lobed leaves (resembling a hand) are so definitive of maples that lobed leaves on other plants are often described as "maplelike." Colorful fall foliage is their chief attraction; the small spring flowers often go unnoticed unless backlit by morning or evening sun; their "parachute" fruits, or samaras, can also be ornamental.

HOW TO GROW

Maples need moisture-retentive but well-drained soil. While other maples can take sun or part shade, the red Japanese maples need dappled shade, since they will turn green in deep shade but burn in hot summer sun. Give them soil richly amended with organic matter, plenty of water during drought, and protection from strong winds. Leaf tips may be browned by wind or late-spring frosts, although this damage is mainly cosmetic. Amur maple is tolerant of drought, wind, shade, and some alkalinity. Small maples will adapt to containers but grow more slowly. Maples are bleeders, so wait until fall or winter to do any pruning. Propagate from seeds planted immediately after collecting.

A. palmatum var. *dissectum*   P. 43

a. pal-MAY-tum var. dy-SEK-tum. Japanese Maple. The Japanese maples— some sources list more than 150 cultivars—are known for their graceful form, deeply dissected deciduous leaves, reddish purple flowers and fruits, and intense fall colors. This botanical variety has finely dissected leaves and forms a 6-foot-tall mound 10 feet across with fall foliage that is brilliant yellow, orange, and red. 'Dissectum Atropurpureum' and 'Nigrum' (more often sold as 'Ever Red') have reddish purple leaves. 'Filigree' has green leaves specked with gold and cream. Two selections have received the prestigious Gold Medal of the Pennsylvania Horticultural Society: 'Tamukeyama', 13 feet tall with dissected leaves that are crimson in spring and purple in fall, and 'Waterfall', a green-leaved form valued for its weeping shape. Zones 6 to 8.

A. tataricum ssp. ginnala

P. 43

a. tuh-TAR-ih-kum ssp. gih-NAY-luh. Amur Maple. This deciduous subspecies can grow to 20 feet tall or more, but is frequently multistemmed and shrublike in habit. The 1½- to 3-inch toothed leaves have three lobes, the middle one longer than the other two. The yellow-white spring flowers are fragrant, and the fall foliage is yellow and red in full sun. You can prune it heavily to a desired shape. For a smaller plant (about 5 feet) look for 'Durand Dwarf'. 'Flame' has red summer fruits and bright red autumn leaves. Some naturalists report problems with this species being invasive in the Midwest, so avoid planting it adjacent to natural areas. Zones 3 to 7

✿ Aesculus

ES-cue-lus. Horse-chestnut family, Hippocastanaceae.

This genus includes 15 deciduous shrubs and trees from northern temperate areas, grown for handsome palmate leaves and upright panicles of flowers, followed by 1- to 3-inch round fruits. The shrub species are native to open woods in the southeastern United States. Both of those listed here have received the Pennsylvania Horticultural Society's Gold Medal.

HOW TO GROW

Give these shrubs sun or part shade and soil that is acidic, well drained, and rich in organic matter. They need little pruning (although bottle-brush buckeye can be pruned to the ground). Propagate from seed (each capsule bears only one or two, shiny and dark brown), which ripens in hot summers, planting them outdoors as soon as you collect them and leaving them to germinate in spring. You can also start bottlebrush buckeye from root cuttings or by dividing suckers.

A. parviflora

P. 44

a. par-vih-FLOR-uh. Bottlebrush Buckeye. This southern U.S. native shrub spreads so wide—15 feet compared to a 9- to 12-foot height—that one plant is about all any garden can handle. In a large space, one is a hedge all by itself. The palmately compound leaves have five to seven leaflets up to 9 inches long that turn bright yellow in autumn. The white cylinder flowers, set off by pink stamens and red anthers, are borne in upright clusters up to 1 foot high, appearing in late summer. In warm areas it develops smooth brown fruits. Zones 5 to 8.

A. pavia
P. 44

a. PAY-vee-uh. Red Buckeye. Palmately compound leaves of five to seven lance-shaped leaflets are crowned in late spring by 6-inch cones of red tubular flowers that attract hummingbirds and can be used as cut flowers. This species is more treelike than *A. parviflora*, often with a single trunk and growing slowly to 15 feet. *A. pavia* var. *splendens* is considered more resistant to sunscorch than the species. *A. pavia* var. *flavescens* has yellow flowers, while 'Atrosanguinea' has deeper red flowers than the species. Zones 5 to 8.

❦ *Aloysia*

al-OY-shuh. Verbena family, Verbenaceae.

In this genus there are 37 deciduous or evergreen shrubs native to rocky soil in the southwestern United States and South America. The single species that is commonly grown is considered an herb, since its lemon-scented foliage is used in potpourri and teas. The oil is used in colognes and other commercial scents.

HOW TO GROW

Give lemon verbena moderately moist and fertile soil in full sun. Where it is not hardy, you can grow it in a container, fertilizing it monthly spring through fall with an organic fertilizer. Some growers recommend pruning it back by half in midsummer and again in fall. Lemon verbena can be trained as a standard. Indoors in winter (where it will drop its leaves), stop feeding it and keep it barely damp. It is especially susceptible to spider mite and whiteflies. Propagate from softwood cuttings.

A. citriodora (syn. A. triphylla)
P. 45

a. sit-tree-oh-DOR-uh. Lemon Verbena. This deciduous species will reach 8 feet or taller in frost-free areas. The lemon-scented leaves are 2 to 4 inches long, narrow and lance shaped in whorls of three. In late summer, tiny white or pale lavender flowers bloom in 5-inch spikes from the leaf axils, but are not at all showy. Zones 8 to 11.

❦ *Amelanchier*

am-eh-LAN-kyer. Rose family, Rosaceae.

About 25 deciduous trees and shrubs native to North America, Europe, and Asia. Several species and cultivars—all very similar—are grown for starry white early-spring flowers, colorful autumn foliage, and small edible fruits. They are often classified as small trees, but their tendency to sucker makes them upright shrubs. The common name, "serviceberry" or "sarvice," is attributed sometimes to their early-spring bloom time, which coincided with the ground thawing enough for burials, and sometimes to the berries being used for wine in church.

HOW TO GROW

Give serviceberry sun or part shade and moisture-retentive but well-aerated acid soil. (*A. alnifolia* is more tolerant of alkaline soil than other species.) These plants are excellent at the edge of a wood or other moist, natural area such as a streambank, where their delicate flowers will be reflected and birds will flock to their fruits. (The fruits are said to make terrific pies if you can rescue any.) Serviceberries don't tolerate stressors such as drought or pollution and are susceptible to problems that plague other members of the rose family, such as Japanese beetles. They don't require or even like regular pruning, but you can remove suckers in winter if you want a more treelike shape. Propagate from root cuttings or seeds that are never allowed to dry out.

A. alnifolia   P. 45
a. al-nih-FOH-lee-uh. Alder-leaved Serviceberry. Also called Saskatoon, this northwest U.S. native is a suckering shrub averaging 12 feet tall, with 2-inch oval leaves, racemes of ¾-inch white flowers, red or yellow fall foliage, and purple-black berries. 'Regent' grows only 4 to 6 feet tall and has especially sweet fruit. Zones 4 to 5.

A. canadensis
a. kan-uh-DEN-siss. Shadblow Serviceberry. Native to the eastern United States, shadblow forms a thicket of suckering shoots up to 20 feet tall. The 4-inch leaves are initially gray and hairy. The white flowers are in erect racemes more than 2 inches long, followed by ½-inch blue-black fruits. Fall leaves are yellow, orange, and red. Zones 4 to 7.

A. stolonifera
a. stoh-lon-IF-er-uh. Running Serviceberry. This species differs from others primarily in stature, reaching only 6 feet tall and narrower. The leaves are white and hairy underneath when young. Zones 4 to 8.

❦ Andromeda
an-DROM-uh-duh. Heath family, Ericaceae.

Of two species of low evergreen shrubs from cool areas of the Northern Hemisphere, one is commonly grown for its small urn-shaped flowers and needlelike leaves. It is one of those valuable shrubs that takes happily to poorly drained areas and is useful for naturalizing.

HOW TO GROW
Bog rosemary needs a shady home in moist, peaty, acid soil. Adding peat to sand will create an ideal medium. This shrub's size makes it useful for a shady rock garden, a pondside bog garden, or the front of a damp, wooded border. Mulch it with leaf mold and prune after flowering only to keep it shapely. Propagate from softwood cuttings, layering, or suckers.

A. polifolia (syn. A. rosmarinifolia)   P. 46
a. pawl-ih-FOH-lee-uh. Bog Rosemary. Only about a foot tall and 8 inches wide, it may be erect or slightly floppy. The leaves are pointed and leathery, like the culinary herb rosemary, inspiring its common name. White or pale pink flowers appear in umbels of two to five, in spring to early summer. Zones 2 to 6.

❦ Aralia
uh-RAYL-yuh. Ginseng family, Araliaceae.

Some 40 deciduous and evergreen trees, shrubs, and perennials native to the Americas and Asia. The deciduous shrubs grown in gardens have dramatic spiny stems, large pinnately compound leaves that provide bright fall color, and mops of white flowers followed by dark fruits that birds love.

HOW TO GROW
Most aralias are native to mountain woods and appreciate fertile, humusy, but sharply draining soil, where they are sheltered from wind.

Site your plant in either sun or shade where a thicket of spiny stems can be admired but won't become a problem because of close proximity to passersby. The texture and habit can offer eye-catching contrast to smoother or more horizontal plants. You may want to remove suckers, especially green-leaved ones that appear around the base of variegated cultivars. Root stem cuttings or suckers, or plant stratified seeds.

A. elata (syn. *A. chinensis*) P. 47

a. eh-LAH-tuh. Japanese Angelica Tree. Growing 20 feet tall and suckering as wide, its spiny stems sprout leaves to 4 feet long with 80 or more leaflets that turn purple, orange, or yellow in fall. In late summer, it is topped with fluffy white flower clusters up to 2 feet across, then swags of black fruits. 'Variegata' has white-margined leaves, edges of 'Aureovariegata' are yellow; both are somewhat smaller than the species. Zones 4 to 9.

A. spinosa P. 47

a. spin-OH-suh. Devil's Walking Stick. Sometimes called Hercules' club, this eastern U.S. native grows to 15 feet with leaves up to 5 feet long radiating from its top like an umbrella. It may be slightly less hardy than the Asian species. The 2-foot flower clusters are more cone shaped and appear mid-summer. Zones 4 to 9.

❧ *Arbutus*

ar-BEW-tus. Heath family, Ericaceae.

Of 145 species of evergreen trees or shrubs from the western United States, the Mediterranean, and Central America, only one can qualify as a garden shrub. This species straddles the fence between tree and shrub, but is worth considering for its mix of attractive bark, foliage, and flowers and fruits that appear together.

HOW TO GROW

Strawberry tree will tolerate drought once established, but give it humus-rich soil to start. While it prefers sun it can tolerate some shade, as well as alkaline soil and salt. It will need protection from wind, however, perhaps in a shrub border where its fall flowers and fruit will stand out. This shrub doesn't require pruning, but gardeners wanting to control its size can trim it in late winter. Sow seeds when ripe (the year after flowering) or take semiripe cuttings in late summer.

A. unedo
P. 48

a. EW-nee-doh. Strawberry Tree. Grows 15 to 20 feet tall and wide with shaggy reddish brown bark. The narrow leathery leaves are shallowly toothed and 2 to 4 inches long. In autumn, white urn-shaped flowers (sometimes tinged pink) appear in 2-inch panicles, while the ¾-inch fruits from the previous year are ripening from yellow to red. Look for 'Compacta', which grows to only 6 to 8 feet, or 'Elfin King', which may stop growing at 5 feet. Zones 7 to 10.

❦ Arctostaphylos

ark-toe-STAF-ih-los. Heath family, Ericaceae.

Of 50 species of mostly evergreen shrubs or small trees, primarily from western North America, only a few are beginning to be appreciated by gardeners. In addition to lustrous green leaves, they have urn-shaped flowers and attractive berries. Those categorized as shrubs make good low to medium ground covers on banks or other challenging sites.

HOW TO GROW

Bearberries, or manzanitas, will grow in poor, dry sandy soil ranging from acid to alkaline, in sun or shade, and tolerate salt and wind. They can be difficult to establish, however. Start shrubs in fall after a good rain, planting those intended as ground covers from quart-sized containers, spaced a foot apart. Pruning shrub tips lightly will encourage growth, but don't prune prostrate branches or species. Start semiripe cuttings in summer or layer in fall.

A. densiflora 'Howard McMinn'

a. den-sih-FLOR-uh. Sonoma Manzanita cultivar. This native Californian forms a dense mound 5 feet high and 7 feet wide, with peeling dark red bark and glossy elliptic leaves. Tiny urn-shaped pink to white flowers hang in clusters from late winter to early spring, followed by tiny reddish brown apple-shaped fruits. 'Sentinel' is more erect. Zones 7 to 10.

A. manzanita

a. man-zuh-NEET-uh. Common Manzanita. This shrub from the Sierra Nevada and Coast ranges varies from 6 to 20 feet tall and about half as wide, but averages 12 feet high. It is known for its crooked reddish purple limbs. The leaves are wide ovals, while the late-winter flowers bloom in clusters of white or pink, followed in fall by rounded white fruits that turn red. Zones 8 to 10.

A. patula

P. 49

a. PAT-ew-luh. Green Manzanita. This California native spreads with an irregular crown to 6 feet high and wide with smooth red-brown bark, rounded leathery leaves, and pink or white flower panicles up to 3 inches long in spring or early summer. It may be difficult to find. Zones 7 to 9.

A. uva-ursi

PP. 49, 50

a. OO-vuh-UR-see. Common Bearberry. Also called kinnikinick, this 6- to 12-inch-high evergreen ground cover is native to northern California and the Northeast as well as northern Eurasia. It has 1-inch glossy green leaves that turn bronze or red in winter. Clusters of ¼-inch pink-tinged white flowers in mid- to late spring are followed by round, brilliant scarlet berries. Plants usually grow 2 feet across but can spread much wider. An excellent seaside plant that tolerates salt and performs best in dry, sandy soil. Numerous cultivars have been selected. 'Emerald Carpet' tolerates shade, and 'Vancouver Jade' has pink flowers and strong autumn color. Gardeners in the southern United States (Zone 7) should look for 'Massachusetts'. Zones 2 to 6.

❦ Ardisia

ar-DEES-juh. Myrsine family, Myrsinaceae.

Among the 250 evergreen trees and shrubs in this genus, from warm to tropical areas of the Americas and Asia, only a couple are commonly grown in gardens. They are eye-catching throughout the year, with whorls of glossy leaves, star-shaped flowers, and lasting bright red fruits.

HOW TO GROW

Native to damp woods, ardisias need rich, organic, well-drained acid soil and shelter from strong sun and wind. In moist, shady conditions they spread quickly by root runners to form a tall ground cover. Temperatures of 20°F and lower can kill leaves, especially of the variegated varieties, although plants will resprout from the roots. Pruning is minimal, but shrubs may need pinching to keep them from getting leggy. These plants propagate most easily by division, but also can be reproduced from stem cuttings collected in early spring or seeds sown in spring.

A. japonica P. 50

a. juh-PON-ih-kuh. Marlberry. Growing only 18 inches tall or less but spreading indefinitely, this Asian species has glossy, toothed leaves up to 3½ inches long, held in whorls. The foliage resembles that of a hellebore. Clusters of ½-inch pink or white star-shaped flowers bloom in late summer, followed by round ¼-inch bright red berries that persist into winter. It spreads quickly, so that its value as a ground cover is limited only by its variable cold hardiness. Variegated forms may have white, cream, yellow, or pink markings. Zones 7 to 9.

Aronia

ah-ROH-nee-uh. Rose family, Rosaceae.

This is a genus of only two species, which are both deciduous woodland shrubs from the eastern United States. They are grown primarily for their stunning fall color and berries.

HOW TO GROW

Native to swamps and moist banks, chokeberries adapt to drier soils ranging from neutral to acid, and even to low fertility. Fruiting is best in full sun. They tend to sucker and become leggy, a trait that is less apparent when they are massed for a huge splash of fall color. If you have space to accommodate their inevitable spread, they are ideal for naturalizing. They are prone to insects and diseases that disfigure other members of the rose family. Pruning back by a third or more will control spread and stimulate new growth. Propagate from dormant suckers, softwood cuttings in summer, or seeds planted in autumn.

A. arbutifolia 'Brilliantissima' P. 51

a. ar-bew-tih-FOH-lee-uh. Red Chokeberry cultivar. This selection grows 6 to 8 feet tall and 3 to 5 feet wide, with lustrous, oval, finely toothed 3- to 4-inch leaves that are hairy and gray on the undersides, with autumn leaves predominantly a brilliant red. The late-spring flowers are white in 2-inch corymbs, upstaged by the abundant bright red fruits, which can be persistent but are a favorite of mockingbirds. This cultivar received a Gold Medal from the Pennsylvania Horticultural Society in 2000. Zones 4 to 9.

A. melanocarpa P. 52

a. mel-an-oh-KAR-puh. Black Chokeberry. This species is similar to red chokeberry but only 3 to 5 feet tall, spreading to twice as wide. The fall fruits are larger and dark purple. Most cultivars have reddish purple foliage in autumn. 'Autumn Magic' has a mix of red and purple leaves. 'Morton' (trademarked as Iroquois Beauty) is a dwarf growing to 3 feet. Zones 3 to 8.

❦ *Asimina*

ah-SIM-in-uh. Custard-apple family, Annonaceae.

Other members of this family are tropical trees and shrubs, some of which produce exotic fruits such as the cherimoya. This temperate genus includes eight deciduous or evergreen shrubs or small trees that are found in rich, moist southeastern U.S. woods. But the only species familiar to most gardeners is the pawpaw, valued for its handsome leaves and custardlike fruits. Because pawpaws—the largest fruits native to North America—don't ship well, only gardeners and their friends can enjoy their unique taste and texture.

HOW TO GROW

Give pawpaws rich, moisture-retentive but well-drained neutral to acid soil. They grow naturally in part shade but develop better form and fruit in full sun. For fruit, plant more than one. Large specimens can be difficult to transplant because of their long taproot. They should not need pruning. Start new plants from stratified seeds that have been nicked to soften the hard seed coat.

A. triloba   P. 52

a. try-LOH-uh. Pawpaw. Also called custard apple, pawpaw grows into a pyramid about 20 feet tall and wide and may sucker. The alternate, oblong leaves droop from the branches and can be 12 inches long and half as wide. They somewhat resemble those of magnolia, to which they're distantly related, but have prominent veins. In fall, they turn yellow-green or bright yellow before dropping. The unusual dark purple-red flowers, which are somewhat hidden among emerging leaves, have six petals, the three outer ones much larger. Fruits are roughly oval, 2 to 5 inches long, turning from yellow-green to purple or dark brown. Cooked or eaten raw, they have a banana taste and creamy consistency and contain large beanlike seeds. Cultivars have been selected for higher-quality fruit or fewer seeds. Zones 5 to 8.

ꆤ Atriplex

AT-rip-lex. Goosefoot family, Chenopodiaceae.

This genus contains about 100 annuals, perennials, and evergreen or deciduous shrubs and subshrubs, found in deserts, along coasts, and in salt marshes throughout the world. The shrubs grown in gardens are chosen for their gray or silvery leaves and toughness in adverse conditions.

HOW TO GROW

Give saltbushes full sun where they are sheltered from cold winds. They thrive in poor to moderately fertile, dry soil and tolerate salt and summer wind. They require only good drainage, needing little water once established. Useful in a shrub border or as a hedge or windbreak, they don't require pruning, although some species adapt to shearing. Propagate saltbush from seed in spring or early summer, or from softwood cuttings in summer.

A. canescens   P. 53

a. kan-ESS-enz. Four-wing Saltbush. This evergreen western U.S. native grows 6 feet tall and 8 feet wide with narrow gray leaves that roll back slightly at the margins. The inconspicuous summer flowers are greenish white in 2-inch clustered spikes. More eye-catching are the fruits with the four long wings that give this plant its common name. Zones 7 to 9.

A. lentiformis

a. lent-ih-FORM-iss. Quail Bush. Native to alkaline soils in the West, this dense, deciduous shrub is often spiny, hence another common name, white thistle. It grows anywhere from 3 to 10 feet tall, usually spreading somewhat wider. The blue-gray oval leaves are up to 2 inches long. A subspecies, *A. lentiformis* ssp. *breweri* (Brewer's saltbush) is semievergreen, usually about 6 feet tall and spineless, and tolerates shearing. Zones 9 to 10.

A. nummularia

a. num-ew-LAR-ee-uh. A rounded evergreen with pale gray leaves up to 2½ inches long, this Australian species tolerates some shade, as well as drought in summer and floods in winter. The small flowers bloom in panicles from spring to summer. Zone 10.

❦ *Aucuba*

ah-KOO-buh. Dogwood family, Cornaceae.

There are three or four evergreen, dioecious species in this genus, native from the Himalayas to East Asia. One species is popular in southern gardens for its handsome leathery, often variegated leaves, and shade tolerance. In spite of its membership in the dogwood family, the common names spotted laurel and Japanese laurel more accurately reflect the appearance of its evergreen foliage.

HOW TO GROW

Variegated aucubas, particularly, should have some shade all year. All should have shade in the south of their range, and in the north, protection from winter sun and wind. They tolerate dry soil, heavy clay, air pollution, and salty wind and can even be grown under trees. Use them to brighten dark corners, as an unusual medium-high hedge, or in containers. They need little pruning. Trim hedges in spring to control growth, and remove any solid green branches on variegated selections. Aucuba roots easily from cuttings all year.

A. japonica   P. 54

a. juh-PON-ih-kuh. Japanese Aucuba. Usually growing to about 6 feet (occasionally up to 10 feet or more) and slightly narrower, aucuba bears ⅓-inch purple flowers in early to midspring, the males in upright terminal panicles to 4 inches long and the female in shorter panicles in the leaf axils. In midautumn females bear elliptic bright red fruit ½ inch long, up to five in a cluster. The gold-flecked 'Variegata', or 'Gold Dust', was introduced to the trade before the species. 'Sulfur' ('Sulfurea Marginata') has wide yellow edges. Zones 7 to 10.

❦ *Baccharis*

BOK-ar-us. Aster family, Asteraceae.

This genus includes some 350 species of dioecious, deciduous or evergreen shrubs and perennials native to North and South America. The species described here is still not widely known among gardeners, but arouses interest wherever it grows because of the unusual wispy white seed heads that cover it in fall. Gardeners who discover it appreciate its adaptability to infertile soil and seaside conditions.

Groundsel bush tolerates moderate to poor, sandy or salty soils in full sun. Use it as a windbreak, a seaside planting, or for naturalizing. Does not need pruning but can be cut back by a third to stimulate growth. Sow seed in spring or take softwood cuttings in summer.

B. halimifolia P. 54

b. hal-ih-mih-FOH-lee-uh. Groundsel Bush. Semievergreen to deciduous, it is also called sea myrtle because its 3-inch leaves have an elongated oval shape and leathery texture similar to plants in the *Myrica* genus. The foliage differs in having more prominent, coarser teeth and can be gray-green as well as dark green. The small white flowers bloom in open clusters in late summer, after which female plants develop clouds of unusual silky white seed heads. Zones 5 to 9.

🌿 *Berberis*

BER-ber-iss. Barberry family, Berberidaceae.

This genus encompasses more than 450 species of spiny-stemmed evergreen or deciduous shrubs from Africa, South America, and the Northern Hemisphere. Many are useful in gardens for fall foliage, colorful fruits, and small yellow or orange spring flowers.

HOW TO GROW

Barberries need well-drained soil in full sun for the best fruit and fall color. The small species are ideal for rock gardens, the larger ones as decorative or barrier hedges. Evergreen species can be pruned lightly after flowering. On mature deciduous shrubs, one-third of old branches can be trimmed back to stimulate growth and reshape. Root from softwood cuttings in summer, or sow seeds in fall after removing them from the pulp. *B. vulgaris* (common barberry) is considered an invasive pest by naturalists in 26 states from coast to coast and should be avoided. Also troublesome, from New England west to Wisconsin and south to Tennessee and Kentucky, is *B. thunbergii* (Japanese barberry), of which there are dozens of cultivars widely available. Gardeners who live in the area described should consider other barberries.

B. × *chenaultii*

b. × shen-OH-ee-eye. Chenault Barberry. This cold-hardy evergreen hybrid, developed in France in the 1930s, grows 3 to 4 feet tall and slightly wider, with shiny dark green leaves that turn bronzy red with the first frosts. Zones 5 to 8.

B. darwinii   P. 55

b. dar-WIN-ee-eye. Darwin Barberry. An upright evergreen to 10 feet high and wide then spreading, with spiny, glossy, 1½-inch dark green leaves. It bears 2-inch racemes of gold to orange flowers in early spring, then pea-sized dark turquoise berries. Zones 7 to 9.

B. gladwynensis 'William Penn'

b. glad-win-EN-siss. The habit is a dense 4-foot mound. High-gloss leaves to 4 inches turn bronze in winter, and some will fall in the north of its range. Bright yellow midspring flowers are followed by ½-inch yellow fruits tinged with purple. Zones 6 to 9.

B. julianae   P. 55

b. jool-ee-AY-nee. Wintergreen Barberry. Forms a mass of upright shoots 8 to 10 feet tall and wide, with spiny, lustrous evergreen leaves that are pale underneath. In late spring it bears clusters of yellow flowers, sometimes tinged red, followed by ⅜-inch glaucous blue-black fruits. In the northern part of its range, its leaves may show signs of winter damage in exposed areas. Nevertheless, along with *B.* × *chenaultii,* it is considered the hardiest of the evergreen barberries. Looks better left unpruned. Zones 6 to 9.

B. koreana

b. kor-ee-AY-nuh. Korean Barberry. A vigorous deciduous barberry to 6 feet or taller, with many stems and sometimes suckering. Oval 1- to 3-inch leaves turn reddish purple in fall. Midspring yellow flowers appear in 3- to 4-inch racemes followed by ¼-inch bright red oval berries. Zones 3 to 7.

B. × *mentorensis*

b. × men-tor-EN-siss. Mentor Barberry. Fast growing and dense, with an upright bearing when young then becoming more rounded, to 5 feet tall and wider. Popular for creating an impenetrable, semievergreen hedge that does not need pruning. The dark green leathery leaves show yellow, orange, and red in fall. Yellow spring flowers, solitary or paired, are occasionally followed by reddish brown fruits. Zones 5 to 8.

B. × ottawensis 'Superba'

b. × aw-tuh-WEN-siss. A rounded deciduous shrub 6 to 8 feet high and wide, valued for purple-red foliage that turns bright red in fall. The spring flower clusters are pale yellow tinged with red, and berries are ⅜-inch red ovals. Zones 5 to 9.

B. verruculosa
P. 56

b. veh-roo-kew-LOH-suh. Warty Barberry. Named for the bumps on its stems, this species makes a dense mound 3 to 5 feet high and across, with small evergreen leaves that develop a burgundy tinge in autumn. The solitary golden yellow flowers are followed by blue-black glaucous fruits. Zones 6 to 9.

❦ Brugmansia

broog-MAN-see-uh. Nightshade family, Solanaceae.

This small genus numbers only five species of evergreen shrubs and trees that are at home in scrubland and along streamsides in the Andes of South America. They are closely related to the annuals and perennials in the genus *Datura* and have similar dangling trumpet flowers with five reflexed lobes, blooming in late spring to summer.

HOW TO GROW

Outdoors, grow brugmansia in fertile, moisture-retentive but well-drained soil in full sun. They are huge, dramatic plants that almost demand to be treated as specimens. They can tolerate some wind, drought, and salt, but not pollution, and will show some frost damage even in mild-winter climates. Gardeners in temperate climates grow them in containers and overwinter them indoors, where their soil should be kept barely damp. They can get by with light pruning but can be cut to within a few inches of the ground for rejuvenation. Propagate from seeds or cuttings taken spring through summer.

B. × candida
P. 56

b. × KAN-dih-duh. This hybrid can grow 6 feet in a single season, eventually reaching 15 feet with somewhat soft stems. The dull leaves, which have coarse teeth and wavy edges, can be up to a foot long. The heavy-textured white trumpet flowers can be single or double and more than 8 inches long, with a powerful nighttime fragrance. They begin blooming in summer and can continue well into autumn. Zones 10 to 11.

❧ *Brunfelsia*

broon-FEL-see-uh. Nightshade family, Solanaceae.

This is a genus of about 40 species of evergreen shrubs and small trees native to the tropical Americas. It includes only one species that is widely grown by gardeners indoors and out for handsome foliage and flowers that change color from the time they open until they drop.

HOW TO GROW

Brunfelsia needs some pampering. Make sure it has rich, moist soil with excellent drainage, and keep it well fed and watered with protection from midday sun. It can be pruned in spring to improve shape or restrict size. Indoors, give it bright indirect light. Water lightly in winter, then resume feeding and repot if needed in late winter. Propagate with softwood cuttings in spring or summer.

B. pauciflora (syn. *B. calcina*)   P. 57

b. paw-sih-FLOR-uh. Yesterday, Today, and Tomorrow. This bushy shrub ranges in height from 3 to 10 feet, with a width about half that. The oval leaves are 3 to 6 inches long, dark green, leathery, and glossy. From spring through summer it produces cymes of pansy-shaped flowers, 2 inches across, with five wavy petals. The blossoms open purple, fading to lavender and then white, suggesting the plant's common name. Established plants growing in the ground can survive temperatures into the 20s (Zone 9), but will be defoliated. Zones 9 to 11.

❧ *Buddleia*

BUD-lee-uh. Logania family, Loganiaceae.

This is a well-populated genus of about 100 species, mostly evergreen to deciduous shrubs plus a few trees, vines, and herbaceous perennials from Asia, Africa, and the Americas. About a dozen species have made their way to gardens, but only two are widely available. Both have clusters of fragrant flowers on slender, arching branches.

HOW TO GROW

Plant buddleia in full sun and relatively fertile, moisture-retentive soil. It can tolerate some drought, but not wet feet. Use it in a shrub or herbaceous border or make it the centerpiece of a butterfly garden. Deadhead it regularly to remove unsightly dead flowers and encourage more blooms. *B. davidii* is becoming invasive on the East Coast, and any possibility of self-seeding needs to be controlled. After the last frost in spring but before new growth begins, prune this species, which blooms on new growth, back to strong buds near the ground. It can be encouraged to take on either upright or more spreading shapes. *A. alternifolia,* which blooms on the previous season's growth, should be pruned after flowering in summer and can be espaliered or trained to a single stem with attractive peeling bark. Propagate buddleia from seeds or semiripe cuttings in summer.

B. alternifolia P. 57

b. al-tern-ih-FOH-lee-uh. Fountain Buddleia. Slender, arching shoots form a fountain 10 to 12 feet tall and wide with alternate, 3-inch willowlike gray-green leaves that turn yellow in fall. In midsummer, dense clusters of fragrant, trumpet-shaped, lilac purple flowers are packed along the slender stems in the leaf axils of the previous season's growth. The leaves of 'Argentea' have silvery white hairs. Zones 5 to 9.

B. davidii P. 58

b. dav-ih-dee-eye. Butterfly Bush. This fast grower sends its shoots up to 10 feet and spreads wider, although it is usually kept to about half that height with annual pruning. The opposite, lance-shaped leaves up to 10 inches long are white underneath and appear gray-green from a distance. They often remain on the plant through fall. The strongly honey-scented terminal flowers appear in cone-shaped spikes from mid- to late summer and are butterfly magnets. Sometimes called summer lilac for the frequently lavender flowers of the species, it has cultivars offering numerous other color choices, many with orange eyes: 'Black Knight' (purple-black), 'Dartmoor' (deep lilac, multibranched flower panicles), 'Honeycomb' (yellow), 'Pink Delight' (bright pink), and 'Royal Red' (purple-red). 'Harlequin' has variegated foliage. 'Nanho Blue', 'Nanho Purple', and 'Nanho White' are smaller at 4 to 5 feet. It will survive to Zone 4 but die to the ground each year. Zones 6 to 9.

B. 'Lochinch' P. 59

This vigorous hybrid is 6 to 8 feet tall with a more compact mound shape, gray-green leaves, and lavender blue flowers. Zones 6 to 9.

B. globosa

b. gloh-BOH-suh. Orange Ball Tree. This species from Chile and Peru is still difficult to find, but is worth seeking for its unusual flowers. For warm-climate gardeners it may offer a noninvasive alternative to *B. davidii.*

Open and lank and ranging from 6 to 15 feet tall, it has deciduous to semievergreen lance-shaped leaves and holds its bright yellow flowers in ¾-inch balls. Zones 7 to 10.

❦ *Buxus*

BUCKS-us. Boxwood family, Buxaceae.

Among 70 species of evergreen shrubs and trees from Europe, Asia, Africa, and Central America, a handful have been cultivated for their usually small, tough, evergreen leaves and amenability to pruning. Boxwood is notoriously slow growing. Its distinctive aroma and formally pruned shapes are a hallmark of many historic gardens.

HOW TO GROW

Boxwoods need relatively neutral, well-drained soil generously amended with organic matter. They will tolerate full sun but handle stress — drought, dry wind, rapid temperature fluctuations — better in part shade. These conditions, or winter sun, can bronze leaves. To reduce winter scorching or ice damage, water heavily in fall and tie up branches by spiraling twine around the shrub from the bottom. Mulch in summer to keep the shallow roots cool. Use small boxwoods to edge walkways or formal herb or ornamental beds, and larger ones for hedging or topiary. Prune heavily in early spring, or lightly in summer. Thin the interior annually to prevent fungal diseases. Propagate from stem cuttings July through December.

B. microphylla   P. 60

b. my-kro-FIL-luh. Littleleaf Box. Forms a dense mound 3 feet tall and wide, with oblong leaves usually less than 1 inch long. 'Compacta' (sometimes listed as 'Kingsville Dwarf') is slower growing, to only 10 or 12 inches tall and 18 inches wide, with ½-inch leaves less than ¼ inch wide. 'Green Pillow' grows 2 feet tall and 3 feet wide and has larger leaves. Zones 6 to 9.

B. microphylla var. *koreana* × *B. sempervirens*

b. my-kro-FIL-uh var. kor-ee-AY-nuh × b. sem-per-VEER-enz. These hybrids are better adapted to the cold, dry, windy winters of the Midwest, most of them growing 2 to 3 feet tall. They include 'Glencoe' (Chicagoland Green), 'Green Ice', and 'Green Mountain', which is 5 feet tall and 3 feet wide and may survive in Zone 4. Others, Zones 5 to 7.

B. sempervirens

P. 61

b. sem-per-VEER-enz. Common Boxwood. A rounded bushy shrub to 15 feet tall and wide that can be trained as a tree. 'Suffruticosa', the edging box or dwarf boxwood, has a dense mound form, small round leaves, and grows only an inch a year to 3 to 5 feet. 'Graham Blandy' is narrow and upright at 9 feet by 18 inches. 'Pendula' has weeping branches, and 'Vardar Valley' is 6 feet high by 10 feet wide with blue-green foliage. 'Elegantissima' has a creamy white margin. Zones 6 to 8.

❦ Callicarpa

kal-lih-KARP-uh. Verbena family, Verbenaceae.

The 140 evergreen and deciduous shrubs in this genus are mainly from the tropics and subtropics, but four or five cold-hardy deciduous species are grown for their small, usually purple but occasionally white fruit clusters.

HOW TO GROW

Give beautyberries moderately fertile, well-drained soil in dappled shade or sun. American beautyberry will even grow under pines, but fruiting is most dramatic when they are grouped in full sun in hot climates. Beautiful in a shrub border or open woods. Flowers appear on new growth; pruning low to the ground regularly in early spring will help them maintain a compact shape. Propagate from softwood cuttings. Give seeds warm stratification and plant in spring.

C. americana

c. uh-mair-ih-KAY-nuh. American Beautyberry. A coarse and open shrub native from Maryland to Florida, beautyberry can reach 8 feet tall and 6 feet wide, but regular pruning will hold it to half that. The oval, toothed, mid-green leaves may reach 6 inches long. In early to late summer, tiny lavender pink flowers appear in the leaf axils, followed by bright purple berry clusters. 'Lactea' has white flowers and fruits. Zones 7 to 10.

C. bodinieri var. giraldii 'Profusion'

P. 61

c. boh-din-ee-EH-ree var. jeer-ALL-dee-eye. Chinese Beautyberry. This selection of a Chinese variety reaches 6 to 10 feet with arching branches. The showy flowers give way to heavy clusters of 30 to 40 iridescent purple-pink berries encircling the branches. In early spring and fall, leaves have a purple cast. Zones 5 to 9.

C. dichotoma   P. 62

c. dy-KOT-oh-muh. Purple Beautyberry. Fountainlike and branching to the ground, this Asian species grows 4 to 5 feet tall with a wider spread. Amethyst berries appear in September or October on short stalks along the branches, either on bare branches in the North or above the leaves in the South. This species, which has received a Gold Medal from the Pennsylvania Horticultural Society, has a white-fruited form, *C. dichotoma* var. *albifructus.* Zones 6 to 9.

C. japonica

c. juh-PON-ih-kuh. Japanese Beautyberry. Erect and rounded, 4 to 6 feet tall and wide, with arching branches. 'Leucocarpa' has heavy white fruit and yellow fall leaves. *C. japonica* var. *luxurians* has larger leaves and reddish violet fruit clusters. Zones 5 to 9.

❧ Callistemon

kal-LIH-steh-mun. Myrtle family, Myrtaceae.

The name of this Australian genus comes from two Greek words meaning "beautiful" and "stamen." Gardeners on America's West Coast grow many of the 25 species of evergreen trees and shrubs for the flower spikes' colorful and prominent stamens.

HOW TO GROW

Callistemons grow in neutral to acid, moderately fertile soil in full sun. Most need little water, and some species will tolerate alkaline soil and salt. They can be pruned hard when young to be used as hedges, espaliers, or to coax them into more treelike shapes. Sow seed in spring or root semiripe cuttings in late summer.

C. citrinus   P. 62

c. sih-TRY-nus. Common Bottlebrush. Variable to 10 or 15 feet tall and wide. The 4-inch lance-shaped leaves are coppery when new; bright red bottlebrush flower spikes attract hummingbirds in spring and summer. 'Jeffers' grows 6 to 8 feet tall with purple-pink flowers. Zones 8 to 11.

C. 'Little John'   P. 63

This dwarf selection, often sold as *C. viminalis* 'Little John', has a rounded form 3 feet tall and wide, with brilliant red flowers that rebloom throughout the year. Zones 8 to 11.

C. salignus

c. sal-IG-nus. White Bottlebrush. Left to grow as a shrub, this species can reach 15 or 20 feet tall, although it is sometimes trained as a tree. Most gardeners grow it for its stunning new leaves, which verge on magenta. The flowers are cream colored to pale yellow. Zones 8 to 11.

❦ Calluna

kal-OO-nuh. Heath family, Ericeae.

There is only one species in this genus of low, evergreen shrubs but more than 500 cultivars. A dominant feature of moors in Europe, heather is also found from Siberia to the Azores islands in the North Atlantic. The upright but flexible branches have tiny overlapping leaves, often with hairs that give them a gray cast. Some of the little bell flowers never open from bud. Subtle variations in foliage and flower color — white, pink, purple, to red — bring year-round interest to gardens in the ideal climate.

HOW TO GROW

Heather prefers poor, acid soil but must have sharp drainage. Sandy soil amended with peat moss is excellent. It becomes leggy in too much shade but can't tolerate full sun or exposure to wind in the southern portion of its range. In winter, mulch where snow cover is unreliable. Like other heath family members heather is shallow rooted, so weed carefully. After flowering, prune back flowered shoots. Propagate by layering.

C. vulgaris   PP. 63, 64

c. vul-GAIR-iss. Scotch Heather. Cultivars range from 4 to more than 24 inches tall and spread up to 2 feet across. Most bloom in summer, but some have flowers in December or even January. Flowers are sometimes double, and foliage comes in shades of green or silver, gold or bronze, sometimes taking on a striking red hue in winter. 'County Wicklow' is double pink, 'Kinlochruel' is double white, and 'Gold Haze' has gold foliage and white flowers. Zones 4 to 7.

❦ Calycanthus

kal-ih-KAN-thus. Sweetshrub family, Calycanthaceae.

There are only two species of these deciduous native American shrubs, usually found in woods and along streams, and grown in gardens for their unusual, fruit-scented flowers. Thanks to taxonomists, a scentless Asian species has recently joined them.

HOW TO GROW

Give sweetshrubs fertile, moisture-retentive soil that is rich in organic matter, in full sun toward the north of their range and part shade in the south. Site them along a path or near a seating area where their fragrance can be enjoyed. Because they flower on the current season's growth they can be pruned close to the ground in early spring. Start from stratified seeds. Cuttings show genetic variation; some root readily, while others are more difficult.

C. chinensis (syn. Sinocalycanthus chinensis)

c. chin-EN-siss. Chinese Spicebush. Grows 6 to 9 feet tall with huge glossy leaves. The 3-inch white spring flowers are tinged with pink and have yellow centers but no fragrance. Zones 7 to 8.

C. floridus

P. 64

c. FLOR-ih-dus. Carolina Allspice. Also called sweet bubby and strawberry shrub, this sweetshrub is native from Pennsylvania to Florida. It averages 8 feet tall and spreads 10 feet wide. Dark green leaves up to 5 inches long are rough to the touch and fragrant when crushed, turning yellow in fall. The 2-inch maroon flowers, which have straplike petals and may smell like strawberries, bananas, or pineapples, bloom late spring into early summer. Buy the shrubs in bloom if possible, since some seed-grown plants may be largely lacking in scent. A persistent leathery pod holds numerous dark brown seeds. Zones 5 to 9.

C. occidentalis

c. ox-ih-den-TAL-iss. California Allspice. This West Coast native is similar to the eastern version but grows larger with longer leaves. Zones 6 to 9.

❧ Camellia

ka-MEEL-yuh. Tea family, Theaceae.

This genus encompasses more than 250 evergreen shrubs and trees from Asian woodlands. Most popular in gardens are hybrids averaging 15 feet tall to about 10 feet wide. They are cherished in the southern United States for their winter to early-spring flowers that look like roses from a distance. Most are unscented, but come in an array of forms: semidouble,

double, anemone, peony, and rose, as well as single. Tea is made from one species, *C. sinensis.*

HOW TO GROW

Give camellias deep, rich, acid soil in part shade. Sun will burn the plants and deep shade will reduce flowering. At the northern range of hardiness, site against a warm wall or other protected place; the shrubs are most subject to winterkill immediately after transplanting from containers. Mulch annually with leaf mold or shredded bark. Camellias make show-stopping specimens and hedges. They can be pruned heavily, but late-season fertilization or pruning can heighten vulnerability to frost. Propagate by air layering or from seeds, which appear in 1-inch woody capsules.

C. japonica P. 65

c. juh-PON-ih-kuh. Japanese Camellia. The 2- to 4-inch alternate leaves are serrated, leathery, and shiny dark green. The species grows slowly to 10 to 15 feet tall and 5 to 10 feet wide, usually rather pyramidal and formal. The 2- to 5-inch-diameter flowers of red, pink, or white appear singly at the ends of branches and can turn brown and mushy if they bloom during a frost. Zones 7 to 10.

C. oleifera

c. oh-lee-IF-er-uh. Tea-oil Camellia. This species stands out for having fragrant flowers and additional cold hardiness. It was used by William Ackerman of the U.S. National Arboretum to breed a line of camellias that can be grown a zone farther north. All tend to be compact with small leaves and bloom in late fall. They include 'Polar Ice' (white, anemone form), 'Winter's Charm' (lavender pink, anemone form), 'Winter's Dream' (pink, semidouble), 'Winter's Rose' (pale pink, double rose), and 'Winter's Star' (reddish purple, single). Zones 6 to 9.

C. reticulata

c. reh-tih-kew-LAY-tuh. These open and lanky shrubs can grow more than 30 feet tall but are usually about 10 feet tall and 8 feet wide. The name "reticulata" recognizes the net of veins on the dull green leaves. The species, from China, bears single rosy red flowers more than 4 inches across; most of the popular cultivars have even larger semidouble flowers with wavy inner petals. 'Captain Rawes' is a cold-hardy rose red; 'Crimson Robe' has bright red flowers and is more attractive out of flower than some others. Zones 8 to 10.

C. sasanqua

c. sas-SANK-wah. Sasanqua Camellia. A bit smaller at 6 to 10 feet tall, it also has smaller leaves and flowers than *C. japonica*. It is somewhat more open, with fuzzy stems, and is also slightly less cold hardy. The flowers, which bloom in late fall or early winter, are white, single, cup-shaped, and fragrant. Zones 7 to 10.

❦ Carissa

kah-RISS-uh. Dogbane family, Apocynaceae.

About 20 evergreen shrubs and small trees with often spiny branches compose this genus. The leaves are glossy, and the fragrant flower clusters are followed by bright red berries that turn dark purple.

HOW TO GROW

Grow this shrub in any soil, in full sun for best fruit. It is a good coastal plant since it tolerates sand, salt, and drought, as well as wet conditions. Weed carefully around its shallow roots. Spines make it a good hedge for deterring pets and wild mammals, or it can be espaliered. Sow seed in spring or propagate by semiripe cuttings in summer. Although this is definitely a tropical species, the sweet-scented flowers induce many gardeners to grow it in a container to overwinter indoors.

C. macrocarpa   P. 66

c. mak-roh-KAR-puh. Natal Plum. Bushy and 8 to 18 feet tall, with spines at the end of the twigs as well as along the branches. The 2-inch fragrant white flowers are like jasmine's with five petals, and they bloom throughout the year. You can collect the 1- to 2-inch red berries to make tart sauces and jellies, but birds like them too. There are many prostrate and dwarf forms, and a thornless one, 'Boxwood Beauty'. Zone 10.

❦ Carpenteria

kar-pen-TEER-ee-uh. Hydrangea family, Hydrangeaceae.

There is just one species in this genus, an evergreen shrub that grows only on scrubby slopes and in pine forests in the foothills of California's Fresno County. But it looks as if it was born for a garden, with a neat, almost formal habit and anemonelike flowers that bloom against glossy leaves.

HOW TO GROW

This shrub can grow in a range of soils in sun or light shade. With some shade, it will tolerate drought once established. Its deep root system can make it somewhat difficult to transplant so site it carefully as a hedge or in a border. After it has flowered, prune some of the oldest shoots to the base to restore the plant's shape and encourage new growth. Propagate by softwood cuttings in summer or by layering.

C. californica P. 66

c. kal-ih-FOR-nih-kuh. Bush Anemone. The bush anemone grows slowly to about 6 feet tall and wide with light brown peeling bark. The handsome leathery leaves are lance-shaped to narrow ovals 4 to 5 inches long. Fragrant white five-petaled flowers, which bloom mid- to late summer, can be up to 3 inches across. As the common name implies, they look just like anemones, with a cup shape and central yellow boss, or cluster of stamens. Zones 8 to 10.

❦ *Caryopteris*

kar-ee-OP-ter-iss. Verbena family, Verbenaceae.

The genus include six deciduous shrubs and perennials from woods and hot dry slopes of the Himalayas and East Asia. Gardeners usually grow one of the hybrids that have been developed for aromatic silvery leaves and delicate, late-season blue flowers that are irresistible to butterflies.

HOW TO GROW

The soil should be well drained, loose, and only moderately fertile, in full sun or part shade. Excellent mixed in an ornamental bed or butterfly garden, or used as a low hedge. Treat as a herbaceous perennial by pruning close to the ground in early spring. (They may die back to the ground in the North.) Propagate from softwood cuttings.

C. × clandonensis P. 67

c. × klan-doh-NEN-siss. Blue-mist Shrub. This mounded, flexible-branched shrub grows to 3 feet tall and somewhat wider and bears pleasantly fragrant 2-inch oval or lance-shaped leaves, slightly toothed with silver hairs underneath. The blue or lavender terminal and axillary flowers appear in late summer and early fall. The petals are delicately fringed, giving members of the genus the common name bluebeard. Some popular cultivars are 'Heavenly Blue' with dark blue flowers, 'Longwood Blue' with masses of violet blue flowers and silvery leaves, and 'Worcester Gold' with yellow foliage. Zones 5 to 9.

❦ Cassia

KASS-ee-uh. Pea family, Fabaceae.

This huge genus encompasses more than 500 species of annuals, herbaceous perennials, and deciduous to evergreen trees and shrubs from throughout the world, primarily the tropics. About half of these have been recategorized as *Senna* by some taxonomists. Pinnately compound leaves give them a delicate air. Virtually all the shrubs have clusters of yellow to gold pealike flowers.

HOW TO GROW

Give cassia full sun. Many of the shrubs are native to desert areas and will tolerate relatively dry, infertile soil as long as it is well drained. Infrequent but deep watering during drought is a good idea. Pruning needs vary among species. Propagate from seeds or semiripe cuttings collected in summer.

C. artemisiodes (syn. *Senna artemisiodes*)

c. ar-tem-iss-ee-OY-deez. Feathery Cassia. This evergreen from Australia grows from 3 to 5 feet tall. It has 1-inch gray needlelike leaves and clusters of six to eight sulphur yellow flowers that bloom from winter to midspring, sometimes continuing into summer. Deadhead or shear lightly to prevent seed formation. Zone 10.

C. bicapsularis (syn. *Senna bicapsularis*) P. 67

c. by-kap-soo-LAR-iss. This evergreen grows to 10 feet tall with thick, rounded leaflets. Yellow flowers in spiky clusters bloom from midfall to late winter; both flowers and top growth are frequently zapped by frost. Zone 10.

C. didymobotrya

c. did-ee-moh-BOH-tree-uh. An evergreen from East Africa, with a lanky habit to about 10 feet tall and 2-inch leaflets with up to 16 pairs of leaves. The yellow flowers bloom in upright clusters up to a foot long from early winter until midspring. Best reserved for informal gardens. Zone 10.

❧ *Ceanothus*

see-an-O-thus. Buckthorn family, Rhamnaceae.

There are more than 50 deciduous and evergreen shrubs in this genus, mostly from woods or dry slopes in the western United States. The leaves are toothed and veined, and in spring they can be all but smothered under clusters of flowers that range from white through all shades of blue and blue-violet. A couple of species native to the eastern and central United States are considered somewhat less showy but are valuable for dry, infertile soils.

HOW TO GROW

These plants bloom best in full sun but tolerate considerable shade. Sharply draining soil is a must, however. Shrubs most often die from overwatering and related fungal disease and root rot, but are tolerant of drought and slightly alkaline soil. They fix their own nitrogen so do not need a fertile site. Give them some protection from cold winds. Low-growing ceanothus are suitable for ground covers or rock gardens, taller ones for shrub borders. Training them against a wall offers shelter from wind and cold. Prune evergreens lightly after flowering; deciduous forms can be cut back close to the ground. The large roots of eastern species can make them hard to transplant when mature. Propagation is difficult.

C. americanus   P. 68

c. uh-MAIR-ih-KAY-nus. New Jersey Tea. In spite of being named for the Garden State (where it was allegedly used as a substitute during the colonists' boycott of British tea), this deciduous species is native from southern Canada to the central and southeastern states. Low, broad, and dense at 4 feet tall and 5 feet wide, it produces small white flowers in 1- to 2-inch terminal panicles in midsummer. The leaves, dark green in summer, may add some yellow to the landscape in fall. A good plant for inhospitable conditions. Zones 4 to 8.

C. cultivars   P. 68

The average cultivar of western species is evergreen and broadly spreading, 5 to 6 feet tall and 10 to 12 feet wide. Some are as low as 1½ feet and others may grow to 20 feet. Blue flowers range from powder blue through violet and dark indigo, in spiky clusters 3 to 5 inches long in spring. On evergreens the leaves are often glossy and can be toothed much like a holly's. Among the best are 'Concha', which grows to about 7 feet tall and wide with dense foliage and dark blue flowers and tolerates water in summer; and 'Ray Hartman', which can reach 20 feet tall with 3-inch leaves and medium-blue flowers in 3- to 5-inch clusters. Gardeners often train it as a small tree. Most ceanothus cultivars, Zones 8 to 10.

C. × delilianus 'Gloire de Versailles'

c. × del-il-ee-AN-nus. French hybrid cultivar. This is one of the most cold-hardy blue-flowered selections, growing densely to only about 3 feet with finely toothed, deciduous leaves. Light blue flowers appear in 4-inch clusters in axils and on branch tips from midsummer to fall. Zones 7 to 10.

C. ovatus

c. oh-VAWT-us. Inland Ceanothus. A slightly smaller, denser plant than *C. americanus,* native from New England to the central United States, with shiny leaves, tiny white flowers, and red seed capsules in summer. Provides food for quail and other birds. Zones 4 to 6.

C. thyrsiflorus

c. thur-sih-FLOR-us. Blue Blossom. Native to California and southern Oregon, this is one of the hardiest evergreens, large and vigorous at up to 20 feet tall and wide with arching branches. It combines glossy leaves with 3-inch spring flower spikes that range from light to dark blue. There is a prostrate form, *C. thyrsiflorus* var. *repens,* and a cultivar, 'Skylark', that grows to only 6 feet. Zones 8 to 10.

❦ Cephalanthus

sef-al-AN-thus. Madder family, Rubiaceae.

Of about 10 deciduous and evergreen trees and shrubs found in wetlands in North and Central America, Asia, and Africa, one species is grown in gardens for small fragrant off-white flowers that grow in sputniklike balls.

HOW TO GROW

Soil should be rich and moisture retentive, in full sun. A good plant for a natural pondside. Midsummer flowers appear on the most vigorous young stems. Prune buttonbush to the ground at least every two to three years when buds swell in spring to keep it from becoming treelike and unkempt. Propagates easily from seeds or soft or hardwood cuttings.

C. occidentalis

P. 69

c. ox-ih-den-TAL-iss. Buttonbush. Native from Canada to Florida, this open-branching, usually deciduous shrub averages 6 feet tall and 8 feet wide, with glossy oval or elliptic leaves to 6 inches long. May be evergreen in the southernmost part of its range. The 1-inch ball flowers appear late summer to fall, depending on heat. Ducks and other waterfowl love to feed on the clusters of nutlets. Look for it at a nursery that specializes in natives. Zones 5 to 11.

❦ Cephalotaxus

sef-al-oh-TAX-us. Plum-yew family, Cephalotaxaceae.

Among about nine evergreen, usually dioecious conifers from Asia, a couple of species are becoming more popular in gardens for their unusual leaf texture and exfoliating bark.

HOW TO GROW

Plum yew needs part shade and soil that is fertile, organically rich, moisture retentive, and relatively neutral. In the North it tolerates full sun. It takes heat and is not attractive to deer, but needs protection from wind. The delicate brushy texture makes it a suitable accent, but it's also striking in masses, as a background for flowering plants, or contrasting with broad-leaved evergreens. It does not require pruning but can be trimmed back hard. Propagate from stratified seeds, or terminal shoots in summer.

C. harringtonia

P. 69

c. hair-ing-TOH-nee-uh. Japanese Plum Yew. Highly variable in size and habit, from 10 to 20 feet tall, spreading or more treelike. Linear, pointed leaves ⅛ inch wide and 1½ inches long are arranged in spirals, banded gray underneath. The common name comes from the 1-inch oval fruits on females, which are most often reddish brown but sometimes olive green. Cultivars selected for more predictable shape include 'Duke Gardens', 3 to 5 feet tall and wide; and 'Fastigiata', which forms a fat column 10 feet tall and 7 feet wide with longer-leaved bottlebrush branches. 'Prostrata', 2 to 3 feet tall and sometimes slightly wider, received a Gold Medal from the Pennsylvania Horticultural Society. Zones 5 to 9.

❦ Cercis

SUR-sis. Pea family, Fabaceae.

The eastern redbud is known to gardeners and nongardeners alike for its little magenta flowers that herald spring. The genus includes five other species of deciduous shrubs and small, usually multitrunked trees native to woods or hills in North America, Asia, and the Mediterranean. The flowers are short stalked or stalkless, usually pink or purple but sometimes white, covering the branches in spring. The leaves are heart shaped, and the flowers are followed by flattened pods. The species described here has the most shrublike habit.

HOW TO GROW

Transplant redbud when young to deep, rich, moisture-retentive soil in full sun or part shade. Useful in shrub and mixed borders. Water during droughts and avoid mechanical injury, which makes this genus susceptible to canker and verticillum wilt. Propagate from seed that has been scarified and cold stratified.

C. chinensis   P. 70

c. chih-NEN-siss. Chinese Redbud. A multistemmed shrub with erect branches that are smothered with rosy purple flowers in early spring before leaves emerge. Generally less than 10 feet tall but can reach 15 feet tall and wide. Choose 'Avondale' for compact size and shape and a profusion of intense pink flowers, 'Alba' for white flowers. Zones 6 to 9.

❦ Cestrum

SESS-trum. Nightshade family, Solanaceae.

This big genus includes some 175 species of evergreen and deciduous woodland shrubs found from Mexico to South America. About a half dozen are available to gardeners. Hummingbirds are passionate about the tubular or funnel-shaped flowers, often powerfully fragrant; the red, white, or purple berries draw other birds as well.

HOW TO GROW

Plants these shrubs in fertile soil, well amended with organic matter, in part sun or shade. Use them in a border or train them against a wall to protect them from frost, which will often freeze them to the ground.

Pinch often to maintain an attractive shape, and prune heavily after flowering or fruiting. Propagate from cuttings in summer.

C. nocturnum

P. 70

c. nok-TERN-um. Night Jessamine. An evergreen shrub to 12 feet tall, grown for pale green to ivory flowers that are intensely fragrant at night. They bloom in late summer or early fall in axillary clusters. Where not hardy they are grown in containers for overwintering indoors. Zones 10 to 11.

✿ Chaenomeles

ky-noh-MAY-leez. Rose family, Rosaceae.

All three species of these deciduous, often spiny shrubs from mountain woods in Asia have been the object of tinkering by breeders to develop variations on form and flower color. The early spring blossoms are cup shaped with five petals and up to 60 stamens. They can be single or double, solitary or clustered. In autumn they bear green or purple fruits that are aromatic and edible. They sometimes split open; the genus name means "gaping apple."

HOW TO GROW

Give flowering quince moderately fertile soil. It does best in full sun but tolerates some shade and some lime, as well as pollution and drought. Smaller species can be used for ground cover and underplanting larger shrubs, while upright species can be espaliered. They are not particularly exciting out of bloom. The branches are popular for forcing and arrangements. Prune after flowering, removing at least a third of old branches, to promote the next season's flowering. Propagate from stratified seed, or semiripe cuttings in fall.

C. japonica

c. juh-PON-ih-kuh. Japanese Flowering Quince. This low-growing thorny shrub rarely reaches 3 feet tall but is often twice as wide, with glossy 2-inch leaves. Flowers are clusters of orange to red in early to midspring. A good choice for northern gardens, where it usually spends winter buried by snow (thus safe from the attention of hungry rabbits). Zones 5 to 8.

C. speciosa

P. 71

c. spee-cee-OH-suh. Flowering Quince. Variable habit from upright to rounded or spreading, 6 to 10 feet or more high and wide, with shiny brown bark. Flowers are red or orange, with some cultivars offering white, pink, or peach. It makes a good barrier hedge, but visual interest is limited to the flowering season. The sour fruits are cooked for preserves. Zones 5 to 8.

C. × *superba*   P. 71

c. × soo-PERB-uh. A compact hybrid of *C. speciosa* and *C. japonica,* averaging 5 feet high and 6 feet wide, twiggy, thorny, and suckering. Its longer-blooming flowers are 2 inches across with a similar range of colors. The fruit is larger and ripens later. Somewhat less drought tolerant. There are a few thornless cultivars, such as 'Cameo' (peachy pink) and 'Pink Lady'. Zones 5 to 9.

❦ *Chamaecyparis*

kam-eh-SIP-ar-iss. Cypress family, Cupressaceae.

There are eight species of these evergreen coniferous trees, seven from Asia and one from eastern North America, characterized by sprays of flattened, scalelike leaves. The first two species listed here have been the source of most garden cultivars available in the United States. Cultivars of the native *C. thyoides* are becoming more common. Although most forms are trees 20 or even 50 feet tall, there are numerous dwarf forms that can be used as shrubs.

HOW TO GROW
The ideal conditions for false cypresses include moist, well-drained, acid to neutral soil in full sun. They will tolerate some lime, however. Although winter wind may burn them, they can handle the salt-laden breezes of seaside gardens and the salt exposure of street plantings. Yellow-needled cultivars require some shade but will revert to green in heavy shade. *C. thyoides* and its cultivars will grow in wet soils. Small cultivars are used for rock gardens, taller ones as accents or to lend evergreen color and texture to a shrub border. They adapt to container culture if well watered and fertilized. Pinch back tips for denser branching. Heavier pruning can be done during the growing season, but avoid cutting into old wood. Dwarf selections must be propagated by grafting.

C. obtusa 'Nana Gracilis'   P. 72

c. ob-TOO-suh. Hinoki False Cypress cultivar. Grows slowly to 6 feet high and half as wide, first broadest at the base and then more cone shaped, with concave sprays of dark foliage. Fruits are ½-inch cones, brown, and round. 'Nana' is half as tall, and 'Nana Lutea' has golden leaves. Zones 5 to 8.

C. pisifera P. 72

c. pis-IF-er-uh. Japanese False Cypress cultivars. 'Squarrosa Minima' forms a fluffy globe less than 3 feet across with feathery gray-green foliage. 'Filifera Aurea Nana' has delicate "thread leaf" golden foliage and grows to about 3 feet tall. Zones 4 to 8.

C. thyoides

c. thy-OY-deez. Atlantic White Cedar cultivars. 'Red Star' grows slowly to form a dense column 10 to 15 feet tall, developing fine purple-red foliage in autumn and winter. 'Heatherbun' is a 4-foot mound. Like most forms of this species, they will tolerate wet feet but not heat. Zones 4 to 7.

Chimonanthus

ky-moh-NAN-thus. Sweetshrub family, Calycanthaceae.

Of six species of deciduous and evergreen shrubs native to Chinese woodlands, one has been brought to gardens for its exceedingly fragrant flowers that appear on bare branches in early to late winter.

HOW TO GROW

Although wintersweet can tolerate more moisture than most shrubs, it will do best in loamy soil with good drainage, in full sun to part shade. Site it against evergreens or a wall, outside a window or along a walk where it can be enjoyed on a cold day. Prune off old branches after flowering; hard pruning keeps it from becoming leggy. Sow seeds in May or June or take softwood cuttings in summer.

C. praecox P. 73

c. PREE-coks. Wintersweet. A deciduous, multistemmed slow grower to an average of 12 feet tall and 10 feet wide. Lance-shaped 2- to 5-inch glossy leaves turn yellow in fall. Outer petals of the 1-inch winter flowers are sulphur yellow and slightly transparent, inner petals are brownish purple. Zones 7 to 9.

ᴡᶠ *Chionanthus*

ky-oh-NAN-thus. Olive family, Oleaceae.

This genus, which gets its name from Greek words meaning "snow flower," contains more than 100 evergreen and deciduous trees and shrubs from streambanks and other moist areas of the eastern United States and Asia. Two deciduous species are coveted by gardeners because of the dramatic "beards" of white flowers that they sport in late spring. On the females the flowers are followed by dark blue fruits. The elliptic leaves are somewhat glossy and may provide yellow foliage in fall.

HOW TO GROW

Give fringe trees neutral to acid soil that is deep, fertile, and moist but well aerated, in full sun to part shade. It flowers and fruits best where summers are long and hot. Requires no pruning but can be limbed up for a more treelike shape. Seeds have double dormancy (needing warm then cold stratification) so take patience to germinate.

C. retusus P. 74

c. reh-TOO-suss. Chinese Fringetree. Open and spreading slow grower to 15 to 25 feet tall and wide, with some individuals tending more toward a tree form than others. The late-spring flowers are fragrant, blooming in upright panicles up to 7 inches long at the end of new shoots. Female plants develop ½-inch dark blue drupes, and furrowed or peeling gray bark provides winter interest. Zones 6 to 8.

C. virginicus P. 75

c. ver-JIN-ih-kus. Fringetree. Also called grancy graybeard and old man's beard, this native of the eastern United States grows slowly to 12 to 20 feet tall and wide and bears its late-spring to early-summer flowers in pendent clusters of three flowers, up to 8 inches long. Flowers of different sexes are borne on separate plants, with the male having longer petals. The bark is smoother than that of the Chinese species, but may become more furrowed with age. In late summer, egg-shaped ½-inch fruits ripen to dark blue on female plants. Birds invariably find these tasty morsels, even though they are usually hidden by foliage. Zones 5 to 9.

❦ *Choisya*

CHOY-zee-uh. Citrus family, Rutaceae.

There are eight or nine species of these evergreen shrubs, which are from canyons and rocky slopes of the southwest United States and Mexico. Only one is commonly cultivated, both for attractive foliage and long-lasting white clusters of flowers that resemble orange blossoms.

HOW TO GROW

Plant the Mexican orange in light but fertile, sharply draining acid soil in full sun. It does best where nights are cool. In hotter areas, give it light shade. It makes a good screen or informal hedge and can be massed or trained against a wall for protection from cold. Make sure that it gets ample air circulation. Prune anytime to reshape; remove old branches to stimulate growth. Propagate from semihard cuttings in summer.

C. ternata   P. 75

c. ter-NAH-tuh. Mexican Orange Blossom. This is a compact moderate grower to 9 feet tall and wide. Glossy, aromatic bright green leaves form fans, composed of three leaflets, up to 6 inches across. White 1-inch flowers, which can begin appearing in very early spring and last almost until summer, are in flat-topped clusters at the end of bright green branches. The yellow-green foliage of 5-foot 'Sundance' makes it an outstanding shade plant, although it rarely flowers. Zones 8 to 10.

❦ *Cistus*

SIS-tus. Rock-rose family, Cistaceae.

This genus of about 20 generally low-growing evergreen shrubs from the Mediterranean has yielded many garden species, appreciated for their spring flowers and tolerance to drought and other adverse conditions. Silky saucer-shaped flowers with four or five petals may be solitary or bloom in flat-topped clusters, most often white or pink, with bright yellow stamens and sometimes a spot of another color at the base.

HOW TO GROW

Rock roses thrive in moderately alkaline soil of poor to average fertility and a structure that is loose and quickly draining. Most can grow in rocky soil and in salt spray and wind, but will react adversely to humidity. These are good fire-retardant plants for high-risk areas, and they also help control erosion when planted on slopes. They can become leggy, so tip-prune frequently, shear lightly, or periodically remove a few older branches. Propagate from seeds or take cuttings in summer.

C. × corbariensis (syn. C. × hybridus) P. 76

c. × cor-bah-ree-EN-siss. White Rock Rose. Spreading or rounded and averaging 4 feet high and wide, with fragrant 2-inch gray-green wavy leaves. Profuse 1½-inch late-spring flowers, which open from red buds, are white with yellow centers. Zones 8 to 10.

C. ladanifer

c. lah-DAN-if-er. Laudanum. Upright to 5 feet high and wide, with sticky, aromatic, blue-green leaves to 4 inches long. In early to midsummer it bears white flowers up to 4 inches across, often with a dark red blotch at the base of each petal, on the end of sideshoots. Zones 8 to 10.

C. × purpureus P. 76

c. × pur-PEWR-ee-us. Orchid Rock Rose. Usually 3 feet tall and wide with upright shoots. Cymes of three 3-inch dark pink flowers with a maroon base bloom in summer. Zones 8 to 10.

C. × skanbergii

c. × skan-BERG-ee-eye. Growing 2 to 3 feet tall but up to 8 feet wide, this hybrid has gray-green lance-shaped leaves. The powder pink 1-inch late-spring flowers bloom in terminal cymes. Zones 8 to 10.

❦ Clerodendrum

klee-roh-DEN-drum. Verbena family, Verbenaceae.

From this large genus—some 400 trees, shrubs, and vines from tropical and subtropical Asia and Africa—a few are known as houseplants. These two shrub species are admired by collectors of unusual plants for their fragrant tubular flowers.

HOW TO GROW

Glory bowers require rich, loamy, moisture-retentive soil in sun to part shade. They require supplemental water in drought. Shrubs need only minimal pruning except for *C. bungei,* which should be pruned back to near the ground in spring and pinched throughout the season. Start from seeds in spring, propagate from suckers or root cuttings in winter.

C. bungei

c. BUN-gee-eye. Glory Bower. This evergreen grows quickly to 6 feet high, spreading by suckers. Hard annual pruning will keep it to a compact 3 to 4 feet. Broad oval, toothed leaves are 8 to 12 inches long, ringed with purple when young, red-brown and fuzzy underneath, and unpleasantly musky if crushed. The sweet-scented dark pink flowers, tubular with five flaring lobes, bloom late summer to fall in rounded terminal panicles 6 to 8 inches across. Zones 8 to 10.

C. trichotomum

P. 77

c. try-KOH-toh-mum. Harlequin Glory Bower. A deciduous suckering multistemmed shrub or tree 10 to 15 feet tall with oval 5-inch leaves that are soft and hairy. The fragrant white flowers, blooming in clusters up to 8 inches across, are set off by ½-inch red calyxes that persist with shiny blue-green fruits. This species can freeze to its base and recover. *C. triochotomum* var. *fargesii,* which may be hardier, is smaller with green calyxes that turn pink. Zones 7 to 10.

ꙮ Clethra

KLETH-ruh. Summersweet family, Clethraceae.

About a half dozen of this genus's 60 deciduous and evergreen trees and shrubs, native to East Asia and eastern North America, are grown in gardens for their fragrant racemes of tiny white to pink late-summer flowers.

HOW TO GROW

Clethra takes about anything but alkaline soil—sun or shade, loam or sand, wet conditions or moderate drought. Full sun will produce more flowering. Use clethras in mixed borders, woodland gardens, masses, or near patios and porches where you can enjoy their pleasant scent. Pruning is unnecessary unless you want to cut back older shoots or remove suckers to control spread. The small seeds may turn black before they are ripe, about midfall, but when ready they germinate readily. Softwood cuttings root easily; hormone treatment may make them more vigorous.

C. alnifolia
P. 77

c. al-nih-FOH-lee-uh. Summersweet. An upright deciduous eastern U.S. native, to 8 feet tall and wide, with 4-inch oval leaves that sometimes turn yellow in fall. In late summer or early autumn it produces sweetly scented ½-inch flowers in upright, 4- to 6-inch racemes. The species is sometimes called sweet pepperbush for the persistent fruit capsules that resemble a string of peppercorns. 'Hummingbird' grows to only 4 feet with heavy flowering. That cultivar received an award from the Pennsylvania Horticultural Society, as did 'Ruby Spice', which has pink flowers that retain their color. The pink blooms of 'Rosea' fade to white, while those of 'Fern Valley Pink' are especially fragrant. Zones 4 to 9.

C. acuminata

c. ah-kew-mih-NAY-tuh. Cinnamon Clethra. Native from West Virginia to Alabama, it grows lankier than *C. alnifolia* to 12 feet tall and wide with leaves to 6 inches long. Terminal racemes 3 to 8 inches long bloom earlier in summer. The cinnamon brown bark may be smooth or exfoliating. Give it full sun if at all possible. Prune away its lower branches and suckers, or prune it back severely in spring to keep flowers at eye and nose level. Zones 5 to 8.

C. barbinervis
P. 78

c. bar-bih-NER-viss. Japanese Clethra. This unusual deciduous Asian species can grow 20 feet tall and wide with a candelabra-like habit. Leaves, arranged in whorls at the end of branches, can turn red, maroon, and yellow in fall. In late summer, the long dangling flower clusters are slightly arched. Smooth, exfoliating cinnamon-colored bark keeps things interesting in the winter. Zones 6 to 8.

❦ Comptonia

komp-TOH-nee-uh. Wax myrtle family, Myricaceae.

The single member of this genus is a deciduous shrub native to sandy, peaty infertile soils of eastern North America. Although not common, it is sought by garden connoisseurs for its shiny, fernlike, aromatic leaves.

HOW TO GROW

An ability to fix its own nitrogen allows sweet fern to thrive in poor to average, sandy or gravelly acid soil, in part shade to full sun. Add peat to help retain moisture, but sharp drainage is essential. Useful in natural gardens or for holding sandy banks. Sweet fern can be tricky to transplant; buy it as a container-grown shrub. It does not need pruning except for removing suckers to control spread. Propagate from rooted suckers in early spring.

C. peregrina P. 78

c. pair-eh-GREEN-uh. Sweet Fern. Forms a suckering shrub 2 to 4 feet high and at least twice as wide. The 4½-inch leaves are ½ inch wide and deeply indented, resembling a fern frond but glossy and fragrant when crushed. Inconspicuous yellow-green catkin flowers appear in midspring, followed by brown burlike fruits. Zones 2 to 6.

❦ *Convolvulus*

kon-VOLV-yew-lus. Morning glory family, Convolvulaceae.

Of some 250 annuals, perennial vines, and evergreen shrubs from throughout the world, one is the rampantly invasive field bindweed *(C. arvenis)*, and some of the other herbaceous forms are known for their invasive potential. This shrub species is well behaved, however, and valued for its silvery leaves and white morning glory flowers.

HOW TO GROW

The bush morning glory is easy to grow in light, dry soil in full sun. It makes a good rock garden plant or addition to an evening garden. Prune severely after flowering to keep it from becoming leggy. Sow seeds in spring or propagate from softwood cuttings in spring, semiripe cuttings in summer.

C. cneorum P. 79

c. nee-OH-rum. Silverbush. The species name is derived from a Greek word for "dwarf." This compact, rounded, bushy evergreen grows quickly to 2 to 4 feet high and wide, with silky, silver-gray, lance-shaped leaves 2 inches long. Emerging from pink buds in axillary clusters beween late spring and summer, the funnel-shaped white flowers have yellow centers. Zones 8 to 10.

❦ *Coprosma*

kop-ROZ-mah. Coffee family, Rubiaceae.

Of some 90 evergreen shrubs and trees, primarily from New Zealand, several are grown in gardens for their attractive foliage and ability to thrive in difficult situations. Only the species listed here is commonly available.

HOW TO GROW
Grow coprosma in neutral to acid, moderately fertile soil in full sun or part shade. It is relatively drought tolerant. This taller species makes a good hedge, screen, or espalier. Spreading forms are used as ground covers or to hold banks. Most require frequent pruning, up to twice a year, to keep them from becoming leggy and unkempt. They tolerate seaside sites, where little pruning will be needed. Propagate from semiripe cuttings in late summer.

C. repens P. 79

c. REP-enz. Mirror Plant. A dioecious shrub that grows rapidly to 10 feet tall and 6 feet wide. In shade it can develop an open, awkward habit unless pruned regularly. The common name comes from the high gloss of its 3-inch oval or oblong leaves. If you have both male and female plants, the inconspicuous greenish white flowers may be followed from summer to fall by ½-inch orange-red, sometimes yellow, berries. There are several variegated forms. Zones 8 to 10.

❦ *Cornus*

KOR-nus. Dogwood family, Cornaceae.

Whether you re a gardener or not, you undoubtedly know either *C. florida* (flowering dogwood), which brightens springtime woods in the eastern United States, or its West Coast equivalent, *C. nuttallii* (Pacific dogwood). In all, the genus contains about 45 shrubs and trees, primarily deciduous species from northern temperate regions. Many are multiseason plants with beautiful bracts in spring, handsome growth habits, colorful fall foliage, and berries that attract birds. Their leaves often have a distinctive veining that makes them looked quilted. Some develop brightly colored stems in winter.

HOW TO GROW

Dogwoods are adaptable but prefer highly organic, neutral to acid, moist yet well-aerated soil in sun to part shade. *C. mas* can take some lime or clay. The species that are grown for colorful winter stems like full sun and tolerate waterlogged soil, making them ideal for pondsides. They should have the oldest stems removed annually, since the best color occurs on new growth. Other species can be sited at the edge of a woodland, or make striking specimens in a lawn, and need little pruning. Dogwood seeds need to be stratified; pagoda dogwood is doubly dormant. Softwood cuttings need to overwinter in their propagating medium. Those grown for colorful twigs can be propagated from suckers.

C. alba   PP. 80, 81

c. AL-buh. Tartarian Dogwood. With strongly upright stems to 8 or 10 feet tall and spreading about as wide, this species is often called red-twigged dogwood because of its bright red winter shoots. The opposite 4-inch leaves turn red or orange in fall. Tiny white flowers bloom in flat 2-inch clusters in late spring to early summer; the fruits are white tinged with blue. It will sucker and form thickets. May not perform well in the South. There are numerous variegated selections. Zones 2 to 8.

C. alternifolia   P. 82

c. al-ter-nih-FOH-lee-uh. Pagoda Dogwood. This eastern North America native is a large shrub or small tree up to 20 feet tall and somewhat wider, with a strongly horizontal habit. In fall, the 2- to 5-inch alternate leaves may become purple-red. The late-spring flowers are yellow-white and fragrant, in 2-inch cymes, followed by blue-black fruits. 'Argentea' is a striking variegated form. Zones 3 to 7.

C. amomum

c. uh-MOH-mum. Silky Dogwood. Native to wet areas from Canada to Florida, this somewhat coarse dogwood can grow 10 or 15 feet tall. The off-white flowers bloom in flat-topped clusters in late spring, followed by pale blue berries that turn black if birds don't eat them. It's useful for naturalizing, or massing in soils too wet for most other shrubs. Zones 5 to 8.

C. mas   PP. 82, 83

c. MAHS. Cornelian Cherry. A Eurasian species, 15 to 20 feet tall and roughly as wide, cornelian cherry is multistemmed and rounded, branching to the ground unless limbed up. The opposite leaves are glossy, sometimes turning purple in fall. In late winter before the leaves, small bright yellow flowers bloom with early daffodils in numerous ¾-inch umbels, followed in summer by edible bright red fruits. 'Golden Glory' is a good choice for northern gardeners, while 'Spring Glow' is recommended in the South. Zones 4 to 8.

C. officinalis

c. oh-fiss-in-AL-iss. Japanese Cornel Dogwood. This rarely seen shrub or small tree is similar to *C. mas,* but many consider it even more attractive in bloom. It also develops exfoliating bark of orange, brown, and gray. Zones 4 to 8.

C. racemosa

c. rass-eh-MOH-suh. Gray Dogwood. From the American East and Midwest comes this upright species, 10 to 15 feet high and wide. Multistemmed and suckering, it can be pruned to a single trunk. Opposite 4-inch leaves may turn purple-red. The late-spring flowers are flat white clusters; white berries are borne on red stalks. A drought-tolerant choice for naturalizing. Zones 4 to 8.

C. stolonifera (syn. C. sericea)

c. stoh-lahn-IF-er-uh. Red Osier Dogwood. An eastern U.S. species that may not do well in the heat of the South, it can grow 7 feet tall and 10 feet or more wide, spreading by stolons. Upright twigs range from bright red to a dark purple-red; leaves are opposite, to 5 inches long. The white late-spring flowers are flat 2-inch clusters, and early fall berries are white, sometimes tinged blue. 'Silver and Gold', a Pennsylvania Horticultural Society award winner, has bright yellow stems and leaves with an irregular cream-colored band around the edge. Zones 2 to 8.

❧ Corylopsis

kor-ih-LOP-sis. Witch hazel family, Hamamelidaceae.

This is a small group of deciduous Asian shrubs, many of which have been tapped by gardeners for their bell-shaped fragrant yellow flowers. They hang from branches in clusters before leaves emerge in early or midspring.

HOW TO GROW

Winter hazels like acidic, fertile, moisture-retentive but well-aerated soil and part shade. They need protection from wind, hot sun, and late frosts, but rarely any pruning. They work well in shrub borders but can also deserve specimen status. Propagate by layering or softwood cuttings allowed to overwinter before replanting.

C. glabrescens
P. 83

c. glab-RES-enz. Fragrant Winter Hazel. Averaging 10 feet high and wide, open and spreading with a somewhat flattened top. The 2- to 4-inch oval leaves are yellow-green to gold in fall. Pale yellow midspring flowers with silky bracts hang in 1-inch racemes. Zones 5 to 8.

C. pauciflora
P. 84

c. paw-sih-FLOR-uh. Buttercup Winter Hazel. A dainty spreading shrub 4 to 6 feet tall and 8 feet wide, with smaller leaves that are silky underneath. Each inflorescence has fewer pale yellow flowers than does *C. glabrescens,* but each individual flower is larger and more open. Zones 6 to 8.

C. spicata
P. 85

c. spih-KOT-uh. Spike Winter Hazel. This species, 6 feet tall and 10 feet wide, is distinguished by crooked branches, and the flowers have pink stamens and darker anthers. New leaves are purple to pink, eventually becoming blue-green. Zones 5 to 8.

✿ Corylus

KOR-ih-lus. Birch family, Betulaceae.

Edible nuts are a big draw in this genus, containing about 10 species of deciduous trees and shrubs from North America, Europe, and Asia. The prominent yellow male catkins make them visually appealing as well.

HOW TO GROW

Give filberts fertile, well-drained soil in full sun or part shade. They adapt well to alkaline soils. In late winter, the first year after planting, head back stems to 2 feet to encourage branching. Then in following winters, head back side shoots and tips by about a third. Removing older branches in the center of the shrub will stimulate growth, reduce chances of disease, and make harvesting easier. Remove vigorous suckers to ground level. Propagate species by stratifying seeds.

C. americana

c. uh-mair-ih-KAY-nuh. American Filbert. This eastern U.S. native is a multi-stemmed shrub growing to 15 feet tall and 12 feet wide. In early spring it produces prominent yellow-brown male catkins up to 3 inches long. In fall you can collect the ½-inch edible nuts. Zones 4 to 9.

C. avellana   P. 86

c. ah-vel-LAY-nuh. European Filbert. Upright to 15 or 20 feet and suckering, this species is often used for commercial nut production. Drooping yellow catkins to 2½ inches appear in late winter. 'Contorta', also called Harry Lauder's Walking Stick, has twisted, curly stems, good for dried arrangements and winter interest in the landscape. Look for clones of this plant, grown from cuttings or layering, since grafted plants will produce uncurly suckers that spoil its silhouette. Zones 3 to 8.

C. cornuta

c. kor-NOO-tuh. Beaked Filbert. A smaller shrub, 4 to 8 feet tall and wide, native from Canada to Missouri and Georgia, with 1-inch catkins. It gets its common name from a "beak" that forms around the ½-inch nuts. Zones 4 to 8.

C. maxima 'Purpurea'

c. MAX-ih-muh. Purple Giant Filbert. Reaching 20 feet tall and 15 feet wide, this species has larger leaves and fruits, and the cultivar sports dark purple new foliage, with catkins and fruit also purple tinged. Zones 4 to 8.

❦ *Cotinus*

koh-TY-nus. Sumac family, Anacardiaceae.

There are only two species of these deciduous trees or shrubs, which hail from the Mediterranean, China, and the southeast United States. Gardeners prize them for their flamboyant fall color and feathery fruiting panicles that look like gray or pinkish puffs of smoke.

HOW TO GROW

Give smoke tree moderately fertile soil in sun to part shade. The popular purple-leaved varieties require full sun. Although the shrub doesn't require pruning, hard cutting back produces larger leaves. Propagation is difficult; try planting seeds in fall.

C. coggygria

P. 86

c. koh-GIG-ree-uh. Smoke Tree. This Asian species is 15 feet tall and wide, with 6-inch fruiting panicles that turn from green to tan to gray. The 3-inch leaves are yellow, orange, and red in autumn. Numerous cultivars offer burgundy or purple leaves, more predictable fall color, or pinkish to purple inflorescences. Zones 5 to 8.

C. obovatus

c. ob-oh-VAH-tus. American Smoke Tree. Oversized for a shrub at up to 30 feet high and 25 feet wide, this southeastern U.S. native is worth considering if you have a large garden. Its fruiting panicles can be a foot long, and the fall foliage is intense red, orange, and purple. Zones 4 to 8.

❦ Cotoneaster

koh-TOH-nee-ass-ter. Rose family, Rosaceae.

This genus, which deserves a prize for most often mispronounced, contains more than 200 deciduous to evergreen shrubs and trees native to temperate areas of Europe, Asia, and North Africa. Bees are drawn to their small white or pink-tinged flowers, which bloom in late spring or early summer, but most species are grown for the berries, usually red or orange.

HOW TO GROW

Give cotoneasters poor to moderately fertile soil in full sun. Most can withstand wind and some drought once established. Evergreens will tolerate shade but will not fruit as heavily. Pruning is not required and can spoil the natural grace of some, but plants can be pruned hard if needed to reshape or increase density. Variable habits within this group lend themselves to ground covers, draping down the sides of raised beds, training against walls, or using in borders or as hedges. Several species—particularly *C. microphyllus, C. pannosus,* and *C. lacteus*—have become invasive in northern and central California, so gardeners in that state are encouraged to look for substitute shrubs. Cotoneaster can be propagated with hormone-treated softwood cuttings in early summer.

C. adpressus

c. ad-PRESS-us. Creeping Cotoneaster. A deciduous, compact species with a stiff habit, to 18 inches high and spreading to 6 feet. The leaves have wavy margins and turn red in fall, with small red fruits. The white flowers are tipped with pink. This species is especially tolerant of a wide range of pH and adapts to seaside conditions, although it is prone to mites where weather is hot and dry. Zones 5 to 8.

C. apiculatus
P. 87

c. ah-pik-ew-LAY-tus. Cranberry Cotoneaster. Deciduous, low and spreading to 3 feet high and 8 feet wide. Alternate glossy ½-inch leaves turn red or bronze-purple in fall. Solitary white flowers are followed by round red ⅓-inch fruits. Zones 4 to 7.

C. dammeri

c. DAM-er-eye. Bearberry Cotoneaster. This 8- to 12-inch-tall evergreen makes a fast- growing ground cover for banks, rocky soil, and other difficult conditions, but after several years needs pruning to keep from looking ragged. The fruits, which can be unreliable, look like tiny apples. Cultivars have been selected for vigor, better fruiting, and greater or lesser height. Zones 5 to 8.

C. divaricatus

c. dih-var-ih-KAY-tus. Spreading Cotoneaster. Erect, rounded deciduous shrub 6 to 8 feet tall with wider spread. The 1-inch-long, ½-inch-wide leaves are especially dark and glossy, turning orange to red in fall with egg-shaped dark red ⅓-inch berries. It is less pest-prone than other cotoneasters. Zones 4 to 7.

C. horizontalis
P. 87

c. hor-ih-zon-TAL-iss. Rockspray Cotoneaster. A spreading deciduous species to 3 feet tall and about 6 feet wide. Trained against a wall to accentuate the distinctive herringbone pattern of its leaves, it may grow 8 feet high. The leaves turn red in fall and persist into winter. Spring pink-tinged flowers give way to small round red fruits. 'Robustus' is a faster grower. This species is especially prone to diseases such as fireblight and rust. Zones 5 to 7.

C. lacteus (syn. C. parneyi)

c. LAK-tee-us. Parney Cotoneaster. A dense, gracefully arching evergreen 6 to 10 feet tall and wide. The 2-inch leaves have deep veins. White flowers are followed by abundant red fruits in 3-inch clusters. Zones 7 to 9.

C. lucidus

c. LOO-sih-dus. Hedge Cotoneaster. An upright rounded deciduous shrub 6 to 10 feet tall and wide, with yellow and red autumn foliage, pinkish white flattened flower clusters, and round blue-black fruits. Zones 4 to 7.

C. multiflorus

c. mul-tih-FLOR-us. Many-flowered Cotoneaster. This deciduous fountainlike shrub resembles a Vanhoutte spirea in flower. It can grow to 15 feet tall and wide with gray-green leaves and long arching branches. It holds its showy clusters of 3 to 12 white flowers upright on the stem, followed by red fruits. Zones 4 to 7.

C. salicifolius (syn. C. flococcus)   P. 88

c. sal-iss-ih-FOH-lee-us. Willow-leaved Cotoneaster. A spreading and arching evergreen, 10 to 15 feet tall, with somewhat hidden woolly 2-inch flower clusters and bright red berries. It may need pruning to keep the base from becoming leggy and can self-sow to become invasive. More desirable are low-growing cultivars, including 'Emerald Carpet', 'Repens', and 'Scarlet Leader'. Zones 6 to 8.

❦ Cryptomeria

krip-toh-MAIR-ee-uh. Bald-cypress family, Taxodiaceae.

This genus is represented by a single species of coniferous evergreen from Asia, valued for the appealing spiral pattern of its leaves, graceful conical habit, and peeling red-brown bark. There are numerous cultivars small enough to be used as shrubs.

HOW TO GROW

Cryptomerias prefer deep, fertile, humus-rich, acid soil with ample moisture, in sun or light shade. On some selections, needles may turn purple-bronze in winter. Protect them from wind. Use the dwarf selections in rock gardens or in a shrub border. They do not adapt well to containers. Pruning should not be needed. Propagation is difficult, but most successful with relatively thick hardwood cuttings in winter.

C. japonica   P. 89

c. juh-PON-ih-kuh. Japanese Cryptomeria. The species can eventually reach 60 feet tall or more. Three popular small cultivars are 'Elegans Compacta', broadly rounded at 3 to 6 feet tall with feathery new foliage, generally bluish green with a purple tinge in winter; 'Globosa Nana', with a domed or pyramid shape, 2 to 5 feet high and roughly as wide; and 'Vilmoriniana', a 1- to 2-foot dwarf with soft gray-green summer foliage that turns purple-bronze in winter. Zones 5 to 8.

❦ Cyrilla

sigh-RILL-a. Cyrilla family, Cyrillaceae.

The only species in this genus is a deciduous to evergreen shrub that grows naturally from the southeast United States to South America. In a garden it will lend interest throughout the seasons with an attractive foliage pattern and fall color, fragrant flowers, and handsome bark.

HOW TO GROW
Leatherwood should have rich, moisture-retentive acid soil in sun or part shade with shelter from wind. It needs little pruning, although mature plants can sucker. Sow seeds in fall or take semiripe cuttings.

C. racemiflora   P. 90
c. rass-eh-mih-FLOR-uh. Leatherwood. This native grows 3 to more than 10 feet tall and wide, smallest where summers are cool. Its leaves, which sometimes appear in whorls, turn orange and red in fall and may linger in the South. The fragrant white flowers are also held in a whorl—a 3- to 6-inch raceme of lizard-tail spikes that bloom in late summer or fall. Removing suckers and lower stems will reveal smooth brown bark and interesting twisted branches. Zones 6 to 10.

❦ Cytisus

sigh-TISS-us. Pea family, Fabaceae.

About 50 species of deciduous or evergreen shrubs from Europe, western Asia, and northern Africa. The palmate leaves are usually opposite with three leaflets, the flowers pealike followed by linear pods that can be downy.

HOW TO GROW
Tolerant of poor, acidic soil; may become chlorotic in alkaline soil. Tends to be short-lived. Needs minimal pruning, but you can cut back flowered

shoots to a new bud or sideshoot if you avoid cutting into old wood. Seeds may need to be soaked in hot water, but sometimes self-sow. Take cuttings with a heel in late summer and overwinter in sand. *C. scoparius* has become a pest in the West, Northeast, and Mid-Atlantic and should be avoided.

C. battandieri

c. bah-ton-dee-AIR-ee. Pineapple Broom. Deciduous, erect shrub to 15 feet tall and wide with hairy silver palmate leaves. Dense terminal racemes of yellow flowers look and smell like pineapples, followed by hairy pods. Zones 7 to 9.

C. × praecox

P. 90

c. × PREE-coks. Warminster Broom. Deciduous and dense, to 4 feet tall and wide, with many long upright shoots and undivided leaves. Midspring flowers are pale yellow. Cultivars offer white, salmon pink, or peach-colored blossoms. Zones 6 to 9.

❦ Daboecia

dab-oh-EE-kee-uh. Heath family, Ericaceae.

There are two species of these dwarf evergreen shrubs, native to European coastal cliffs and heaths, which are grown in gardens for their colorful pitcher-shaped flowers.

HOW TO GROW

Give this heath rich, acid soil in full sun. Use the plants as ground covers, or for underplanting taller acid-loving shrubs. Trim lightly in spring to maintain their tidy habit. Propagate by layering or taking semiripe cuttings in midsummer.

D. cantabrica

P. 91

d. kan-TAH-brih-kuh. Irish Heath. Also called connemara or St. Dabeoc's heath, this little shrub grows 12 to 20 inches tall and about twice as wide, with upright shoots of narrow evergreen leaves. From summer through fall, clusters of rosy purple urn-shaped flowers bloom above the leaves. Zones 7 to 8.

❦ *Daphne*

DAF-nee. Daphne family, Thymeleaceae.

Heady fragrance is the primary claim to fame for landscape shrubs in this genus. It embraces some 50 species, deciduous to evergreen, from Europe, Asia, and North Africa.

HOW TO GROW

Most daphnes will grow in either full sun or part shade, and all require fertile, well-amended soil that stays cool and moist at the roots. They have a reputation for being difficult and often die suddenly for unknown reasons after thriving for years. Pruning should be kept to a minimum. Seeds (which are poisonous) need cold treatment; you can also propagate daphne by layering in spring or taking soft or semihard cuttings.

D. × burkwoodii   P. 91

d. × berk-WOOD-ee-eye. Burkwood Daphne. This dense, semievergreen, upright hybrid grows 3 to 4 feet high and wide and is the source of many cultivars. The clusters of sweetly fragrant late-spring flowers (it can rebloom in early fall) are white, sometimes tinged with pink or lavender. The 1½-inch leaves are linear and often variegated. 'Carol Mackie' has cream margins and flowers of palest pink. 'Somerset' is slightly bigger with brighter pink flowers. Zones 4 to 7.

D. caucasica   P. 92

d. kaw-KASS-ih-kuh. Caucasian Daphne. This deciduous daphne is 4 to 5 feet tall and wide. The intensely fragrant white flowers are heaviest in late spring but can continue sporadically until fall, followed by black or red berries. The pale green leaves are 3 inches long. A Pennsylvania Horticultural Society award winner. Zones 5 to 7.

D. cneorum   P. 92

d. nee-OH-rum. Rose Daphne. Sometimes called garland flower, this rock-garden evergreen grows only 8 inches tall with ½-inch dark green leaves and branches that trail along the ground or over a wall. The fragrant flowers, which vary from white to rose pink, appear in abundant clusters in late spring, reblooming in late summer. Zones 4 to 7.

D. genkwa
P. 93

d. GENK-wah. Lilac Daphne. Clusters of lilac-colored flowers, lacking noticeable fragrance, appear in mid- to late spring before the leaves on this 3- to 4-foot upright shrub. Not as widely available as some other daphnes, it is less heavily branched but provides winter interest with copper bark. Zones 6 to 8.

D. mezereum

d. meh-ZEE-ree-um. February Daphne. This semievergreen or deciduous daphne may live up to its common name by blooming in late winter or wait until early spring. The clusters of two to four fragrant, rose- or lilac-colored flowers are followed in early summer by red fruits. Usually under 4 feet tall, it grows upright with pale green or grayish leaves. Zones 5 to 8.

D. odora
P. 94

d. oh-DOR-uh. Winter Daphne. This dense rounded daphne, 4 to 6 feet tall, blooms in late winter or earliest spring with large wonderfully fragrant purple-pink or white flowers. Considered more shade tolerant but less cold hardy than other daphnes, it has glossy dark evergreen leaves and occasional red berries. Zones 7 to 9.

❦ Decaisnea

deh-KAYS-nee-uh. Lardizabala family, Lardizabalaceae.

There are just two species in this genus, both hailing from woods in western China. Gardeners who enjoy growing a conversation piece should consider this shrub for its huge tropical-looking leaves and odd, drooping fruits.

HOW TO GROW

Provide sun or part shade in fertile soil with protection from strong winds. In the landscape, blue-bean is destined to be a focal point. It needs minimal pruning. Sow seeds in fall.

D. fargesii
P. 94

d. far-JEE-see-eye. Blue-bean. This upright, open, deciduous shrub can grow more than 15 feet tall and wide. In late spring it produces 1-inch bell-shaped yellow-green flowers in 12- to 18-inch panicles, followed by the decidedly more dramatic bluish bean pods. The 3-foot-long pinnate leaves show a hint of blue when they emerge. Zones 7 to 9.

❦ *Deutzia*

DOOT-see-uh. Hydrangea family, Hydrangeaceae.

This genus encompasses more than 60 species of mostly deciduous shrubs from East Asia, grown for their airy sprays of white or pink spring flowers and often delicate, arching habit. Some develop exfoliating bark with age.

HOW TO GROW

Give deutzias full sun or light shade and moderately fertile soil. They tolerate some alkalinity and pollution but not much drought. They can become ragged, so give them a hard pruning to within 6 inches of the ground every two to three years. Propagate with softwood cuttings.

D. crenata 'Nikko'   P. 95

d. kreh-NAH-tuh. By far the most popular deutzia, sometimes listed under *D. gracilis*, 'Nikko' grows only 2 feet tall but spreads to 4 feet wide, making it excellent in a rock garden or as a ground cover. In late spring the branches drip panicles of starry white flowers, and in fall the dainty leaves turn burgundy. Winner of the Pennsylvania Horticultural Society Gold Medal. Zones 5 to 8.

D. gracilis

d. GRASS-ih-liss. Gradually growing 3 to 5 feet tall in an erect, graceful mound, its upright panicles or racemes of white flowers are slightly fragrant. Zones 4 to 8.

D. × lemoinei

d. × lem-WON-ee-eye. Lemoine Deutzia. A dense shrub growing to an average of 6 feet tall and wide, this hybrid is considered the most reliably cold-hardy deutzia. The pure white flowers bloom in late spring and the foliage often provides good yellow fall color. Zones 4 to 8.

D. × magnifica

d. × mag-NIF-ih-cuh. Showy Deutzia. This upright hybrid, which grows 6 feet or taller, is considered outstanding for its dense 3-inch panicles of double flowers. Zones 6 to 8.

D. scabra

d. SKAB-ruh. Fuzzy Deutzia. Growing to 8 feet with exfoliating bark and reliable blooms, this species is coarser than some others in the genus. Zones 5 to 8.

🌿 *Diervilla*

dy-er-VILL-uh. Honeysuckle family, Caprifoliaceae.

There are three species of these suckering deciduous shrubs, all native to North America, grown for their dense habit, sulphur yellow summer flowers, and extreme toughness.

HOW TO GROW

Adaptable to a wide range of soils, the bush honeysuckle prefers sun but will take some shade. Because it spreads by underground stolons, it makes a good choice for difficult situations such as hillsides and windy sites. Problems are rare. Give it some mulch for cool roots and rejuvenate as needed by pruning close to the ground in early spring. Propagate from suckers or softwood cuttings.

D. lonicera 'Copper'

d. lahn-ISS-er-uh. Bush Honeysuckle cultivar. This selection of a 2- to 3-foot native has coppery new leaves produced throughout the growing season, as well as yellow flowers and fall foliage. Zones 3 to 8.

D. sessilifolia   P. 95

d. sess-il-ih-FOH-lee-uh. Southern Bush Honeysuckle. This species is 3 to 5 feet tall and suckers to 5 feet across. The tubular yellow flowers appear in flattened 3-inch terminal clusters, among lance-shaped leaves up to 7 inches long. 'Butterfly' has deep yellow flowers. Zones 4 to 8.

🌿 *Disanthus*

dis-AN-thus. Witch hazel family, Hamamelidaceae.

Brilliant fall color has made a rising star of this deciduous species from the woods and mountains of Asia, the only member of its genus.

HOW TO GROW

Disanthus needs rich, moisture-retentive, slightly acid soil in light shade, especially in the southern part of its range. Plant it as a specimen in a spot where you can admire its autumn show. It won't tolerate wind or drought and may develop fungal diseases in high humidity. It rarely needs pruning. Propagate from seeds or cuttings.

D. cercidifolius   P. 96

d. ser-sih-dih-FOH-lee-us. The habit is open and upright to 10 feet high with a rounded crown spreading as wide. The leaves don't look like others in the witch hazel family but are heart shaped like those of the unrelated redbud and 4 inches across. Blue-green in summer, in fall they may simultaneously show yellow, orange, red, and purple. The spidery purple-red flowers, which appear at the same time, have a slightly unpleasant scent. Zones 5 to 8.

❦ *Edgeworthia*

ej-WORTH-ee-uh. Daphne family, Thymelaeaceae.

From an East Asian genus come three species of deciduous to evergreen shrubs, grown for unusual tubular flowers.

HOW TO GROW

Plant in moist, rich soil in sun or dappled shade. Rarely needs pruning. Plant seeds in autumn or take semiripe cuttings in summer.

E. chrysantha   P. 96

e. krih-SAN-thuh. Averages 5 feet high and wide with narrowly oval blue-green tropical-looking deciduous leaves more than 5 inches long. The yellow tubular flowers appear in late winter in terminal clusters of 30 to 40. There is considerable confusion about names in this genus, with this species sometimes sold as *E. paperifera*, with white flowers and a yellow "mouth." Zones 8 to 10.

❦ *Elaeagnus*

el-ee-AG-nus. Oleaster family, Elaeagnaceae.

A genus of 45 deciduous or evergreen trees and shrubs, primarily from Asia, grown for silvery leaves, small but intensely fragrant flowers, and berries that attract wildlife.

HOW TO GROW

Several of the Asian species, notably *E. angustifolia* (Russian olive) and *E. umbellata* (autumn olive), have escaped cultivation in many areas, displacing native trees and birds' nesting sites in fields and along streams.

They have succeeded in spreading because they are tolerant of wind and poor, dry, even salty soil, as are the species listed here. They can become chlorotic in highly alkaline soil. They do not need pruning, except to remove solid green branches on variegated selections. Propagation is easy by cuttings taken in summer or from rooted suckers.

E. commutata

e. kom-mew-TAY-tuh. Silverberry. A thicket-forming deciduous shrub 6 to 12 feet tall and wide, this species is native to the American Midwest and eastern Canada. It has reddish brown shoots and broad, elliptic, showy silver leaves. The silvery yellow-white ½-inch fragrant flowers appear in late spring and are followed by red berries. Zones 3 to 6.

E. × ebbingei   P. 97

e. × eb-BIN-gee-eye. This hybrid, 10 to 12 feet tall and wide, has silvery speckled, semievergreen to evergreen leaves. The small creamy flowers appear in fall. 'Gilt Edge' has yellow-gold leaf margins. Zones 7 to 9.

❦ Eleutherococcus

eh-loo-thur-oh-KOK-us. Ginseng family, Araliaceae

This genus was formerly called *Acanthopanax*. Only a few of its 30 members, mostly deciduous Asian trees, shrubs, and occasionally vines, are grown in gardens. These are valued for their dramatic foliage and fall fruits.

HOW TO GROW

This species will tolerate poor, dry soil and sun or shade. Good for a screen or security hedge in polluted cities. Prune as needed to keep its form upright or to remove suckers. Propagate by seeds, softwood cuttings, or suckers.

E. sieboldianus   P. 97

e. see-bold-ee-AY-nus. Five-leaf Aralia. This spiny shrub, 8 feet tall and wide, has arching branches and bright green palmate leaves with three to seven leaflets. The late-spring umbels of star-shaped greenish flowers give way to round black fruits. 'Variegatus' has creamy white margins. Zones 4 to 8.

❦ *Embothrium*

em-BOTH-ree-um. Protea family, Proteaceae.

A genus of eight evergreen shrubs and trees from woods of Central and South America. If you have room for it, the species listed here is worth seeking out and attempting to grow for the spectacular fiery red-orange tubular flowers that give it its common name.

HOW TO GROW

Grow in full sun or part shade in neutral to acid, moisture-retentive soil where it is protected from wind. The plant is native to the Chilean Andes and thrives only in relatively mild climates such as the Pacific Northwest. It needs little pruning. Sow seeds in spring, or root from greenwood cuttings or suckers.

E. coccineum   P. 98

e. kok-SIN-ee-um. Chilean Firebush. Upright, freely branching and suckering shrub 10 to 30 feet tall and 15 feet wide. The leathery, narrow oval leaves grow to 4 inches or more. Waxy flowers, which appear in late spring and early summer, are intensely orange-red 2-inch tubes, in dense terminal and axillary racemes. Zones 8 to 10.

❦ *Enkianthus*

en-kee-AN-thus. Heath family, Ericaceae.

This genus, the name of which means "pregnant flower," contains about 10 species of primarily deciduous shrubs and trees from East Asia. They are increasingly making their way into gardens because of their interesting habits, clusters of bell-shaped flowers, and arresting fall color.

HOW TO GROW

Good in open woods with sun or part shade in neutral to acid, humus-rich soil. An excellent companion in a shrub border with acid-loving broad-leaved evergreens. Pruning is rarely needed. Propagate from seeds or softwood cuttings.

E. campanulatus   P. 98

e. kam-pan-yew-LAY-tus. Redvein Enkianthus. Generally ranging from 8 to 15 feet tall and wide, this species is narrow and upright with layered branches. The elliptic leaves are held in whorls at the ends of branches and turn bright yellow, orange, and red in fall. The slightly fragrant creamy flowers with pink to red veins hang in graceful clusters of 5 to 15 in late spring as the leaves unfurl. 'Red Bells' has slightly redder flowers and stays somewhat smaller. There are several selections with pink to red flowers. Zones 5 to 8.

E. cernuus var. rubens

e. SER-noo-us var. ROO-benz. This variety is 6 to 8 feet tall. Its leaves have a purple tinge in summer and turn purple-red in autumn. The flowers are reddish purple with toothed lips. Zones 5 to 8.

E. perulatus

P. 99

e. pur-yew-LAY-tuss. White Enkianthus. Still difficult to find, this species grows slowly to 6 feet and eventually wider, with a striking layered habit. In late spring, dangling clusters of the urn-shaped white flowers bloom before the leaves emerge. The autumn color is intense scarlet. Zones 5 to 8.

✿ Erica

AIR-ih-kuh. Heath family, Ericaceae.

More than 700 species of these evergreen shrubs occur in moors and heaths in Europe and temperate parts of Asia and Africa. Most are grown as shrubby ground covers, for their needlelike whorled leaves and terminal racemes of bell-shaped flowers. A collection of species and cultivars provides color through most of the year. There are a few treelike species.

HOW TO GROW

Most heaths demand acidic soils of peat and sand in open sunny sites. They're good for low hedges, rock gardens, and as companions for azaleas and rhododendrons. Prune spring bloomers after flowering, fall bloomers in spring to about an inch above the previous season's growth. Give tree heathers a light trim. Propagate by semiripe cuttings or layering.

E. arborea

P. 99

e. ar-BOR-ee-uh. Tree Heath. To 12 feet tall with honey-scented white flowers in the spring. Half as tall are E. arborea var. alpina, which is anise scented with profuse flowering, and 'Albert', which has yellow foliage but rarely blooms. 'Estrella Gold' is chartreuse and 4 feet tall. Zones 7 to 10.

E. carnea

P. 100

e. KAR-nee-uh. Winter Heath. This species from eastern Europe is the best choice for the Northeast. With a prostrate habit, usually around 6 inches tall, plants spread quickly to smother weeds. Flowers, which have protruding anthers, begin budding in summer and can take nine months to finish blooming, depending on the climate. The needlelike leaves can be dark or pale green, gray-green, or golden, some tipped with cream or pink. Flowers include white, pink, magenta, and bicolors. Zones 5 to 7.

E. × darleyensis

e. × dar-lee-EN-siss. Tolerant of alkaline soil, this hybrid grows in mounds 2 feet tall, producing white to rosy flowers in late winter or early spring. It performs best in the Southeast. There are many cultivars with slightly varying foliage hues or more predictable bloom colors. Zones 7 to 8.

E. vagans

e. VAY-ganz. Cornish Heath. Also called wandering heath for the ground-hugging branches that can develop on this 2-foot-tall mound. Purple-pink flowers bloom midsummer to early fall. Zones 5 to 8.

❦ *Escallonia*

es-kal-LONE-ee-uh. Currant family, Grossulariaceae.

Approximately 50 species of evergreen shrubs, most from South America, grown for their shiny, often aromatic foliage and long-blooming funnel-shaped, five-petaled flowers.

HOW TO GROW

Escallonia doesn't tolerate highly alkaline soil, temperature extremes, or wind and is suitable primarily for the Northwest or mild coastal regions. (It doesn't mind salt.) It needs full sun and is happy against a sunny wall or in a hedge. Although it doesn't require pruning it can be pruned hard to correct shape or restrict growth. Propagate with semihard cuttings.

E. × exoniensis 'Frades'

P. 100

e. × ek-soh-nee-EN-siss. This hybrid selection is a dense shrub growing 12 or more feet tall with relatively small, glossy leaves. Profuse pink or rosy flowers cover it most of the year. It is often espaliered. Zones 8 to 9.

E. × langleyensis 'Apple Blossom' P. 101

e. × lang-lee-EN-siss. Pink Escallonia cultivar. Dense but sprawling if not controlled, growing to 4 or 5 feet with large leaves. Profuse pale pink flowers with a white eye appear for many weeks from late spring to early fall. Zones 8 to 9.

E. rubra

e. ROO-bruh. This upright, compact species grows anywhere from 8 to 15 feet tall with glossy dark green leaves and profuse 3-inch panicles of deep red flowers. 'C. F. Ball' will stay under 3 feet with some attention. Zones 8 to 9.

❦ Euonymus

yew-ON-eh-mus. Bittersweet family, Celastraceae.

This genus comprises some 175 species of deciduous to evergreen shrubs, trees, and climbers, mainly from Asia. Several species are popular in gardens because they dependably provide bright fall color or interesting seed displays. Unfortunately, some of those most often grown — *E. elatus* and *E. europeaeus* — have escaped into the wild.

HOW TO GROW

As a rule, euonymus should have full sun and moisture-retentive soil. While evergreen species will tolerate some shade, those with variegated foliage won't develop their best coloration without plenty of sunlight. Use them as specimens, in the shrub border, or in masses. The native species is good for naturalizing where you need some fall interest. None require pruning, but some are prone to scale and fungal diseases. Propagate with ripe seeds, softwood cuttings of deciduous species, and semiripe cuttings of evergreens.

E. alatus P. 101

e. uh-LAY-tus. Winged Euonymus. This species has escaped cultivation in the East and upper Midwest, and even cultivars will self-sow. Gardeners in those regions should avoid it, or choose cultivars that produce little seed. The species grows 10 to 15 feet tall and wide, with 3-inch toothed leaves that turn fuchsia red in fall. Insignificant yellow-green early-summer flowers give way to capsules of orange-red seeds. 'Rudy Haag' grows slowly to 4 or 5 feet but has inconspicuous fruits. Zones 4 to 8.

E. americanus
P. 102

e. uh-mair-ih-KAY-nus. Strawberry Bush. This native of the eastern United States, 4 to 6 feet tall with a loose suckering habit, is often called hearts-a-bustin' in honor of its surprising fall fruits. Red and bumpy, they split open to reveal orange-red seeds. Not otherwise showy, so situate it at the edge of a wood or other out-of-the-way spot. Zones 6 to 9.

E. europaeus 'Red Cap'
P. 102

e. ew-roh-PAY-us. European Spindle Tree cultivar. The species, although not necessarily its cultivars, is invasive in the East and upper Midwest. Growing fast to 12 to 25 feet tall and wide, the cultivar is notable for abundant fall fruits that are reddish pink with exposed orange seeds (arils). Zones 4 to 7.

E. japonicus
P. 103

e. juh-PON-ih-kuss. Japanese Spindle Tree. Growing 12 to 16 feet tall and 6 feet wide, this evergreen species has been the source of a wide array of variegated cultivars. There are dwarf and variegated forms, such as 'Silver King', which grows to 6 feet tall and 3 feet wide with off-white leaf margins. Zones 6 to 9.

❦ Exochorda

ex-oh-KOR-duh. Rose family, Rosaceae.

A small group of deciduous shrubs from central and East Asia, these bushes go through a Cinderella-like transformation in spring when they explode with virginal white flowers. The common name, pearlbush, comes from the appearance of their swelling buds.

HOW TO GROW

While they prefer loamy acid soil, most pearlbushes are adaptable. Plant them in a shrub border in sun or part shade with plants that provide a longer season of interest, since they are rather nondescript when out of flower. After flowering, cut back a third of the old shoots to promote flowers and maintain the shape. Propagate by softwood cuttings in summer.

E. giraldii

e. jer-AL-dee-eye. Redbud Pearlbush. Usually up to 10 feet tall and wide, this species from northwest China has pinkish new leaves that retain red veins. The upright clusters of 1-inch flowers bloom in late spring. A variety, *E. geraldii* var. *wilsonii*, is more upright with green veins and larger flowers, to 2 inches across. Zones 6 to 9.

E. × *macrantha* 'The Bride'   P. 103

e. × mak-RAN-thuh. A compact, bushy form with arching branches, this selection rarely grows more than 4 feet tall (the species can grow to 15) although it may spread somewhat wider. In midspring it is smothered in 4-inch racemes of 6 to 10 white flowers. Zones 4 to 8.

❦ *Fallugia*

fal-LOO-gee-uh. Rose family, Rosaceae.

This genus boasts only one species, a deciduous shrub native to the southwest United States and Mexico. It is being eagerly adopted by dry-climate gardeners for its white roselike flowers and interesting seed heads.

HOW TO GROW

Apache plume prefers dry, sandy soil in full sun, and hot dry summers. Excellent in a shrub or mixed border of other drought-tolerant species. Needs little care of any kind. Propagate by seeds.

F. paradoxa   P. 104

f. pair-uh-DOKS-uh. Apache Plume. Usually 5 to 8 feet tall, it has tiny, pinnately dissected deep green leaves that are semipersistent. Slightly arching branches peel as they age. The white single-rose flowers last throughout the season, and more interest is provided by feathery achenes (seed heads) from which it gets its common name. Zones 6 to 10.

❦× *Fatshedera*

× fats-HED-er-uh. Ginseng family, Araliaceae.

A hybrid between plants in two genera—*Hedera* (ivy) and *Fatsia*—useful for its dramatic foliage and dual nature as a shrub or climber.

HOW TO GROW

Grow in reasonably fertile soil in sun to moderate shade, as a freestanding shrub or trained against a wall. Does not require pruning except to control growth; you may want to grow it in a container to overwinter as a houseplant. Propagate from softwood cuttings or heel cuttings.

× *F. lizei*   P. 104

× F. liz-AY-eye. As a shrub, it forms a loose mound 5 feet high and 10 feet wide, but will climb to 10 feet if trained as a vine. The leathery, dark green leaves are palmate with five to seven leaflets and up to 10 inches across. In fall, rounded flower panicles are greenish white and sterile. Zones 8 to 10.

ᴡ *Fatsia*

FAT-see-uh. Ginseng family, Araliaceae.

At most there are three species of these evergreen shrubs or small trees, all from East Asia, grown for dramatic-looking foliage and autumn flowers and fruits.

HOW TO GROW

Fatsia is adaptable but prefers fertile, quickly draining soil and dappled to deep shade, with protection from cold wind and hot sun. Native to coastal areas, it tolerates salt spray and pollution. Lends a tropical air to swimming pools, patios, and entryways and adapts to container culture. Remove any suckers and prune back hard if plants become spindly. Otherwise prune lightly to retain shape and foliage display. Propagate from seeds or semihard cuttings in midsummer.

F. japonica   P. 105

f. juh-PON-ih-kuh. Rounded and suckering, to 6 or 8 feet tall and wide. The palmate leaves have 7 to 11 deep lobes. Fall flowers are tiny and white in spherical clusters, followed by little round black berries. There are forms with gold or white variegated leaves. Zones 8 to 10.

ᴡ *Forsythia*

for-SITH-ee-uh. Olive family, Oleaceae.

A genus of seven primarily deciduous shrubs from eastern Asia (with one from southeast Europe), widely grown for their early-spring display of yellow flowers with four flaring petals. The stems leaf out as blossoms fall and, on some forsythias, will root where they touch the ground.

HOW TO GROW

Give forsythia average soil in full sun or dappled shade. It adapts to a wide range of pH and urban insults, such as compacted soil. Grow on a hillside, as a specimen or in masses where its weeping habit can be best displayed. Forsythia is a favorite to force for indoor flowers in late winter. Northern gardeners should select cultivars for bud hardiness. Prune to the ground after flowering or remove the oldest stems. Seeds are not hard to germinate and softwood cuttings root readily, but layering is the easiest route to propagation.

F. 'Arnold Dwarf'. Grown primarily for its stature, only 3 feet tall and about 7 feet wide, and not a heavy flowerer. The bright green leaves are serrated. Good for banks and other bare areas since it roots itself readily. Zones 5 to 8.

F. × *intermedia*

f. × in-ter-MEE-dee-uh. This hybrid, which averages 10 feet tall, is the source of the most popular cultivars. 'Beatrix Farrand' is relatively upright and is smothered with deep yellow flowers, but less bud hardy than some others; 'Lynwood' ('Lynwood Gold') is upright to 7 feet and considered one of the most reliable for uniform bloom on the stems; 'Spectabilis' bears masses of bright yellow flowers in its axils; 'Spring Glory', which has big sulfur yellow flowers, is a good choice for southern gardeners because it needs less cold than others to flower well. Zones 6 to 9.

F. ovata

f. oh-VAH-tuh. Early Forsythia. Compact and blooming earlier than other forsythias, this species is used to breed new cultivars for cold hardiness. 'Northern Sun' grows 8 to 10 feet high and not quite as wide with sulphur yellow flowers. Zones 4 to 8.

F. suspensa var. *sieboldii*   P. 105

f. suh-SPEN-suh var. see-BOLD-ee-eye. Weeping Forsythia. Left as a shrub, it grows 8 to 10 feet high and often wider. Some gardeners train its pendulous branches against a wall where the golden yellow flowers can be admired 15 or more feet above the ground. Zones 6 to 8.

F. viridissima 'Bronxensis'   P. 106

f. ver-ih-DISS-ih-muh. Green-stem Forsythia cultivar. A good bank cover, growing only 1 foot high but 2 to 3 feet wide, with small, serrated, bright green leaves and pale yellow flowers. Zones 6 to 8.

ᵂᵉ *Fothergilla*

foth-er-GIL-luh. Witch hazel family, Hamamelidaceae.

In this genus there are just two species, both deciduous shrubs from the eastern United States. In spring they have white, honey-scented bottlebrush flowers. The real show comes in fall, when the foliage turns a rainbow of colors. The leaves, sometimes blue-green, are veined in the same manner as the related witch hazel.

HOW TO GROW

Provide rich, moisture-retentive acid soil in full sun (for best bloom and coloring) or part shade. Good along foundations or with azaleas and rhododendrons. Fothergilla needs minimal pruning. Propagation is difficult; seeds need double-dormancy treatment, cuttings require bottom heat (for suckers or root cuttings) and mist (for softwood cuttings in summer).

F. gardenii

f. gar-DEEN-ee-eye. Dwarf Fothergilla. Usually 3 feet tall and wide but sometimes reaching 5 feet. The white flowers, which consist entirely of showy stamens in 1- to 2-inch cylindrical spikes, open in midspring before the leaves. On some selections the foliage is a pronounced blue-green. In fall it turns yellow, orange, and red. 'Blue Mist' won a Gold Medal from the Pennsylvania Horticultural Society. Zones 5 to 9.

F. major   P. 106

f. MAY-jer. Large Fothergilla. Up to 10 feet tall and about as wide, this species often has larger flowers than the dwarf species and blooms slightly later, as its leaves are emerging. Its foliage is blue-green in the North, darker green in the South. It is less drought tolerant than its smaller relative. 'Mt. Airy' was selected for consistent fall coloring, often including reddish purple, and heavy flowering. Zones 4 to 8.

ᵂᵉ *Fouquieria*

foh-KEE-ree-uh. Ocotillo family, Fourquieriaceae.

This genus includes about 10 deciduous, upright-stemmed succulent or spiny shrubs or trees, native to low arid hillsides of the southwest United States and Mexico. In the desert landscapes where it is at home, it provides a dramatic silhouette and bright tubular flowers.

HOW TO GROW

Grow ocotillo in poor to average, sharply draining sandy soil in full sun. Highlight its shape against the sky or a wall, or plant several as a security hedge or screen. It doesn't tolerate overwatering and rarely needs pruning. After prolonged drought the canes often look dead but will turn green again after a rain. Propagates easily by cuttings.

F. splendens   P. 107

f. SPLEN-denz. Ocotillo. Grows 10 to 25 feet tall with numerous white-striped thorny branches in a candelabra shape. It has two types of leaves: 2-inch elliptic leaves and shorter spoon-shaped leaves. These appear after rains and fall in a drought, leaving numerous scars. The narrow bell-shaped flowers, which bloom after spring and summer rains, are bright red in clusters 4 to 11 inches long, closing at night and attracting hummingbirds by day. Zones 8 to 11.

❦ Fremontodendron

free-mont-oh-DEN-dron. Chocolate family, Sterculiaceae.

This genus is represented by just two species that can be considered shrubs or trees, evergreen to semievergreen and native to dry woods and mountainsides in the southwest United States and northern Mexico. They are valued by gardeners for long-lasting bright yellow flowers and leathery, lobed, deep green leaves that are felted underneath. The blooms are followed by persistent cone-shaped seed capsules covered by reddish brown hairs.

HOW TO GROW

Give flannel bushes dry soil of poor to average fertility, siting them in full sun where they are protected from wind. Provide sharp drainage, such as on a hillside, with drought-loving companion plants. Flannel bushes are often wall-trained, which shows off their handsome foliage and flowers. They tend to be short-lived. Pruning is minimal except for wall-trained specimens. Propagate by seeds (which may benefit from soaking) or from soft or semiripe cuttings taken in summer.

F. 'California Glory'. Vigorous and upright to 20 feet tall and 12 feet wide, with rounded five-lobed leaves. Bright yellow 2-inch saucer-shaped flowers with an outer red tinge bloom late spring into fall. Zones 8 to 10.

F. californicum
P. 108

f. kal-ih-FORN-ih-kum. Common Flannel Bush. Differs from 'California Glory' in having smaller lemon yellow flowers that appear all at once in mid-spring. Zones 8 to 10.

F. 'Ken Taylor'. Forms a spreading mound 6 feet tall and 10 feet wide with orange-yellow flowers. Zones 8 to 10.

❧ *Gardenia*

gar-DEEN-ee-uh. Coffee family, Rubiaceae.

Even if you don't live where these shrubs will grow outdoors, you know their intensely fragrant, waxy white flowers, probably offered by your nearest grocer as a houseplant. Double forms are employed as corsages. In the garden, they are also prized for their thick, glossy leaves. The approximately 200 members of this genus are evergreen shrubs and trees from tropical Asia and Africa. Most of the widely available cultivars were developed from the single Chinese species listed here.

HOW TO GROW

In the garden, give gardenias dappled to part shade and provide rich, humusy, neutral to acid soil that retains moisture but drains well. Site them near a sidewalk, deck, or window where the fragrance can be savored. They can be espaliered or used as a hedge or screen. Gardenias should be planted shallowly, like azaleas and rhododendrons, or in a container. The roots don't tolerate competition or heavy cultivation, so mulch them well. Feed monthly during the growing season and lessen disease problems by providing adequate air circulation. Indoors, they are prone to whitefly. Deadhead regularly or prune just lightly in spring, unless espaliered. Sow seeds in spring or root softwood cuttings in summer.

G. augusta (formerly *G. jasminoides*)
P. 109

g. ah-GUSS-tuh. To more than 30 feet tall in the wild, in the garden it is more often 5 or 6 feet tall and wide, with a dense and rounded habit. The 3-inch glossy, leathery leaves are usually in whorls of three. Thick-petaled white flowers, 2 or 3 inches across, appear from late spring to midsummer. Single forms have a half dozen petals, but double forms with 12 are most popular. 'August Beauty' blooms into fall; 'Mystery' is upright to 8 feet with flowers to 5 inches across; 'Radicans' has small leaves and grows to 1 foot tall and twice as wide; 'Veitchii' grows to 4½ feet with profuse flowering from midspring to late fall. Zones 8 to 11.

🌿 Garrya

GAIR-ee-uh. Silk-tassel family, Garryaceae.

There are about a dozen species of these evergreen shrubs and trees from the western United States and Mexico, called silk-tassel because of their dramatic winter catkins. Gardeners like them for their handsome foliage and tough nature. The females bear persistent clusters of purple fruits.

HOW TO GROW
Silk-tassel needs only well-drained soil in sun or part shade and shelter from cold wind. Unlike many other western natives, the species listed here can use some supplemental water during summer droughts. Try this species for a showy hedge or screen, or as a specimen plant. You will need both male and female shrubs for fruit. Prune lightly to reshape if necessary. Propagate by seeds or semiripe cuttings.

G. elliptica   P. 109
g. eh-LIP-tih-kuh. Silk-tassel Tree. This shrub or small tree grows quickly to 12 feet tall and wide, with 1½- to 3-inch leaves that are shiny green on top and fuzzy gray underneath. The thin, drooping, yellow or yellow-green catkins can be up to 8 inches long on male plants, but only about 3 inches on the female, which in early summer develops purple fruit in grape-like clusters. 'James Roof' has striking silver-gray catkins, while *G. issaquahensis* has dark, glossy foliage. Zones 8 to 10.

🌿 Gaultheria (syn. Pernettya)

gall-THEAR-ee-uh. Heath family, Ericaeae.

A genus of almost 200 evergreen shrubs from the Americas, the West Indies, and Asia. A few species are grown in gardens for a combination of leathery leaves, small urn-shaped white flowers, and fleshy, long-lasting seed capsules.

HOW TO GROW
Give these shrubs acidic peat-rich soil that retains moisture. They can be grown in full sun only where the soil never dries out. Excellent to face

down rhododendrons or azaleas, along woodland margins, or in shady rock gardens. They require little pruning except for shaping or to restrict growth. Propagate with suckers or semiripe cuttings in summer.

G. mucronata

g. mew-kron-AH-tuh. This popular suckering shrub from Chile and Argentina has upright shoots and glossy dark green leaves only ¾ inch long with a spine at the tip. The white urn-shaped flowers, sometimes tinged pink, are solitary and bloom in late spring to early summer. The ½-inch fruits can be white or reddish purple. Plant several to ensure fruiting. Cultivars include 'Bell's Seedling' (reliable large dark red berries), 'Cherry Ripe' (cherry red fruit), 'Mother of Pearl' (pale pink berries), and 'Snow White' and 'Wintertime' (white berries). Zones 8 to 9.

G. procumbens
P. 110

g. proh-KUM-benz. Checkerberry. Also called creeping wintergreen, this species is native from eastern Canada south to Michigan and Georgia and grows to less than 6 inches high. Shiny dark green 2-inch leaves smell of wintergreen when crushed and blush with the onset of cold weather. Quarter-inch flowers, white with a pink tinge, bloom midspring through fall, while bright red fleshy seed capsules decorate the plant from mid-summer through the following spring. Zones 3 to 6.

G. shallon
P. 110

g. SHAL-lon. Salal. This western U.S. native suckers to form a thicket 5 feet tall and wide, lower and denser in sun. Red shoots set off the thick, glossy, nearly round 4-inch leaves. Arching 5-inch clusters of pinkish flowers bloom in early summer, followed by small purple-black berries that birds enjoy. Zones 6 to 8.

G. × wisleyensis
P. 111

g. × wiz-lee-EN-siss. An upright, suckering hybrid 4 feet high and wide with elliptic leaves 1½ inches long. Two-inch racemes of white flowers bloom in late spring and early summer, followed by ¼-inch reddish fruits. Zones 7 to 9.

✿ Genista

jen-ISS-ta. Pea family, Fabaceae.

Members of this genus are closely related to *Cytisus* and are very similar in appearance, with pealike yellow flowers and bright green branches all year. To add to the confusion, they are also commonly called broom as well as woadwaxen. (Woad is the common name for the herb *Isatis tinctoria,* and, like that plant, members of this genus were once commonly used as dyes.) Most of the 80 or 90 species are deciduous and almost leafless, and a few are spiny. Their natural habitat is rocky and open sites in Europe, North Africa, and western Asia.

HOW TO GROW

Woadwaxens can be a sound choice for challenging conditions, thriving in poor, sandy or gravelly, drought-prone soil in full sun. They must have sharp drainage and don't take well to high humidity. Unlike *Cytisus* and *Spartium* (Spanish broom) species, they are unlikely to become invasive, and they make good substitutes where those plants have become a problem. Good for hedging, as specimens, or planted on banks; small species are ideal for rock gardens. They rarely need pruning; if you do prune them, avoid cutting into mature wood. Propagate by semihard cuttings.

G. lydia   P. 111

g. LID-ee-uh. A potential ground cover at 2 feet tall and 3 feet wide. Arching gray-green stems bear widely spaced linear blue-green leaves and, in early summer, profuse ½-inch yellow flowers in 2-inch racemes. Zones 6 to 8.

G. tinctoria

g. tink-TOR-ee-uh. Dyer's Greenweed. Variable in habit, leaf, and flower throughout its natural range, from Europe to the Ukraine. Spreading or upright to 6 feet and rather spiky, with oblong leaves 1 to 2 inches long. In early summer, bright yellow flowers bloom in upright racemes up to 3 inches high, followed by ½-inch pods. 'Royal Gold' is 2 feet tall and wide. Zones 4 to 7.

❦ Grevillea

greh-VILL-ee-uh. Protea family, Proteaceae.

A genus of 250 Australian evergreen shrubs and trees grown for clusters of slender, tubular flowers that split and curve backward and long styles that give them a spidery look. The foliage is often fine and needlelike.

HOW TO GROW

Give grevillea moderately fertile, neutral to acid soil in full sun. Tolerates drought and heat, but not salt or high levels of phosphorus. Larger species are useful as specimens, against a wall, or in borders with other large shrubs. Use smaller ones at the front of a border to face down bigger shrubs, or in a rock garden. Needs minimal pruning. Propagate with semihard cuttings in summer.

G. banksii

g. BANK-see-eye. Red-flowered Silky Oak. Averaging 12 to 15 feet tall and not quite as wide, with leaves 4 to 10 inches long, deeply lobed and silky gray underneath. The dark red flowers bloom in 3- to 7-inch erect racemes, mainly in spring but intermittently all year. Zones 10 to 11.

G. 'Canberra Gem'.

Vigorous and rounded, from 6 to 8 feet high and sometimes wider, with linear leaves and waxy, bright pink flowers that may bloom heavily into summer. Zones 9 to 11.

G. rosmarinifolia

P. 112

g. rohs-mar-reen-ih-FOH-lee-uh. Compact, 5 to 6 feet tall and wide, with linear leaves that look like those of rosemary, and 3-inch racemes of red and cream (occasionally pink or white) flowers from autumn into early spring. Zones 9 to 11.

❦ Grewia

GREW-ee-uh. Linden family, Tiliaceae.

The 150 deciduous and evergreen trees, shrubs, and climbers in this genus are native to Australia, Africa, and Asia. The South African species listed here is grown for its small mauve flowers and adaptability to a wide variety of uses.

HOW TO GROW

Give grewia fertile, moisture-retentive soil in full sun or part shade. It tolerates some wind and salt but not drought. Occasional light pruning will increase its bushiness, and it can be pruned hard to control its size or shape. Prune it to grow vertically in a treelike shape, as an espalier, or across an arbor. Train it to grow horizontally as a bank cover, or shear it as a hedge or even a topiary. If you want it to serve in several of these capacities, propagate it with cuttings collected in spring.

G. occidentalis (syn. G. caffra)

P. 112

g. ox-ih-den-TAL-iss. Lavender Starflower. If left unpruned, lavender starflower grows to 10 feet or more with similar spread. The 3-inch oval leaves have rounded teeth. In summer, star-shaped pink and purple flowers with yellow centers bloom in axillary cymes. They are followed by 1-inch four-lobed fruits that are gold and then purple. Zones 8 to 11.

❦ *Hamamelis*

ham-uh-MEEL-liss. Witch hazel family, Hamamelidaceae.

You may be more familiar with this plant for the soothing, astringent extract made from its bark. The common name comes from an Anglo-Saxon word, *wych*, meaning "to bend" and referring to its former use in dowsing for water. As an ornamental, witch hazel has an equally valuable role to play. There are only five species, from North America and eastern Asia—all deciduous and ranging in habit from spreading shrubs to small trees—but many garden-worthy hybrids and cultivars. Their fragrant, straplike flowers bloom in what are often the bleakest weeks of fall or winter, and the autumn foliage can be colorful as well. The leaves have shallow teeth and paired veins.

HOW TO GROW

Give witch hazel moisture-retentive, moderately fertile soil in full sun or part shade. *H. vernalis* may tolerate some alkalinity, but most species prefer acid soil. Take note of the bloom time of the variety you choose, and site it to catch morning or evening sun where it can be seen from a window or frequently used path. Branches can be forced to bloom indoors. Pruning should be minimal, but you can control size and shape by pinching. Seeds take a full year to ripen after the flowers bloom, then "explode" from the pod, so need to be closely monitored if you want to collect them. The seeds require warm then cold stratification to germinate. You can also propagate witch hazels from cuttings taken in midspring.

H. × intermedia   P. 113

h. × in-ter-MEE-dee-uh. May grow 15 to 20 feet tall, often spreading wider, upright and sparsely branched. The flowers of this hybrid, which appear in mid- to late winter on bare branches, are not as fragrant as those of most species. Fall foliage is yellow on yellow-flowered plants but can be reddish purple on the red-flowered forms. Flowers of 'Arnold Promise' are large and bright yellow. Those of 'Diane' (a Pennsylvania Horticultural Society award winner) are red, and 'Ruby Glow' blooms reddish copper. Flowers of 'Jelena' are red at the base fading to orange and then yellow at the tips. Zones 5 to 9.

H. mollis
P. 114

h. MAHL-iss. Chinese Witch Hazel. A more compact species, 10 to 15 feet tall, spreading to 20 feet or more. Its yellow flowers, with reddish brown calyx cups, are especially fragrant and appear in late winter or early spring. Fall foliage ranges from clear yellow to orange-yellow. 'Pallida' has pale yellow flowers and has been honored by the Pennsylvania Horticultural Society. Zones 5 to 9.

H. vernalis

h. ver-NAL-iss. Vernal Witch Hazel. A native of gravelly streambanks in the Ozarks, usually about 10 feet tall and spreading wider, this species is multistemmed and may sucker heavily to form colonies. The red to yellow flowers, which bloom in late winter as the persistent leaves finally begin to fall, are generally considered the most fragrant of all. The fall foliage is bright yellow. Zones 4 to 8.

H. virginiana
P. 114

h. ver-jin-ee-AY-nuh. Common Witch Hazel. A widespread eastern native, this understory shrub is usually 15 to 20 feet tall, somewhat less in width. The habit is open crowned with crooked branching that adds to winter interest. Fragrant yellow flowers appear late fall to early winter, sometimes hidden by the leaves as they turn yellow. Zones 3 to 8.

❦ Hebe

HEE-bee. Figwort family, Scrophulariaceae.

This genus, named for Hebe, the Greek goddess of youth, contains about 100 species of evergreen shrubs, mostly from coastal areas of New Zealand. Many are low growing or prostrate, and in mild areas they make good ground covers or rock garden plants. Often called shrubby veronicas, for their spiky flowers' resemblance to those of that more herbaceous genus, they sometimes have colored or variegated foliage.

HOW TO GROW

Give hebes good drainage in full sun; part shade is better in the hottest part of their range. Soils should be poor to average, neutral to alkaline. They tolerate pollution, salt, and coastal wind, but not dry heat. The largest species listed here can be used as low hedges as well as rock garden plants. Deadhead; prune lightly if needed. Propagate semiripe cuttings with bottom heat, in late summer.

H. 'Alicia Amherst'

Upright to about 4 feet tall, with glossy 4-inch leaves. Somewhat hardier than other hebes, it produces 3-inch racemes of deep violet flowers in late summer or fall. Zones 9 to 10.

H. 'Amy'

Growing to 4 feet tall, 'Amy' has bronze-purple foliage in winter and on new growth. Violet purple flowers in 2-inch spikes bloom in late summer. Zones 9 to 10.

H. 'Autumn Glory'   P. 115

Spreading and 2½ feet tall, with a reddish purple edge to the leaves and bright purple flowers that bloom from midsummer into winter. Zones 9 to 10.

H. diosmifolia

h. dy-ahs-mih-FOH-lee-uh. This rounded shrub grows 2 to 5 feet tall and wide, with leaves smaller than most species, an inch or less long and ¼ inch wide. Rounded clusters of white to lavender flowers bloom in summer at the branch tips. Zones 9 to 10.

H. speciosa

h. spee-cee-OH-suh. A rounded shrub 3 to 6 feet tall with large glossy leaves up to 4 inches long and 2 inches wide. Summer flower spikes are brilliant hues of cerise to purple. Zones 9 to 10.

❦ Helichrysum

hel-ih-KRIS-um. Aster family, Asteraceae.

This genus consists of about 500 annuals, perennials, and evergreen shrubs and subshrubs from dry sunny sites in Africa, Asia, and Europe. The shrubby species included here are valued for their silvery gray foliage.

HOW TO GROW

Give helichrysums sharply draining, poor to moderate soil in full sun. Protect from winter moisture and cold wind. Use them to provide both texture and color contrast among green-foliaged plants. Cut back flowered shoots in spring. Propagate with seeds planted in spring, or root semiripe cuttings in summer.

H. italicum

h. eye-TAL-ih-kum. A 2-foot evergreen subshrub with needlelike, silvery gray, aromatic leaves and small yellow flower clusters in summer and fall. A smaller subspecies, *I. italicum* ssp. *serotinum* (curry plant), is often grown in the herb garden for its spicy scent. Although it smells exactly like curry powder, it is not considered a culinary herb. Zones 7 to 10.

H. petiolare   P. 115

h. pet-ee-oh-LAH-ree. Licorice Plant. This is a tender evergreen shrub from South Africa, often grown as an annual. It makes a good plant for a hanging basket because of its trailing stems, which can reach 4 feet long, and what look like stacks of woolly gray heart-shaped leaves that smell slightly of licorice when crushed. The flowers are insignificant. 'Limelight' has chartreuse foliage, and the leaves of 'Variegata' are marked with white. Zones 10 to 11.

❦ Heptacodium

hep-tuh-KODE-ee-um. Honeysuckle family, Caprifoliaceae.

This single species, a deciduous shrub or tree from the mountains of China, is just being discovered for its multiseason appeal. It was a 1995 recipient of a Gold Medal from the Pennsylvania Horticultural Society. The common name, seven-son flower, refers to the whorl of six small white flowers with another at the tip of the cluster. But the show-stealers are the reddish calyces that persist long after the petals drop.

HOW TO GROW

Grow this shrub in moderately fertile acidic soil in full sun, with some dappled shade in the South. Ideally the soil will be moisture retentive, although *Heptacodium* will tolerate some dryness. Give it a place in the shrub border or use it as a specimen. The flowers are irresistible to both butterflies and bees. Requires minimal pruning. Propagate with soft or semihard cuttings in summer.

H. miconioides   P. 116

h. my-koh-nee-OY-deez. Seven-son Flower of Zhejiang. Grows 15 to 20 feet tall, spreading to half that, with a graceful canopy. Grayish bark exfoliates to show lighter inner bark. The 3- to 4-inch-long oval leaves have prominent veins. Fragrant white flowers appear in late summer and early fall in terminal panicles up to 6 inches long, followed by the persistent calyces that change from green to reddish purple. Zones 5 to 9.

❦ *Heteromeles*

heh-ter-oh-MEEL-es. Rose family, Rosaceae.

Once classified among the photinias so popular as shrubs in the Southeast, this evergreen shrub native to southern California now has its own genus. Although it has other merits, it is grown primarily for bright berries that are attractive to wildlife.

HOW TO GROW

Give this plant well-drained soil in sun or part shade. Fairly tolerant of both wind and drought, it looks better if it gets some supplemental water in summer but will develop root rot if the soil is too wet. Use it for screening or plant it on a slope. It needs minimal pruning, but removing old branches will produce more berries. Propagate from seeds or cuttings.

H. arbutifolia   P. 116

h. ar-bew-tih-FOH-lee-uh. Christmas Berry. Also called toyon and California holly, this dense shrub will grow 25 feet high in its native chaparral, but usually remains under 10 feet tall in gardens. Glossy, leathery, dark green leaves are 2 to 4 inches long and sharply toothed. Small white flowers appear in flat terminal clusters in early to midsummer. The bright red egg-shaped berries that inspired its common name appear November through January. Zones 8 to 10.

❦ *Hibiscus*

hy-BIS-kus. Mallow family, Malvaceae.

Among some 200 species of annuals, perennials, and deciduous and evergreen shrubs and trees, only one species is suitable for temperate gardens, and one other is commonly grown in subtropical areas of the United States. They are prized for colorful funnel-shaped flowers, often with contrasting centers and dramatic stamens.

HOW TO GROW

Grow hibiscus in neutral to alkaline soil that has been well amended with organic matter, in full sun. It thrives in long hot summers. Use plants in a hedge, a border, or plant them in masses. They do not require much pruning, but can be pruned heavily in spring for bigger flowers. Propagate by softwood cuttings in late spring.

H. rosa-sinensis
P. 117

h. ROH-suh-sih-NEN-siss. Chinese Hibiscus. This rounded subtropical ever-green species averages 10 feet tall and not quite so wide, although most cultivars grow from 6 to 8 feet tall. The glossy, dark green oval to lance-shaped leaves are up to 6 inches long. From summer through fall, five-petaled red flowers 4 inches in diameter appear in the leaf axils. Cultivars in single or double forms can be white, yellow, orange, and pink, and 5 to 8 inches across. Some gardeners grow this tender species as an annual or in containers for overwintering indoors. Just a few of the many choices include 'All-Aglow', with orange edges verging to yellow and a pink halo around a white center; 'Cooperii', which has red flowers but is grown pri-marily for its white, pink, and green foliage; and 'Hula Girl', long bloom-ing and narrow with red-throated bright yellow flowers. May be root hardy to Zone 8. Zones 9 to 11.

H. syriacus
P. 118

h. sih-ree-AY-kuss. Rose-of-Sharon. This deciduous upright shrub grows to 10 feet tall and 6 feet wide with erect branches. The 4-inch toothed leaves are often three-lobed, and the 2- to 4-inch axillary flowers, which bloom midsummer into early autumn, can be white, rosy pink, or lavender with a red center. In the heat of late summer it can develop powdery mildew where humidity is high and attract mites in dry conditions. The species self-sows readily and is making its way onto lists of invasives in the Southeast, Mid-Atlantic, and Midwest. Popular selections, which may volunteer less eagerly, include 'Aphrodite' (dark pink), 'Diana' (pure white, a Pennsylvania Horticultural Society award winner), 'Helene' (white with a red, radiating eye spot), and 'Minerva' (lavender with a dark red eye). Zones 5 to 9.

❦ Hippophae

hip-POFF-ay-ee. Oleaster family, Elaeagnaceae.

This genus is made up of three species of deciduous, dioecious shrubs and trees from coastal areas and riverbanks in Asia and Europe. Not well known, it offers great potential for growing in seaside gardens and road-side plantings, as well as for ornamental attributes such as narrow silvery leaves and persistent orange fruits.

HOW TO GROW

This plant needs full sun. While happy in poor, sandy soil it probably will do better with some organic matter to keep its roots cool. Sea buckthorn withstands salt, is useful for stabilizing dunes and riverbanks, and will lend winter color to naturalized areas. Not a selection for small gardens; you'll need both male and female plants in order to enjoy the colorful fruits. Rarely needs pruning. Propagate with cold-treated seeds, root cuttings, layering, or suckers.

H. rhamnoides   P. 118

h. ram-NOY-deez. Sea Buckthorn. Variable in size but averaging 20 feet tall and wide, with an irregular open shape and suckering tendency. The 1- to 3-inch willowlike leaves are gray-green and silvery, borne on spiny branches. Inconspicuous yellow-green spring flowers give way to bright orange round to oval berries on the females. Zones 3 to 8.

❧ *Holodiscus*

hol-oh-DIS-cuss. Rose family, Rosaceae.

There are eight deciduous shrubs in this genus, with most of those available for gardeners native to dry woods of the western United States. They are closely related to spirea but bloom later, producing graceful white flower plumes almost a foot long in summer.

HOW TO GROW

Give holodiscus rich, fertile, moisture-retentive soil in sun to part shade. They are ideal for naturalizing in the West, since they can attract birds and need little care. They do not require pruning, but cutting out older stems after they flower will promote growth. Propagate by seeds, semiripe cuttings in summer, or layering.

H. discolor   P. 119

h. DISS-kuh-ler. Ocean Spray. Vigorous and upright, ranging from 3 feet tall in dry soil to 20 feet in rich soil, with arching branches. The triangular 3-inch leaves are wrinkled above, white and fuzzy underneath, with four to eight lobes. The individual midsummer flowers are tiny and cup shaped, appearing in pendulous clusters at the branch tips for many weeks in late spring to early summer. Zones 6 to 9.

❦ *Hydrangea*

hy-DRAN-juh. Hydrangea family, Hydrangeaceae.

Hydrangeas are an old-fashioned favorite, some form of which is always being newly discovered by gardeners. They offer flowers that range from buxom white belles to lacy sapphire "caps," as well as species with burgundy fall foliage and furrowed bark. The genus includes two dozen species of deciduous and evergreen shrubs and climbers from East Asia and the Americas. Flowers of all the common shrub species are good for drying indoors.

HOW TO GROW

Give hydrangeas fertile, moisture-retentive soil in full sun to part shade. These species are all fast growers but vary in their tolerance to sun, wind, salt, and drought and in their pruning requirements. See individual species listings. You can start them from seeds in spring, but they are easy to root from softwood cuttings in early summer.

H. arborescens 'Annabelle' P. 119

h. ar-bor-ES-enz. Smooth Hydrangea cultivar. Quickly reaching 3 to 5 feet tall and wide with a suckering habit, this rounded shrub species is considered coarse by some, but the cultivar is noteworthy for summer flowers in rounded clusters up to 12 inches in diameter. In hot summer areas it needs shade and supplemental water. Prune back to low buds in late winter. Zones 4 to 9.

H. macrophylla P. 120

h. mak-roh-FIL-uh. Big-leaf Hydrangea. There are two forms, both averaging 6 feet tall and 8 feet wide. The hortensias have large heavy "mopheads" of sterile flowers, while the lacecaps are airy wheels of tiny fertile flowers surrounded by showier sterile flowers. The blooms, which begin appearing in midsummer, are generally blue if growing in soil with a pH of 5.5 or less, purple in slightly acid soil, or pink if grown in neutral to slightly alkaline soil. Hydrangeas may become chlorotic if the soil is strongly alkaline. There are some white-flowered cultivars. Leaves are 4- to 8-inch toothed ovals, somewhat waxy. This species thrives in the wind and salt of coastal areas but wilts rapidly in a drought. To keep the plant tidy, prune back the previous season's flower heads to the stem's uppermost bud in late winter. 'Blue Billow', which has sapphire blue lacecap flowers, was a 1990 Pennsylvania Horticultural Society award winner. Zones 6 to 9.

H. paniculata

P. 121

h. pan-ih-kew-LAY-tuh. Panicle Hydrangea. Upright and somewhat coarse in texture, but with branches that arch over gracefully, particularly while in bloom. Ranging in size from 10 feet tall to as much as 20 feet with an equal spread, these plants are sometimes trained to a treelike form. The cone-shaped, summer-through-fall flower panicles are 6 to 8 inches long, fading from cream colored to rosy pink. This species is more drought tolerant than *H. macrophylla*. It blooms on new wood and may be pruned in early spring, leaving just a few buds if you want to force larger flowers and a bushier habit. 'Grandiflora', the "peegee" hydrangea, is the most commonly available. 'Tardiva' is a more diminutive form that flowers a bit later. 'Unique' grows 10 to 13 feet tall with a pure white flower panicle up to 16 inches long. Zones 4 to 8.

H. quercifolia

P. 122

h. kwer-sih-FOL-lee-uh. Oakleaf Hydrangea. The common name comes from the lobed leaves, which can be 8 inches long and turn mahogany red in fall, remaining on the plant for many weeks. The late-spring flowers, held in upright panicles to 12 inches high, emerge white and color pink before fading to brown. Winter interest is provided by exfoliating bark. Up to 8 feet tall and wide, it prefers more shade than others. Although said to flower from buds produced the previous season, in reality it can bloom after being killed to the ground by frost. Doesn't require pruning at all, but a proportion of old growth can be removed to reshape or rejuvenate it. 'Snow Queen' (a Pennsylvania Horticultural Society honoree) and 'Snow Flake' are considered more floriferous than the species. Zones 5 to 9.

❦ *Hypericum*

hy-PAIR-ih-kum. Mangosteen family, Clusiaceae.

The yellow flowers of these shrubs are unavoidable in the Pacific Northwest, where they thrive in the mild conditions. The genus contains more than 400 annuals, perennials, and deciduous or evergreen shrubs and small trees, grown primarily for the bright yellow flowers with starry stamens. A weedy Eurasian species, *H. perforatum*, is the source of a popular herbal antidepressant that goes by the common name for most of the genus, St. Johnswort.

HOW TO GROW

Most St. Johnsworts, except for *H. frondosum*, are suited primarily to mild climates. Some will tolerate poor or heavy clay soils but succumb to heat and humidity or cold wind. Most species need excellent drainage and full sun, with minimal pruning. An exception is *H. calycinum*, which can be severely pruned or even mowed to the ground in spring. Other species are planted as tall ground covers, rock garden plants, and for facing down taller shrubs. Propagate from seeds or softwood cuttings in summer.

H. calycinum
h. kal-ih-CY-num. Aaron's Beard. In the Northwest, this species is an almost ubiquitous ground cover along highways and in other public plantings. Evergreen or semievergreen and 1 to 2 feet tall, it spreads by stolons and often becomes invasive. It tolerates shade, where the 4-inch leaves become more yellow-green. Bright yellow saucer flowers 3 to 4 inches across bloom throughout the summer. Zones 5 to 9.

H. frondosum
h. fron-DOH-sum. Golden St. Johnswort. A deciduous southeastern U.S. native growing 3 to 4 feet high and wide, upright and rounded with exfoliating bark and 2½-inch blue-green oblong leaves. Summer flowers are 1 to 2 inches across with a dense mass of stamens, followed by reddish brown seedpods. 'Sunburst' is tolerant of Midwest conditions and compacted clay soil. Zones 6 to 8.

H. 'Hidcote'   P. 122
Taxonomists can't decide if this popular St. Johnswort is a hybrid or a selection of *H. patulum*. Gardeners need only know that it is a dense, bushy evergreen to 5 feet tall and wide with lance-shaped dark green leaves and golden yellow flowers up to 3 inches across, often blooming summer into fall. Zones 6 to 9.

H. kalmianum
h. kal-mee-AN-um. Kalm's St. Johnswort. This cold-hardy species, native to southern Canada and the Upper Midwest, is a dense evergreen growing 2 to 3 feet tall with blue-green leaves in summer and clusters of three 1-inch flowers in midsummer. Zones 4 to 7.

H. patulum
h. PAT-ew-lum. Golden Cup. Semievergreen to evergreen, this Chinese species grows up to 4 feet high and spreads to 5 feet, with 2-inch flowers blooming singly or in flat clusters in midsummer. Zones 7 to 9.

❦ *Ilex*

EYE-lex. Holly family, Aquifoliaceae.

Unless you draw your curtains and hibernate in winter, you need to include at least one holly in your landscape, whether you want glossy leaves that sparkle in the sun or bright berries for the birds. There are many choices among more than 400 evergreen and deciduous shrubs, trees, and climbers from temperate to subtropical climates.

HOW TO GROW

A majority of hollies prefer acid soils, but are otherwise varied in their preferences—from rich humus to sand to waterside conditions—and somewhat adaptable. As woodland natives they tolerate shade, but variegated species in particular do best in full sun. Both male and female plants are needed for berries. Hollies do not require extensive pruning, but can be pruned in late winter or early spring for shaping and to collect berries for arrangements. Propagate from softwood or semiripe cuttings in summer.

I. cornuta   P. 123

i. kor-NOO-tuh. Chinese Holly. A rounded evergreen shrub to 15 feet tall, possibly wider, with rectangular large-spined leaves and ½-inch red berries. 'Burfordii' has a more prominent spine at the tip and berries heavily without pollination. 'Dwarf Burford' stops growing at 6 feet tall. Zones 7 to 10.

I. crenata   P. 123

i. kren-AH-tuh. Japanese Holly. An evergreen boxwood look-alike, on average 10 to 15 feet tall and wide, roughly rounded, with oval, slightly scalloped leaves. The small black fruits are persistent but usually hidden in the foliage. As many as 500 cultivars have been introduced with about 10 percent of them currently available. Most are considerably lower-growing than the species. You can choose forms that are columns, globes, dwarves, or horizontal in habit, and others with yellow berries or golden or variegated foliage. 'Dwarf Pagoda' has small dense leaves and an irregular form. Zones 5 to 9.

I. decidua   P. 124

i. deh-SID-ew-uh. Possumhaw. An upright, deciduous native of the Mid-Atlantic and southeastern United States with glossy oval leaves, 15 to 18 feet tall and 12 to 15 feet wide, upright and then weeping in some specimens. May sucker to form colonies. Attractive gray bark sets off ⅓-inch persistent orange-red fruits. 'Warren's Red' is upright to 20 feet with persistent leaves and red berries plus additional cold hardiness. Zones 4 to 9.

I. glabra

i. GLAB-ruh. Inkberry. An upright evergreen native to the eastern United States, growing to about 8 feet tall and wide, this is a wetland plant that needs moist acid soil and may sucker to form colonies. Oval leaves ¾ to 2 inches long may develop a purple tinge in winter. The tiny berries are generally black. 'Shamrock' is a compact form growing slowly to about 5 feet tall. Zones 5 to 9.

I. × meserveae

i. × meh-SERV-eye-ee. Blue Hollies. Cold-tolerant hybrids of English holly (*I. aquifolium*) and other species, with spiny blue-green oval leaves from ¾ to 2 inches long. Females of the variously named pairs produce ¼-inch bright red fruits. These hybrids demand excellent drainage. Both male and female forms have the word "blue" in their cultivar names. Highly rated, but unrelated, hybrids from the same breeder include 'China Boy' and 'China Girl' — more rounded in habit, more heat tolerant, and with larger fruits than the blue hollies — and 'Dragon Lady', which is pryamid shaped with spiny leaves. Zones 5 to 7.

I. 'Nellie Stevens'. Popular fast-growing evergreen hybrid that forms a wide pyramid about 20 feet tall and half as wide. The glossy leaves have two or three spines to a side. Red berries are plentiful but less persistent than some. Zones 6 to 9.

I. pedunculosa

i. ped-un-kew-LOH-suh. Longstalk Holly. Asian, somewhat irregular evergreen usually 15 to 20 feet high and sometimes as wide with untoothed, glossy, elliptic 1- to 3-inch leaves. The berrylike fruits appear in midautumn on stalks, much like cherries. Zones 6 to 9.

I. serrata

i. sair-AH-tuh. Finetooth Holly. Sometimes called Japanese winterberry because of its resemblance to that native holly, it gets its other common name from the fact that its leaves have barely discernible serrations. This species will grow about 12 feet tall with a spreading habit, but is usually 8 feet or less in gardens. The ⅕-inch persistent red fruits ripen in late summer, and new foliage has a purple cast. 'Sundrops' has yellow berries. Zones 5 to 8.

I. verticillata

P. 124

i. ver-tiss-il-LAH-tuh. Winterberry. A deciduous eastern U.S. native usually 8 to 10 feet tall, sometimes spreading and suckering wider. The dark green leaves are serrated and small. Bright red stalkless fruits cover the branches beginning in late summer, sometimes lasting until spring. Many cultivars and hybrids, with "male escorts" for the berrying females, have been selected for brighter, larger, or more persistent fruit. These include 'Harvest Red' and 'Winter Red'. 'Sparkleberry', a Pennsylvania Horticultural Society award winner, is from a hybrid with *I. serrata*. Zones 3 to 9.

I. vomitoria

i. vom-ih-TOR-ee-uh. Yaupon. An upright, suckering evergreen from the southeastern United States, growing 15 to 20 feet high and 10 to 15 feet tall. The small leaves are glossy, and the persistent red fruits translucent and abundant. Native to swampy areas, it adapts well to drier soil and can take heavy pruning if you want to use it for a foundation shrub, hedge, espalier, or even topiary. The species name refers to Native Americans' use of the leaves as a purgative. Growing only 3 to 4 feet tall are 'Nana' and 'Stokes Dwarf'. Zones 8 to 10.

❦ Illicium

ih-LIH-see-um. Anise family, Illiciaceae.

A host of attributes have made this genus (whose name stems from a Latin word meaning "to attract" and commonly called anise trees despite their shrubby habit) deservedly popular among southern gardeners: thick, glossy, aromatic leaves; unusual flowers with numerous strap-shaped petals; and star-shaped late-summer fruits that turn from green to yellow then brown. There are about 40 species, all evergreen shrubs and trees, from woodlands in the southeastern United States, Southeast Asia, and West Indies.

HOW TO GROW

Ideally, you will give anise trees a moist, rich, acid soil in shade to semishade, with protection from wind. They are useful in difficult wet and shady areas as screening, in masses, or against a sheltered wall. *I. floridanum* may need pruning when young, after it flowers in spring, to guide its shape. Propagate by seeds or semiripe cuttings in summer.

I. anisatum   P. 125

i. an-iss-AY-tum. Star Anise. This Asian species forms a pyramid shape 10 or 12 feet tall, with glossy dark green leaves to 4 inches long. In early spring, pale yellow-green, unscented flowers, 1 inch across and composed of 30 narrow petals, appear in the leaf axils. Zones 7 to 9.

I. floridanum

i. flor-ih-DAY-num. Florida Anise. Also called purple anise, this native of Florida and Louisiana grows upright and compact from 5 to 10 feet tall, occasionally suckering. Dark green 2- to 6-inch leaves held in whorls are similar to a rhododendron's. In midspring it produces 1- to 2-inch fragrant flowers with up to 30 maroon petals. Zones 7 to 9.

I. henryi

i. HEN-ree-eye. Henry Anise Tree. A western Chinese species forming a dense pyramid 6 to 10 feet tall, with whorls of lustrous dark green leaves. The midspring flowers are 1 inch across with 15 to 20 dark pink to red petals. Zones 8 to 9.

I. parviflorum

i. parv-ih-FLOR-um. Small Anise. Native to Florida and Georgia, small anise is similar to the Chinese species but taller at 15 to 20 feet and sometimes suckering. Leaves are olive green, and the midspring flowers that inspired the common name are only ½ inch across. Tolerant of more sun and drier soils. Zones 7 to 9.

❦ *Itea*

eye-TEE-uh. Currant family, Grossulariaceae.

A genus of about 10 shrubs from the eastern United States and East Asia, grown for catkinlike panicles of small white flowers and either evergreen leaves similar to a holly's or deciduous leaves with colorful fall foliage.

HOW TO GROW
The two readily available species are quite different in appearance and cultural needs. Both propagate easily from cuttings or suckers.

I. ilicifolia

i. il-ih-sih-FOL-ee-uh. This Chinese evergreen grows 10 to 12 feet tall and has spiny, lustrous, dark green hollylike leaves 2 to 4 inches long. The tiny greenish white flowers appear in slender racemes mid- to late summer. It needs fertile, moist soil in part shade and out of the wind and requires minimal pruning. Zones 8 to 9.

I. virginica   PP. 125, 126

i. ver-JIN-ih-kuh. Virginia Sweetspire. An eastern U.S. wetland plant growing to 5 feet tall and easily suckering twice as wide, this species is adaptable to drought and almost any other hardship, although it flowers and colors best in moist, fertile soil and full sun. Autumn foliage can be a spectacular mix of red and reddish purple, sometimes with orange or yellow. Excellent at the edge of a wood or pond, or in a border. On mature plants, cut back about one-third of oldest shoots to stimulate new growth. 'Henry's Garnet', which received a Gold Medal from the Pennsylvania Horticultural Society, has large flowers and outstanding fall color. Zones 6 to 9.

❧ Jasminum

jas-MIN-um. Olive family, Oleaceae.

This genus boasts about 200 evergreen and deciduous shrubs and climbers primarily from Europe, Asia, and Africa. The temperate shrubs are cultivated for their yellow, usually fragrant, flowers.

HOW TO GROW

Jasmines are often wall trained, which provides extra warmth, or incorporated into mixed borders. Give them fertile well-drained soil in full sun or part shade. Prune off flowered shoots and remove about one-third of old shoots from established plants to encourage new growth. Propagate from semiripe cuttings.

J. floridum

j. FLOR-ih-dum. Showy Jasmine. An evergreen to semievergreen from China growing to 5 feet tall. The lustrous dark green leaves have three to five leaflets, and the yellow five-lobed flowers bloom in cymes from mid- to late spring. Zones 8 to 10.

J. humile   P. 126

j. HEW-mil-ee. Italian Yellow Jasmine. An evergreen similar to showy jasmine but more upright to about 6 feet, with less glossy leaves. Commences blooming later with slightly fragrant flowers. 'Revolutum' may be more cold hardy. Zones 8 to 10.

J. mesnyi

j. MEZ-nee-eye. Primrose Jasmine. Forms an evergreen mound to 8 feet high and half as wide, with trailing branches and double flowers in early spring. Good for training against a wall. Zones 8 to 10.

J. nudiflorum   P. 127

j. noo-dih-FLOR-um. Winter Jasmine. Deciduous arching or climbing shrub, 4 feet high and 6 feet wide if grown in a border or down a bank, up to 10 or 12 feet high if trained against a wall. Bright yellow axillary flowers are 2-inch tubes with spreading lobes 1 inch across, appearing for a long period in late winter before the foliage. Zones 6 to 9.

❦ Juniperus

jew-NIP-er-us. Cypress family, Cupressaceae.

Of up to 60 evergreen conifers in this group from the Northern Hemisphere, perhaps a dozen species are commonly represented in gardens. Even among the tallest species, there are dwarf cultivars that can be considered shrub-sized with habits that are round, columnar, or low-spreading.

HOW TO GROW

Junipers are ubiquitous because they tolerate almost any soil type—acid or alkaline, sandy or clay—except waterlogged. They can survive drought and wind and some salt. Give them full sun, as they may become too open in shade. Small varieties can be used in rock gardens and containers, or to provide an evergreen accent among perennials. Try taller selections in hedges, shrub borders, or as specimens. Juniper blight can cause tip dieback on many types, and bagworms are often a serious problem. Junipers do not require pruning but can be pruned heavily. Propagation varies with species.

J. chinensis 'Echiniformis'

j. chih-NEN-siss. A dense, pincushion-shaped mound 2 feet tall and a bit wider, with whorls of awl-shaped needles that are blue-green on top and grayish underneath. Does not tolerate heat or poor drainage. Zones 2 to 6.

J. communis 'Repanda'

j. kom-EW-niss. Repanda Common Juniper. Maturing to 15 inches tall, it forms a nearly perfect 9-foot circle. The needles are densely arranged with a soft silvery sheen over the year-round mid-green. Not heat tolerant. Zones 2 to 6.

J. × *pfitzeriana* (syn. *J.* × *media*)

j. × fits-er-ee-AY-nuh. Pfitzer Juniper. This widely planted variety is a hybrid of *J. sabina* and *J. chinensis,* looking much like the former (with 45-degree branches) but sometimes listed as a cultivar of the latter. Growing about 5 feet tall and 10 feet wide, it has scalelike, diamond-shaped, sage green leaves and round, dark purple cones. It performs well in both the North and the South. Cultivars include 'Monlep' (trademarked as Mint Julep), which is slightly more compact with a fountainlike habit and fine foliage; and 'Sulphur Spray', which is about 20 inches tall by 4½ feet wide, with soft green foliage tipped with yellow when new. Zones 4 to 9.

J. procumbens 'Nana'

j. proh-KUM-benz. Japanese Garden Juniper. Forms a ground-hugging mat 1 foot tall and 4 to 6 feet wide (possibly 10 or more after many years) with upturned, spray-shaped branches that form layers. The blue-green foliage often turns somewhat purple in winter. Zones 5 to 9.

J. sabina   P. 127

j. suh-BEE-nuh. Savin Juniper. This species from the mountains of Europe and Asia grows 4 to 6 feet tall and 5 to 10 feet wide with stiffly upturned branches. Among its many low-growing cultivars are 'Broadmoor', growing 2 to 3 feet tall and 10 feet wide with gray-green foliage; and 'Monna' (trademarked as Calvary Carpet), truly carpetlike at 6 to 8 inches high and 10 feet wide. Both are considered blight resistant. Zones 4 to 7.

J. sargentii 'Glauca'

j. sar-GEN-tee-eye. Blue Sargent Juniper. Grows 30 inches tall by 10 feet wide with upright branching and blue-green, camphor-scented foliage that is disease resistant. Zones 3 to 9.

J. squamata 'Blue Star' P. 128

j. skwah-MAH-tuh. Blue Star Juniper. This popular cultivar of the singleseed or flaky juniper from Asia forms a pincushion-shaped mound about 3 feet tall and wide, with silver-blue needles that may turn somewhat purple in winter. Does not perform well in heat and humidity. Zones 4 to 7.

J. virginiana P. 128

j. ver-jin-ee-AY-nuh. Eastern Red Cedar. This central and eastern U.S. native has several cultivars with a spreading habit similar to the Pfitzer juniper. 'Grey Owl' grows to 6 feet tall with horizontal branches, silver-gray foliage, and bluish green fruits. 'Mona' (trademarked as Silver Spreader) is even lower growing, to perhaps 2 feet tall and about 8 feet wide, with foliage that remains silvery all year. Zones 4 to 9.

❦ *Kalmia*

KAL-mee-uh. Heath family, Ericaceae.

Out of flower, the laurel-like leaves of these species look a lot like those of the related rhododendron. But the blossoms of these species are cup shaped with stamens radiating to anther sacs in the flower wall. Dark dots around these sacs inspired the common name calico bush for one species. The taut stamens "shoot" pollen onto visiting bees. There are seven species of these evergreen shrubs, at home in woods and meadows primarily in North America.

HOW TO GROW

Grow kalmia in fertile, humus-rich acid soil in part shade. Growing naturally on slopes, they need a well-draining but moisture-retentive situation in the garden. Excellent for woodland gardens or shady shrub borders. They don't need regular pruning, but leggy plants can be pruned hard to stimulate new growth. Propagation is difficult.

K. angustifolia P. 129

k. an-gus-tih-FOL-ee-uh. Sheep Laurel. Native to the eastern United States and Canada, this shrub averages 2 feet high and spreads by stolons to 10 feet wide. The oblong, leathery leaves are 2 inches long in whorls of three. The early-summer, saucer-shaped flowers range from lavender pink to burgundy, rarely white, in 2-inch clusters. Zones 2 to 7.

K. latifolia
PP. 129, 130

k. lat-ih-FOL-ee-uh. Mountain Laurel. This better-known eastern U.S. native grows slowly to 10 feet tall and wide, fairly rounded and dense at first and then more open and showing gnarled branches. The leathery leaves are up to 5 inches long. The cup-shaped "calico flowers" with 10 stamens are usually pink in bud and open to white but can open deep pink. Among the many cultivars are forms with red buds opening to pink ('Olympic Fire', 'Richard Jaynes'), interior bands ('Bullseye'), or stars ('Carousel'). Zones 4 to 9.

❧ Kerria

KAIR-ee-uh. Rose family, Rosaceae.

There is just one species in this genus, a deciduous shrub from Asia with cheery golden yellow flowers and bright green stems that provide winter interest.

HOW TO GROW
Give kerria moderately fertile soil in full sun to full shade. Part shade will keep flowers from fading. Good for awkward narrow spaces, massing, or in shrub or mixed borders. Prune out dead branches and trim back a portion of flowered branches to keep under control. Suckers can pop up a couple of feet from the parent plant, but the species is not invasive. Pull up the suckers, or use them for easy propagation. Zones 4 to 9.

K. japonica
P. 130

k. juh-PON-ih-kuh. Japanese Kerria. The upright, arching, bright green branches grow 5 to 6 feet tall and can sucker to form a mass 6 or more feet across. Bright green leaves, doubly toothed and slightly pleated, grow to 4 inches long. Golden yellow five-petaled flowers 1½ inch across appear in midspring and sporadically throughout the season. 'Pleniflora' is a double-flowered form with 1- to 2-inch pompon blooms. 'Picta' has white leaf margins. Zones 4 to 9.

❧ Kolkwitzia

kolk-WIT-zee-uh. Honeysuckle family, Caprifoliaceae.

A single species from a single province in China, grown for clusters of pink bell-shaped flowers in mid- to late spring.

HOW TO GROW

Beautybush prefers fertile, loamy, well-drained soil in full sun, but adapts to a wide pH range. It becomes rangy and ragged, so is best situated where it can be somewhat hidden in a shrub border. Prune flowered shoots after blooming is over, and remove a third of old growth annually. Propagate from softwood cuttings.

K. amabilis   P. 131

k. am-AH-bil-iss. Beautybush. A deciduous shrub with an erect and arching habit similar to forsythia, 6 to 10 feet tall and spreading wider if given space. Dull green leaves 1 to 3 inches long may turn slightly yellow or red in fall. The ½-inch midspring pink flowers, which are flaring pink bells with yellow throats, bloom in clusters up to 3 inches across. Zones 4 to 8.

✿ *Lagerstroemia*

lay-ger-STROH-mee-uh. Loosestrife family, Lythraceae

This genus contains about 50 deciduous and evergreen shrubs and trees from Southeast Asia and Australia. Most of those grown in gardens, almost exclusively cultivars or hybrids of the species listed here, are better characterized as multitrunked trees. In the northern part of their range, however, they often die to the ground in winter and remain shrub-sized. For those farther south, there are several selections chosen for their dwarf stature. In summer, crape myrtles produce white or brightly colored panicles of flowers. When out of flower, older specimens can be admired for sinewy trunks, sometimes adorned with colorful exfoliating bark.

HOW TO GROW

Give crape myrtle relatively fertile, moisture-retentive but well-aerated soil in full sun. Use smaller forms in masses, or as hedges, screens, or specimens. Where it is fully hardy, cut it back immediately after flowering, pruning only shoots smaller than finger size. More severe pruning prevents its muscular trunks from taking shape. In the northern part of its range, unfortunately, it may have to be pruned to the ground in early spring. Where hardiness is borderline, in Zone 7, growers should save all pruning except deadheading until early spring when shrubs begin to leaf out. Pruning between late summer and early winter can compromise winter survival. Propagate from softwood cuttings taken during the first flush of growth in spring, or from hardwood cuttings taken in winter.

L. indica cultivars and hybrids
P. 131

l. IN-dih-cuh. Common Crape Myrtle. Forms range to 20 or more feet tall and 15 or more feet wide, but new genetic dwarves are only 2 by 3 feet. Small dark green leaves may turn orange-red or red-purple in fall. Flower colors include white, pinks, lavender, purple, and red, with blooms on some beginning mid-June, sometimes continuing into September. Bark colors include gray, cinnamon, tan, and mahogany. Excellent mildew-resistant, reliably reblooming cultivars from the U.S. National Arboretum (many of them hybrids with *L. fauriei*) can be recognized by names representing Native American tribes. Two new "miniature" forms are 'Chickasaw' (lavender pink) and 'Pocomoke' (deep rosy pink). Semidwarf forms growing to 12 feet or less include 'Acoma' (white), 'Hopi' (light pink), 'Tonto' (fuchsia), and 'Zuni' (lavender). Zones 7 to 9.

❧ *Laurus*

LAH-russ. Mint family, Lamiaceae.

There are just two evergreen shrubs or trees in this genus, one of which is known to most of us primarily for the tough bay leaves that are used in cooking. Those who can grow it outdoors employ it in formal gardens.

HOW TO GROW

Most gardeners grow sweet myrtle in a container, either as a year-round houseplant or to overwinter indoors. It needs full sun, consistent moisture with excellent drainage, and good air circulation. The persistent leaves benefit from an occasional shower or sponge bath. Scale may be a problem indoors. Outdoors, in a formal setting or an herb garden, it can tolerate part shade and hard pruning into a standard or other form, or it can be allowed to take on its natural pyramid shape. Easily propagated from midsummer cuttings.

L. nobilis
P. 132

l. NOH-bil-iss. Sweet Bay. Sometimes called bay laurel, this is the plant whose branches were used in antiquity to honor Olympians and other heroes. Outdoors it may grow to 20 or 30 feet tall, but 5 to 10 feet is a maximum for an indoor-outdoor existence. It may produce inconspicuous yellow-green flowers followed by ½-inch purple or black berries. Of Mediterranean origin, it may survive outdoors in the southern part of Zone 8. Otherwise, Zones 9 to 11.

❦ *Lavandula*

lav-AN-doo-luh. Mint family, Lamiceae

The clean scent of lavender has been used in bath water and soaps for so long that the name of this genus came from a Latin word meaning "to wash." Of 28 species native from the Mediterranean to India, about a dozen are commonly grown for their silvery, aromatic foliage and spikes of fragrant purple flowers that bloom from mid- to late summer. Lavender is often grown in herb gardens for its uses in potpourri, sachets, and cosmetics.

HOW TO GROW

Give lavender full sun and sharply draining neutral to slightly alkaline soil of moderate to low fertility. Use plants for a low hedge or as contrast with green-foliaged perennials. They make a good choice for hiding the bare stems of roses. The tender lavenders can be grown as houseplants if you are careful to avoid overwatering them. Prune lightly after flowering to maintain shape. They are most easily propagated from heel cuttings or by layering.

L. angustifolia   P. 132

l. an-gus-tih-FOH-lee-uh. English Lavender. This is the most commonly grown species, sometimes reaching 3 feet tall and even wider, although many of the popular cultivars are smaller. They include 'Hidcote', 12 inches tall with dark purple flowers; 'Munstead', 18 inches tall and early blooming; and 'Twickel Purple', to 3 feet with tall flower spikes. Zones 5 to 8.

L. dentata

l. den-TAH-tuh. Fringed Lavender. Probably the tallest of the garden lavenders, reliably growing to 3 feet tall and spreading to 5 feet. Sweetly scented, it gets its common name from the bumpy appearance of its toothed gray-green leaves. The flowers are pale lavender with purple bracts. Zones 8 to 9.

L. × intermedia   P. 133

l. × in-ter-MEE-dee-uh. These hybrids, less than 2 feet tall and wide, have broad, hairy leaves, long stems, and relatively open flower spikes. Zones 5 to 8.

L. stoechas
P. 133

l. STOY-kus. French Lavender. This compact, 2-foot-tall species gets both its botanical and common names from its origin on the French Mediterranean Iles d'Hyeres, once known as the Stoechades. From late spring through summer, it bears tiny dark purple flowers arranged in a rectangular cone and topped with upright lavender pink bracts, especially showy in the subspecies *L. stoechas* ssp. *pedunculata*. The aroma is more camphorous than that of other lavenders. Zones 8 to 9.

❦ Lavatera

Lav-uh-TEER-uh. Mallow family, Malvaceae.

This genus includes 25 species of annuals, herbaceous perennials, and deciduous and evergreen shrubs, native to western Europe, central Asia, Australia, and California. The shrubs are grown in gardens for their large five-petaled flowers, usually saucer shaped and similar to hollyhocks.

HOW TO GROW

Tree mallows are generally trouble-free if they have full sun and loose, well-drained soil of moderate fertility. They tolerate salt and ocean breezes but need shelter from cold winds. Use them as a screen, in a shrub or mixed border, or as specimens. Along the coast, they make an attractive windbreak. Prune near the ground when buds swell in spring. Propagate from softwood cuttings in early summer. Plants tend to be short-lived.

L. maritima
P. 134

l. mar-IH-tih-muh. Tree Mallow. Evergreen shrub to 6 feet tall and 3 feet wide, with gray-green lobed leaves. Throughout summer, it produces pale pink flowers, 2 to 3 inches across, with notched petals. The veins and base of each petal are magenta. Zones 8 to 10.

L. thuringiaca

l. thur-in-gee-AH-cuh. Another 6-foot evergreen shrub, this species differs from *L. maritima* in having denser growth and greener foliage. Lavender pink flowers bloom most of the year. 'Barnsley' has light pink flowers with white centers. Zones 8 to 10.

❦ *Ledum*

LEE-dum. Heath family, Ericaceae.

This genus is made up of four species of evergreen shrubs, native to marshes and other wet habitats throughout the Northern Hemisphere. The species listed here offer northern gardeners a rare opportunity to grow a broad-leaved evergreen. The leaves are aromatic, while the five-petaled white flowers have prominent stamens and are borne in long-lasting clusters.

HOW TO GROW

Ledum species are happy only in areas with cool summers. There they can grow in full sun or part shade, as long as they have soil that is rich, acidic, and moisture retentive but well aerated. Peat and sand make an ideal mix. Mulching generously will help keep roots moist and cool. Site these little shrubs in a rock garden or with their relatives, the heaths and heathers. Deadheading after bloom is a good practice. Seeds will germinate readily if sown on peat. You can also propagate ledum from semiripe cuttings in late summer or by layering.

L. glandulosum   P. 134

l. gland-yew-LOH-sum. Trapper's Tea. This western U.S. native can grow to 5 feet but is more often about 3 feet tall, with clusters of white flowers in late spring. Zones 2 to 6.

L. groenlandicum

l. groon-LAN-dih-kum. Labrador Tea. Native to Greenland, Alaska, and Canada, this shrub is bushy and round to 3 feet tall and 4 feet wide. Rusty fuzz covers new shoots and the undersides of the leaves, which are narrow ovals with edges curled under, 2 inches long. The ½-inch white flowers bloom in late spring. 'Compactum' grows only 1 foot tall. Zones 2 to 6.

L. palustre

l. pal-US-tree. Wild Rosemary. Differs from *L. groenlandicum* in having a more erect habit, ranging in height from 1 to 4 feet. The tiny leaves are covered with fuzz. Zones 2 to 6.

❧ *Leiophyllum*

Ly-oh-FIL-um. Heath family, Ericaceae.

The only species in this genus is a suckering evergreen shrub native to woodlands in the eastern United States, often found on mountain slopes. The leaves are small and dainty. In spring, frothy clouds of white spring flowers open from pink buds.

HOW TO GROW

Give box sand myrtle full sun to part shade and acid soil that combines peat and sand for moisture retention with good drainage. Keep the soil moist. Does best where nights are cool. Its low habit makes it ideal for rock gardens, or for facing down azaleas and rhododendrons. To propagate, sow the tiny seeds on peat moss, collect softwood cuttings in late summer, or divide suckers.

L. buxifolium   P. 135

l. bux-ih-FOH-lee-um. Box Sand Myrtle. Native from New Jersey into the Carolinas and Kentucky, box sand myrtle averages 18 inches tall but can range in habit from erect to almost a ground cover. Tends to spread and sprawl to 4 feet or more wide. The ½-inch, shiny dark green leaves bronze in winter. Small white flowers retain a pink edge when they open in May and June. It does well in mountainous parts of the South, but in lower elevations may suffer from heat. Zones 5 to 8.

❧ *Leptospermum*

Lep-toh-SPUR-mum. Myrtle family, Myrtaceae.

This genus includes about 80 evergreen trees and shrubs primarily from Australia. About a half dozen species are grown in gardens for small but profuse spring flowers and aromatic foliage. The common name, tea tree, comes from Captain James Cook's brewing of the leaves to prevent scurvy among his sailors. There are many better-tasting sources of vitamin C, however. Don't confuse this tea tree with *Melaleuca* species, another genus from Down Under. Those leaves are distilled into an oil used externally in herbal medicine, but one species, *M. quinquenervia*, has wreaked environmental havoc in Florida.

HOW TO GROW

Give New Zealand tea tree fertile acidic soil that is moisture retentive but drains well. It tolerates seaside conditions but not cold wind or a combination of heat and humidity. It can become chlorotic in high-pH soils. Give shrubs a light to medium pruning in spring if needed to maintain shape, which should be graceful rather than formal. Don't cut into bare wood. Used in mild climates as a hedge or screen. In Zone 8 it is sometimes grown in a container for overwintering indoors, then moved outdoors to admire on a deck or in a border during its heavy spring flowering. Propagate in summer from semiripe cuttings.

L. scoparium

PP. 135, 136

l. skoh-PAH-ree-um. New Zealand Tea Tree. Grows 6 to 10 feet tall with an upright habit and dense branches of small, almost needlelike, aromatic leaves. Gardeners grow not the species but cultivars, which offer profuse displays of ½-inch flowers, many of them double, in late winter or late spring. They include 'Helene Strybing' (deep pink spring flowers, somewhat silver leaves with a graceful, more open habit), 'Nanum Tui' (a 2-foot dwarf with a cushion shape and pale pink single flowers, darker in the middle), 'Pink Pearl' (6 to 10 feet tall with pink buds that open to double white or pink flowers), 'Red Damask' (large double cherry red flowers from midwinter to spring with leaves tinged reddish purple), 'Ruby Glow' (compact to 6 or 8 feet tall with profuse double red flowers in winter and spring and bronzy foliage), and 'Snow White' (2 to 4 feet tall and spreading with double white, dark-green-centered flowers winter to spring). Zones 9 to 10.

❦ Lespedeza

Les-ped-EEZ-uh. Pea family, Fabaceae.

Includes 40 species of perennials, subshrubs, and shrubs native to the eastern United States, Asia, and Australia, grown for their clusters of bright pealike flowers, and often grown as perennials in the northern part of their range. Arching branches provide winter interest.

HOW TO GROW

If bush clover has good drainage and full sun it will tolerate any soil and actually prefers somewhat sandy soil of low fertility. Where it doesn't die to the ground over winter, it needs a hard pruning in early spring to keep it from becoming unkempt. Site it among other plants in a border; it is late to leaf out in spring but will provide color when other flowers have faded. It's also a magnet for bees and other pollinators. Propagate from seeds soaked in hot water, from softwood cuttings, or dividing clumps in spring.

L. bicolor

l. BY-kuh-ler. Shrub Bushclover. This Asian species grows 6 to 8 feet tall and wide with arching shoots. The palmate, three-part leaves are dark green. Magenta pink flowers bloom in racemes up to 5 inches long from the upper leaf axils in late summer. Root hardy in Zones 4 to 8.

L. thunbergii   P. 136

l. thun-BERG-ee-eye. Thunberg Lespedeza. Also from Asia but less cold hardy, this species is considered more ornamental than *L. bicolor*. In late summer or early fall, rosy purple flowers bloom in racemes up to 2 feet long at the ends of long graceful, arching branches. 'Alba' has white flowers, and 'Gibraltar' is vigorous with deep pink blooms. Zones 5 to 8.

❦ Leucophyllum

Loo-coh-FY-lum. Snapdragon family, Scrophulariaceae.

From the 12 species of these evergreen shrubs, native to the American Southwest, several species and hybrids are being brought into gardens because of their adaptability to drought and for their silvery foliage, which contrasts with bell-shaped summer flowers.

HOW TO GROW

These shrubs thrive in the dry soil and air of their native landscape. They're outstanding in a border of other drought-tolerant shrubs or herbaceous perennials. In the humid Southeast, where they are often grown as hedge plants, they are prone to pests and diseases, particularly scale. Give them excellent drainage in full sun, preferably in slightly acid soil. Leucophyllum tolerates salt as well as hard pruning when reshaping is needed. Excellent in a border or as an unusual hedge. Propagate from cuttings.

L. candidum

l. KAN-dih-dum. Violet Silverleaf. Also called dwarf silverleaf sage, this Texas native grows to 3 feet tall with silvery foliage. 'Thundercloud' has profuse dark purple flowers, and a rounded, compact habit. Zones 8 to 10.

L. frutescens   P. 137

l. froo-TESS-ens. Texas Sage. Also called Texas ranger or cenizo, this is the most commonly grown species of *Leucophyllum*. It will reach 5 to 8 feet tall and wide with open branching. The silvery, woolly leaves are ½ to 1 inch long, while the 1-inch flowers are magenta tubular bells. Cultivars include 'Green Cloud', with green leaves and purple flowers; 'Rain Cloud' (a hybrid with *L. minus*), with gray leaves and lavender blue flowers; and 'White Cloud', with gray leaves and white flowers. Zones 8 to 10.

❦ *Leucothoe*

Loo-KOH-thoh-ee. Heath family, Ericaceae.

A genus of approximately 45 evergreen and deciduous shrubs from wetlands and woodlands, primarily in the United States and Japan. A half dozen species are prized in woodland gardens for their graceful, often arching shape, with branches of some species forming a zigzag. The shiny, leathery leaves are often colored bronze or purple in spring and fall; the white urn-shaped flowers bloom in racemes.

HOW TO GROW
Like other members of the heath family, leucothoe needs rich, acid, moisture-retentive soil that has been well amended with organic matter, and it prefers part to full shade. It does not tolerate drought, heat, drying winds, or soggy soil. These shrubs are good for facing down rhododendrons and other larger relatives, or for use in rock gardens, on slopes, or as edging to help define paths. Pruning is the key to keeping these plants attractive. Cut them back hard after they flower. The leaves are often heavily defaced by leafspot when cultural conditions aren't ideal. Propagate from semihard or hardwood cuttings treated with hormone powder.

L. axillaris
l. ax-il-LAIR-iss. Coast Leucothoe. Growing 2 to 4 feet tall and half as wide, this evergreen bears lustrous leaves to 5 inches long on arching branches. New foliage is bronzed, turning somewhat purple in fall. The white flowers bloom in midspring. Zones 6 to 8.

L. fontanesiana   P. 137
l. fon-tan-ee-zee-AY-nuh. Drooping Leucothoe. Also called doghobble and fetterbush, this southeastern U.S. native evergreen is the most commonly grown species of *Leucothoe*. Reaching 3 to 6 feet tall and wide, its arching branches form a fountainlike shape. The pointed leaves are 3 to 6 inches long. Dangling flower clusters appear midspring in 3-inch racemes.

Drooping leucothoe must have shade in the southern portion of its range. It is sometimes pruned as a ground cover. Among cultivars selected for colored or variegated foliage are 'Scarletta', with leaves that are scarlet when young, bronze in autumn; and 'Girard's Rainbow', which is mottled with pink and cream. Zones 5 to 8.

L. keiskei

l. KEES-kee-eye. Keisk's Leucothoe. A dwarf evergreen from Japan with red spring growth, purple-red in fall, and large flowers that bloom early to midsummer. Zones 5 to 8.

L. populifolia

l. pop-ew-lih-FOH-lee-uh. Florida Leucothoe. Now reclassified in the *Agarista* genus with two natives of Brazil, this species is still usually sold under its former name. An evergreen native from South Carolina to Florida, it has especially graceful drooping branches. Although it can grow 8 to 12 feet tall, it tolerates severe pruning. New reddish growth turns rich, glossy green. In the humid South, it resists leafspot better than other species. The fragrant flowers droop from leaf axils in late spring. Tends to sucker; a good choice for shady banks. Zones 7 to 9.

L. racemosa

l. rass-eh-MOH-suh. Sweetbells Leucothoe. A deciduous species native from Massachusetts to Florida, usually suckering and 4 to 6 feet tall and wide. The 2-inch leaves are slightly toothed and may turn brilliant scarlet in fall before dropping. The cylindrical flowers, in racemes to 4 inches long, may be tinged with pink when they appear in mid- to late spring. Zones 5 to 9.

❦ Leycesteria

Ly-sess-TEER-ee-uh. Honeysuckle family, Caprifoliaceae.

Of six species of deciduous shrubs native to the Himalayas and China, one or two are grown in gardens for showy wine red bracts and ½-inch reddish purple berries that attract birds.

HOW TO GROW

For best flower and fruit color, give these shrubs full sun in rich, well-amended, moisture-retentive soil. They will tolerate some drought as well as wind. Prune hard in late winter to maintain shape and stimulate colorful new growth. *Leycesteria* may die back in winter but will regrow in spring, even if killed to the ground. It looks best in an informal situation, such as a relaxed shrub border or wildlife garden. Propagates easily from seeds planted in a mix of peat moss and sand.

L. formosa P. 138

l. for-MOH-suh. Pheasant-eye. The stems of this shrub, also called Himalayan honeysuckle, are hollow canes similar to bamboo and remain blue-green through winter. They grow 6 feet tall and sucker as wide. The leaves, up to 7 inches long, have small teeth, heart-shaped bases, and taper to a point. In late summer to fall, drooping spikes up to 4 inches long bear small white flowers in deep red bracts, followed by the red berries. Zones 7 to 10.

❦ *Ligustrum*

lih-GOOS-trum. Olive family, Oleaceae.

Of some 50 species of deciduous to evergreen shrubs and trees native to Europe, Asia, and Australia, about 10 are commonly used as hedges and screens. The fragrant white or cream-colored flowers are often pruned off in creating formal hedge shapes. If left unpruned, they are followed by blue-black or dark gray fruits. Some of the species, notably *L. sinense* (Chinese privet), have escaped into natural areas, especially in the Mid-Atlantic and Southeast. That species is no longer recommended, and others should be chosen with care.

HOW TO GROW

Privets are popular because they are trouble-free in a wide range of conditions. (As with other plants, this is also what has led to their becoming invasive.) They grow quickly and thrive in most any soil in sun or part shade and tolerate pollution, salt, and drought, but not soggy soil. Prune after flowering; if flowers aren't desired, prune in spring and early fall. They propagate easily from softwood cuttings.

L. amurense

l. am-ur-EN-see. Amur Privet. A deciduous Chinese species growing 12 to 15 feet tall and 9 to 12 feet wide with 1- to 2-inch dull green leaves and four-lobed white flowers that bloom in racemes in late spring, followed by persistent black berries. Zones 4 to 7.

L. japonicum
l. juh-PON-ih-kum. Japanese Privet. An evergreen to 12 feet high and usually 8 feet wide, with thick, shiny, rounded 2- to 4-inch leaves, paler underneath. Pyramid-shaped panicles of heavily perfumed white flowers bloom for several weeks in midspring. Popular for southern gardens, sometimes pruned as a tree. Dark berries are flat and waxy. Cultivars include variegated and curly-leaved forms. Zones 7 to 10.

L. obtusifolium   P. 138
l. ob-too-sih-FOH-lee-um. Border Privet. A deciduous, multistemmed, twiggy shrub to 12 feet tall and wide. The leaves often turn purple in the fall, and the early to midsummer flowers nod from side branches. *L. obtusifolium* var. *regelianum* (Regel privet) is even more strongly horizontal, with hairier leaves that are held in a flat plane. Zones 4 to 7.

L. ovalifolium
l. oh-val-ih-FOH-lee-um. California Privet. This Japanese species got its common name from popularity as a hedge in California. Also called oval-leaved privet, it is a deciduous to semievergreen shrub forming thickets of upright stems to 15 feet with shiny dark green leaves. Erect terminal racemes of white flowers bloom in early to midsummer. Usually sheared when planted as a hedge. There are many variegated forms. Zones 5 to 8.

L. vicaryi   P. 139
l. vih-KAIR-ee-eye. Golden Privet. This semievergreen grows to 10 feet tall and wide with yellow-green leaves. The coloration is strongest in full sun. Flower panicles appear in midsummer. Zones 5 to 8.

✿ Lindera
lin-DEH-ruh. Laurel family, Laureaceae.

Includes 80 dioecious, deciduous or evergreen shrubs and trees that occur naturally in moist woods and along hillside streams in North America and East Asia. Only two or three of these species are cultivated, but they have year-round appeal. The foliage is aromatic and often brightly colored in fall, with attractive fruit on female plants. Tiny yellow-green flowers appear on naked branches in early spring.

HOW TO GROW
Spicebush must have the same moisture-retentive, well-aerated, organically rich soil it enjoys in the wild, but it adapts to a wide range of pH.

Give it full sun in the North, semishade in the South. Fibrous roots require steady supplemental moisture when newly transplanted. You will need plants of each sex in order to have berries, which are handsome in wildlife and woodland gardens. Keep them near the beaten path, though, where you can brush against the fragrant leaves. Propagate by cleaning seeds and giving warm treatment followed by cold treatment.

L. benzoin

l. BEN-zoh-in. Spicebush. Often found on moist limestone outcrops from Canada to Florida and Texas, spicebush nevertheless thrives in more acidic conditions. It grows 6 to 12 feet tall and wide, denser in sun and more open in shade. In early spring the bare branches are covered with clusters of small yellow-green flowers. When crushed, the light green oblong leaves, berries, and stems emit a spicy scent. In early fall, bright red berries ripen on female plants and attract birds, while leaves turn bright yellow. Zones 5 to 9.

L. obtusiloba

P. 139

l. ob-tuss-ih-LOH-buh. Japanese Spicebush. This Asian species can grow larger than *L. benzoin,* up to 20 feet but usually much smaller. In autumn it has more uniform, lasting, golden yellow coloration, even in shade. Leaves are frequently lobed. The foliage and the fruits, which turn from red to shiny black, are less heavily scented than those of the native species. Zones 6 to 8.

❦ Lithodora

Lith-oh-DOR-uh. Borage family, Boraginaceae.

A genus of seven evergreen shrubs from southwest Europe and the Mediterranean, grown primarily as rock garden plants for their ground-hugging form and terminal flat-topped clusters of intense blue (occasionally white) tubular summer flowers. These plants were formerly classified as *Lithospermum.*

HOW TO GROW

Give *L. diffusa,* the most commonly available species, neutral to alkaline soil with excellent drainage in full sun. Prune lightly after flowering. Propagate from semiripe cuttings in summer.

L. diffusa

P. 140

l. dif-FEW-suh. A prostrate shrub usually 6 inches tall and spreading to 2 feet wide with narrow, oblong, hairy leaves to 1½ inches long. 'Heavenly Blue' and 'Grace Ward' are covered with azure blue, funnel-shaped, ½-inch flowers for a long period in late spring and summer. Zones 6 to 8.

❦ Lonicera

lahn-ISS-er-uh. Honeysuckle family, Caprifoliaceae.

Better known for the vining members among its 180 species, this genus from throughout the Northern Hemisphere also includes deciduous and evergreen shrubs. Like the climbers, they are grown primarily for their tubular, usually fragrant flowers. The berries are popular with birds. Like the common honeysuckle vine, *L. japonica,* many of the shrub species (notably *L. maackii* and *L. tatarica*) have become widely invasive. In most of the country, less troublesome shrubs should be substituted. Most of those in cultivation are native to Asia.

HOW TO GROW

Honeysuckles have become invasive because they are so easy to grow, adapting to most any relatively moisture-retentive, well-draining soil. They bloom best in full sun but also grow in heavy shade, leafing out before taller plants and getting a jump start on the season. If plants become overgrown they can be pruned to the ground and will develop new shoots. Use them as hedges, in the shrub border, in wildlife gardens, or massed for winter or early-spring fragrance. They propagate easily from softwood cuttings.

L. fragrantissima

l. fray-gran-TISS-ih-muh. Winter Honeysuckle. Growing 8 to 10 feet tall and wide, winter honeysuckle is somewhat rounded and holds its broad, oval, 1- to 3-inch leaves late into winter. Half-inch two-lipped flowers are cream tinged with pink and open as early as January and as late as April, more fragrant than pretty. The dark red berries are hidden by foliage. Zones 4 to 10.

L. nitida

P. 140

l. NIT-ih-duh. Boxleaf Honeysuckle. An evergreen species cultivated as a fast-growing, easily pruned, salt-tolerant hedge, rather than for its inconspicuous flowers. Reaches 10 feet tall but is usually kept lower. The common name reflects the leaf shape, similar to boxwood. The dark blue fruits are round and translucent but rarely produced. Shiny leaves may bronze in winter. Cultivars include 'Baggesen's Gold' with golden foliage. Zones 7 to 9.

L. pileata   P. 141

l. pil-ee-AY-tuh. Privet Honeysuckle. A semievergreen with a graceful, spreading, horizontal habit to 3 feet tall and more than twice as wide. Similar to boxleaf honeysuckle except that the leaves are elongated and larger. It does not perform well in the South, but does tolerate seaside conditions. Zones 6 to 8.

L. xylosteum

l. zy-LOSS-tee-um. European Fly Honeysuckle. Forms a mound, 10 feet tall and wide with arching branches. The gray-green leaves are slightly fuzzy, and the yellow and white flowers are followed by dark red berries. Good selection for the Midwest and Plains. 'Emerald Mound' grows to only 3 feet tall and 5 feet wide with bluish green foliage. Zones 4 to 6.

❦ Loropetalum

Lor-oh-PET-uh-lum. Witch hazel family, Hamamelidaceae.

A genus containing only one small evergreen species from Asia, grown for its compact size, graceful form, and unusual early-season flowers. Cultivars offer the bonus of colorful foliage.

HOW TO GROW

Loropetalum needs organically rich, moist, well-drained acid soil in sun or part shade. It tolerates heavy pruning and can be espaliered, but otherwise loses its appealing natural shape with anything but a light trim after flowering. Plant against a sunny wall or in a shrub border. Pink-flowered forms make a striking echo for similarly colored tulips. Needs mild winters and hot summers. Cuttings need hormones and mist to root; bottom heat may prevent rotting.

L. chinense   P. 141

l. chih-NEN-see. Chinese Fringe-flower. Grows 6 to 10 feet tall and wide, with an irregular fountain or vase shape. The spidery white flowers, similar to those of witch hazel, appear in early spring. Several with purple flowers and purple-tinged leaves include *L. chinese* var. *rubrum*, 'Blush', 'Burgundy' (with leaves that develop orange or red streaks in fall), and 'Zhuzhous Fuchsia' (said to be the best at maintaining maroon color through summer heat). Plants have occasional light rebloom in fall. The species is considered hardier than the red-foliaged varieties, possibly into southern Zone 6 with protection. Otherwise, Zones 7 to 10.

❦ *Magnolia*

Mag-NOLE–yuh. Magnolia family, Magnoliaceae

Most gardeners know the tree forms among the 125 species of deciduous and evergreen woody plants, native to North and South America, East Asia, and the Himalayas. There are several forms, all deciduous, of small to large shrubs worth growing for white or colorful early-season flowers.

HOW TO GROW

Give magnolias full sun to part shade and organically rich, moisture-retentive soil that drains well. Most prefer neutral to acid soil; *M. stellata* is an exception among the shrubby magnolias. Plant in a border or against a background where you can enjoy their gray winter branches. For *M. stellata*, avoid southern exposures, which may cause buds to open before danger of frost is past. Prune only dead or misshapen branches, back to the base. Propagate with fresh seeds after cold stratification, or from semihardwood cuttings.

M. liliiflora

m. lih-lee-ih-FLOR-uh. Lily Magnolia. A bushy shrub 10 feet tall and about as wide, the lily magnolia is named for upright flowers that are purple outside and usually white inside, borne in midspring just as its dark green, slightly fuzzy leaves begin to unfurl. May develop mildew in humid climates. There are numerous cultivars with purple to reddish purple flowers. Zones 5 to 10.

M. liliiflora × *stellata*   P. 142

m. lil-lee-ih-FLOR-uh × stel-AH-tuh. Little Girl Hybrids. Developed in the 1950s at the U.S. National Arboretum, these more upright deciduous shrubs all have purple-red flowers, some of them with white on the inside. Bloom is early to midspring with some summer reblooming. Most are 12 feet high and wide. All have girls' names, such as 'Ann', 'Betty', and 'Jane'. Zones 4 to 7.

M. sieboldii P. 142

m. see-BOLD-ee-eye. Oyama Magnolia. Usually maturing at 12 feet high and about 10 feet wide, this deciduous Asian species has fragrant white cup-shaped flowers up to 4 inches across with bright red stamens. Opening in late spring from a big egg-shaped bud, they nod slightly from their stems. Zones 6 to 8.

M. stellata P. 143

m. stel-AH-tuh. Star Magnolia. A popular shrub or small tree for home gardens, it can surprise the owner by growing to 20 feet tall and 15 feet wide, but usually remains smaller. The 4-inch straplike early-spring flowers, often damaged by frost, open from fuzzy buds that give winter pleasure, especially when backlit by morning or evening sun. Cultivars include 'Centennial' (larger flowers with narrow petals twice as numerous as those of the species), 'Rosea' (pink flowers), 'Royal Star' (opens from pink buds, with many petals), and 'Waterlily' (deep pink buds, highly fragrant flowers). Zones 4 to 10.

M. wilsonii

m. wil-SOH-nee-eye. Somewhat treelike to 20 feet tall, and similar to *M. sieboldii* in having pendulous flowers with red stamens. Plant it where you can look up at the late-spring blooms. More shade tolerant than most magnolias. Zones 7 to 9.

❧ *Mahonia*

mah-HOH-nee-uh. Barberry family, Berberidaceae.

This genus of some 70 evergreen shrubs, native to North and South America and East Asia, includes several species that are popular in gardens, especially those with an abundance of shade. They have eye-catching, usually spiky foliage, clusters or spikes of yellow flowers, and, often, colorful berries.

HOW TO GROW

Most mahonias do best in partial or even full shade, especially if the soil is at all dry. The soil should be acidic and full of humus, but well aerated. Most need protection from drying winds. Mahonias are perfect for woodland gardens, shady foundation areas, or borders. Site spiky varieties away from paths, or use them as security hedges. Prune off shoots that are leggy above foliage, or that otherwise spoil the shape. Propagate from stratified seeds, semiripe cuttings in autumn, or suckers.

M. aquifolium P. 143

m. ah-quih-FOH-lee-um. Oregon Grape-holly. Up to 6 feet or taller, this North-west native will sucker and spread to 5 feet. Leathery, spiny compound leaves with up to 12 leaflets on a side emerge light green or bronze and become shiny dark green, bronzing again in fall. The clusters of early to midspring yellow flowers are followed in summer by grapelike clusters of blue fruits that remain through winter. Cultivars include 'Apollo' (2-foot ground cover with golden orange flowers), 'Atropurpurea' (another low grower with reliable red-purple fall color), 'Compacta' (dwarf with leaves that bronze), 'Mayhan Strain' (about 3 feet tall with fewer, closely spaced leaves), 'Moseri' (colorful new growth), 'Smargd' (trademarked as Emerald, with bronzy fall leaves and flower clusters to 4 inches long). Zones 5 to 8.

M. bealei P. 144

m. BEE-lee-eye. Leatherleaf Mahonia. From China, leatherleaf grows to 12 feet tall with foot-long leaves of up to 15 spiny leaflets. Fragrant lemon yellow flowers appear on spikes in late winter to early spring, followed by powdery bright blue berries that birds may harvest. Zones 7 to 9.

M. fortunei

m. for-TOON-ee-eye. Chinese Mahonia. Erect and somewhat stiff to 6 feet tall, with slender leaflets that are more ferny and less spiky than other species. The yellow flowers are in upright racemes in late summer or early fall. Berries seldom appear. Can survive with protection in Zone 7. Otherwise, Zones 8 to 9.

M. japonica

m. juh-PON-ih-kuh. Japanese Mahonia. Similar to *M. bealei* but usually only 6 feet tall and spreading half again as wide, with flowers more relaxed than upright and brighter yellow. The oval berries are bluish purple. Zones 7 to 8.

M. nervosa

m. ner-VOH-suh. Cascades Mahonia. Sometimes called longleaf mahonia, this 12- to 18-inch suckering shrub is native from British Columbia to northern California. The thick, glossy gray-green leaves are bristly with 11 to 23 leaflets up to 3 inches long. A good ground cover with the habit of a stiff fern. Flowers bloom in upright clusters mid- to late spring, followed by purple-blue berries. Zones 5 to 7.

M. repens
P. 144

m. REP-enz. Creeping Mahonia. Also called dwarf Oregon grape, this cold-hardy ground cover is native from northern Mexico and California to British Columbia and east to the Rockies. Rarely growing much higher than 1 foot, it spreads by underground stolons to 2 or 3 feet across. The somewhat dull, blue-green spiny leaves turn purple-bronze in winter. Yellow flowers are in 1- to 3-inch racemes in midspring, and blue-black berries develop in late summer. Zones 4 to 7.

M. × wagneri 'King's Ransom'

m. × WAG-ner-eye. King's Ransom Mahonia. An upright form to 6½ feet, with 8-inch, dark blue-green leaves, dense terminal racemes of spring flowers, and powdery blue-black berries. Develops bronzy, red-purple color in winter. Leaves of 'Undulata' have wavy margins. Zones 6 to 8.

❦ Michelia

my-KEE-lee-uh. Magnolia family, Magnoliaceae.

At the turn of the twentieth century, this shrub was all the rage in the South because of its fruit-scented blossoms. It arrived in the United States from China a century earlier. There are 45 evergreen trees and shrubs in this genus, most from Southeast Asia, but this is the only one common to gardens. When out of bloom it offers handsome foliage.

HOW TO GROW

Give the banana shrub acidic sandy loam, well amended with organic matter, that retains moisture and drains well. It will grow in sun but part shade is best. Mulch with leaf mold to further improve moisture retention; protect it from cold, drying winds. It needs little pruning, but can be espaliered. Plant near paths, patios, or entrances to make the most of its fragrance. Propagate from semiripe summer cuttings treated with hormones.

M. figo
P. 145

m. FY-goh. Banana Shrub. Rounded and dense to 2 feet high and wide, its stems are covered with tan down as are new leaves, which mature to a leathery, glossy green with paler undersides. The magnolia-like midspring flowers are yellow-green tinged with purple and smell richly of fruit. It may grow in the south of Zone 7 with protection. Zones 8 to 10.

❦ Microbiota

My-kroh-by-OH-tuh. Cypress family, Cupressaceae.

This genus contains only one species, a prostrate conifer native to south-east Siberia. Graceful in form, it makes an attractive and useful evergreen ground cover for northern gardeners.

HOW TO GROW

This species needs moist, well-drained soil. It will tolerate some shade, but not heat or poor drainage. Use it to cover bare ground in a difficult spot or at the front of a border. Needs no pruning except to remove damaged branches or redirect growth. It spreads slowly, but indefinitely; a snip or two here and there will keep it from heading in a direction you'd rather it not go. Propagate with heel cuttings, leaving them over winter in a cold frame or other protected spot.

M. decussata   P. 145

m. deh-koo-SAY-tuh. Russian Arborvitae. These ground-hugging plants rarely rise above 1 foot tall, but after many years can spread to 15 feet. The foliage is in flat sprays, bright green in summer and plummy purple in winter. The tiny female cones bear only one seed. Zones 3 to 7.

❦ Myrica

my-REE-kuh. Bayberry family, Myricaceae.

The 50 evergreen and deciduous members of this genus are found in moist or coastal habitats throughout the world. About a half dozen shrubs and small trees are grown in gardens for aromatic foliage and attractive small berries that appeal to birds. The flowers are inconspicuous catkins.

HOW TO GROW

Wax myrtles or bayberries vary in their requirements but are frequently chosen for their ability to withstand challenging situations such as seaspray, drought, or boggy sites. This genus offers a good example of regional genetic variation. To assure cold hardiness, look for plants grown locally or farther north, as *M. cerifera* raised in Florida (for example) may die in a cold Georgia winter. Its coastal origins make it tolerant of less than ideal soil conditions, although it's best to provide humusy, well-draining soil in full sun or part shade. Useful as screens, hedges, background plantings, or for naturalizing. They require little pruning, but respond well to cutting back if you want to control size or shape. Propagate seeds by first removing their waxy coating; two months' cold stratification may help. Propagate *M. cerifera* from semihardwood cuttings in early summer or root cuttings in winter.

M. californica

m. kal-ih-FORN-ih-kuh. California Bayberry. Native from Southern California to Washington State, it can reach 20 feet or more when grown away from coastal winds, but can also remain under 10 feet. Often multitrunked, its branches are dense with glossy, toothed, dark green leaves 2 to 4 inches long. The small purple fruits are persistent if not removed by birds. Tolerates salt, drought, and sandy soil. Zones 6 to 10.

M. cerifera

m. ser-IF-er-uh. Southern Waxmyrtle. This Southeast native evergreen, also called candleberry, can grow more than 30 feet tall in the wild but usually remains 10 to 15 feet tall in a garden. The fragrant, usually narrow, olive green leaves are dotted with resin glands on the underside. Tiny blue-gray berries, almost white with wax, cover the stems fall and winter. Too much shade may make it leggy, but it takes well to pruning, which will expose handsome, smooth, muscular gray bark. It tolerates infertile soil, wet or dry, and possibly a wider pH range than *M. pensylvanica*. Zones 7 to 10.

M. gale

m. GALL-ee. Sweet Gale. This deciduous shrub from Europe, Asia, and cold boggy areas of North America suckers and forms low thickets less than 4 feet high. Male plants have yellow-brown catkins in mid- to late spring, followed by round yellow-brown fruits on the female plants. Fragrant, glossy leaves are dark bluish green. It tolerates saturated soils. Zones 1 to 6.

M. pensylvanica   P. 146

m. pen-sil-VAN-ih-kuh. Bayberry. Native from the northeastern United States to the Mid-Atlantic, it is deciduous in the north and evergreen in the southern parts of its range. It averages 9 feet tall and suckers to form rounded colonies. The fragrant, leathery leaves are gray-green to olive and dotted with resin glands on the undersides. Males bear tiny yellow-green flowers, and the females produce equally small blue-gray waxy berries that may last from September to spring. It tolerates soil that is wet or dry, sand or clay, salty or infertile, but may become chlorotic in alkaline soil. Zones 3 to 6.

❦ *Myrtus*

MUR-tus. Myrtle family, Myrtaceae.

There are only two species of these evergreen shrubs from North Africa and southern Europe. One of them is popular in mild climates for its aromatic foliage — similar to boxwood and often trained in a similar manner — as well as its attractive white flowers and berries.

HOW TO GROW

This myrtle is not particular about soil as long as its drainage is excellent. It does well in full sun or light shade and can be pruned to almost any shape, including espalier, topiary, or limbed up as a tree to expose the attractive branches. In the colder part of its range, plant it against a sunny wall with shelter from wind. It can also be grown as an indoor-outdoor plant, in a loam-based medium with even moisture. Scale and mealy bugs, which can be a problem indoors, should be wiped with cotton swabs dipped in neem or denatured alcohol. Propagate with semiripe cuttings in summer.

M. communis P. 147

m. kom-MEW-niss. Common Myrtle. Upright and bushy, this Mediterranean native usually grows 10 to 12 feet tall and wide but can become much larger with a more arching habit. Pointed oval leaves, glossy and dark green, are 2 inches long and fragrant when crushed. The late-summer solitary flowers are fragrant, white, and ¾ inch across with five petals and a starry brush of stamens, followed by elliptical ½-inch blue-black berries. 'Microphylla' is a dwarf form with especially tiny leaves. There are other compact forms as well as variegated selections. Zone 8 to 11.

❦ *Nandina*

nan-DEEN-uh. Barberry family, Berberidaceae.

A single species of evergreen shrub from China and Japan, grown widely in gardens for its graceful habit and foliage — often bronze-red when young and again in fall — its white flower clusters, and, especially, the red berries that persist through winter.

HOW TO GROW

Nandina will thrive in any moderately fertile soil in sun or shade, although it will produce the most berries if given full sun and kept relatively moist. Use it in masses, as contrast with heavier-foliaged plants, for narrow spaces, and to provide winter interest. Can be pruned to the ground; yearly pruning out of old canes will keep growth dense rather than leggy. Propagates most easily by dividing clumps.

N. domestica   P. 147

n. doh-MES-tih-kuh. Heavenly Bamboo. Unbranched stems to 6 feet tall form clumps similar to bamboo, with leaves divided into slender leaflets. The late-spring or early-summer flowers are white in foot-long panicles. But they are outdone by the heavy clusters of red berries that last from early autumn through winter, often against bronze-purple or red foliage. Cultivars include 'Alba' (white berries), 'Fire Power' (bright red winter foliage), 'Gulf Stream' (mounded form to 3 feet, red leaves in winter), 'Harbour Dwarf' (suckering form to 3 feet, graceful with smaller flower clusters), 'San Gabriel' (under 2 feet tall with narrow leaflets, less cold hardy), 'Umpqua Warrior' (erect, 4 to 6 feet tall), and 'Wood's Dwarf' (very compact at 2 feet, red winter foliage). Often killed to the ground or winterburned in Zone 6. Zones 7 to 10.

❦ *Nerium*

NEE-ree-um. Dogbane family, Apocynaceae.

There is only one species of this genus, an evergreen shrub or small tree found from the Mediterranean to western China. Many cultivars have been developed for gardeners who live in similarly mild climates, where the shrubs produce long-blooming terminal clusters of five-petaled flowers.

HOW TO GROW

Oleanders are tolerant of soils that are dry, salty, or waterlogged, and they thrive in the bright, reflected light typical of waterside or desert gardens. They will also tolerate light shade and are deerproof. They can be pruned as single- or multiple-trunked trees, grown in containers and pruned as standards, or allowed to sucker as a screen or border. In early spring, prune back flowered wood, cutting a proportion of stems to the ground. Other branches can be pruned lightly to restrict size. Pull out any unwanted suckers. Propagates easily from seeds or softwood cuttings.

N. oleander

P. 148

n. OH-lee-an-der. Oleander. Oleander is broad, round, and suckering from 8 to 12 feet tall and wide unless pruned, with stout stems and leathery lance-shaped leaves to 4 inches long. The clusters of pinwheel flowers, usually pink in the species, can start blooming in late spring and last well into fall. They are followed by a 6-inch seedpod. All parts of the plants are poisonous and even smoke from the wood can cause irritation. Cultivars have single or double flowers in white, peach, pink, yellow, and red, and many have been chosen for more compact habits. Popular selections include 'Calypso' (single, cherry red), 'Hardy Pink' (single salmon pink), 'Hardy Red' (single, red), 'Hawaii (single, salmon pink with yellow throat, compact), 'Petite Pink' (grows only 3 to 4 feet tall), 'Sister Agnes' (white, found in both single and double, fast-growing), and 'Tangier' (single, pale pink, 4 to 6 feet). Zones 8 (south) to 11.

❦ Neviusia

Nev-ih-YEW-see-uh. Rose family, Rosaceae.

This genus contains only two rare species of deciduous suckering shrubs. The better known *N. alabamensis* is native to the southeast United States, while a second, *N. cliftonii,* has been more recently discovered in California. Much like a spirea in habit, they are covered with starry balls of white flowers in midspring.

HOW TO GROW

Alabama snow-wreath does best in moisture-retentive, well-drained loam, but adapts fairly well to less ideal situations in sun or part-shade. Grow as a specimen or in the shrub border. Prune assertively after flowering to keep it from becoming shaggy. Propagate from softwood cuttings or divide suckers.

N. alabamensis

P. 148

n. al-uh-BAM-en-siss. Alabama Snow-wreath. Native to isolated areas of the mid-South, this shrub has erect, arching stems to 6 feet high and spreads at least as wide, eventually developing a rounded habit. Spade-shaped leaves are serrated. The unusual showy white midspring flowers consist entirely of feathery stamens. Zones 4 to 8.

❧ Oemleria

om-LER-ee-uh. Rose family, Rosaceae.

A single species of deciduous, dioecious shrub native to western North America. Closely related to the plum, it is one of the first plants of the growing season to leaf out and bloom, with dangling flowers that smell of almonds, followed by dark blue fruits.

HOW TO GROW

Oso berry is easy to grow in any moderately moist and fertile soil with good drainage, in sun or part shade. Both male and female shrubs are needed to produce fruits. Grow it in a shrub border or use for naturalizing. Head back stems or remove suckers to restrict growth. If you want more flowers and fruit, prune old flowered shoots to the ground. Propagate with softwood cuttings in early summer or by dividing suckers.

O. cerasiformis   P. 149

o. keh-rass-ih-FORM-iss. Oso Berry. Upright, eventually arching shoots to 8 feet tall can sucker to form a thicket 12 feet across. The lance-shaped leaves to 3½ inches long are dark green and glossy above, gray-green and somewhat fuzzy underneath. Drooping 4-inch racemes of tiny, fragrant, white bell-shaped flowers appear just after the leaves in late winter or earliest spring. Female shrubs then bear oval ¾-inch blue-black fruits. (The species name means "cherry shaped.") Zones 6 to 9.

❧ Osmanthus

Oz-MAN-thus. Olive family, Oleaceae.

The genus name comes from Greek for "fragrant" and "flower," and the miniscule blossoms are often intensely fragrant far out of proportion to their size. This is a group of about 20 evergreen shrubs and trees from the southeast United States, East Asia, and the Middle East. The flowers, which bloom in spring or fall depending on the species, are often hidden by the dense glossy foliage. They are followed by usually persistent, ½-inch blue-black berries.

HOW TO GROW

Osmanthus does best in soil that is acidic, fertile, moist, and well drained. It tolerates some clay or alkalinity, but not prolonged drought. Although it can be grown in sun or part shade, the foliage may burn if exposed to winter sun and wind. Ideal for hedges and screens, or along walks and entryways where its fragrance can be appreciated. It can take fairly heavy pruning, after flowering, but doesn't require it. Propagate with semiripe cuttings in late spring or early summer.

O. americanus

o. uh-mair-ih-KAY-nus. Devilwood. Native to swampy areas of the southeastern United States, devilwood is unlike other osmanthus in having a more open and loose habit and untoothed leaves. From 2 to 4 inches long, they are lance shaped and shiny olive green. It can grow 15 or 20 feet tall. The aromatic white flowers bloom in midspring. Considered the most cold-hardy species. Zones 6 to 9.

O. delavayi   P. 149

o. del-AH-vay-eye. Delavay Osmanthus. A Chinese species growing slowly to 6 to 10 feet (although some have reached 20 feet), often broader, and rounded. The 1-inch lustrous leaves are toothed, and the fragrant white flowers with reflexed petals are borne profusely in midspring. It produces clusters at the ends of branches as well as in leaf axils, where other osmanthus flowers are often hidden. Zones 7 to 9.

O. × fortunei

o. × for-TOON-ee-eye. Fortune's Osmanthus. This hybrid of *O. heterophyllus* and *O. fragrans* grows slowly to 15 to 20 feet high but is usually kept smaller. The 4-inch leaves are toothed like a holly's, and the fragrant flowers bloom in early to midautumn. Retains its deep green color in hot sun better than some other species. 'San Jose' has narrower leaves. Zones 7 to 9.

O. fragrans

o. FRAY-granz. Sweet Olive. Also called fragrant tea olive, this Asian species can be a huge shrub at 20 or 30 feet tall and wide but is usually about half that size. The shiny green leaves are finely toothed or untoothed, up to 5 inches long. Flowers, considered the most fragrant of the genus, bloom from early fall and sporadically through winter. 'Aurantiacus' has yellow-orange flowers. Zones 8 to 10.

O. heterophyllus   P. 150

o. het-er-oh-FIL-us. False Holly. A Japanese species that will grow to 20 feet tall but is usually less than 10 feet high and slightly narrower. Very dense and rounded, it earned all of its common names—holly olive, holly osmanthus—from the resemblance of its leaves to those of many *Ilex* species: shiny, leathery, and spiny when young, less so as they mature. The intensely fragrant, four-petaled white flowers bloom in early to midautumn, almost hidden by foliage. Cultivars include 'Goshiki' (leaves flecked with yellow), 'Gulftide' (to 15 feet tall and cold tolerant, with shiny, spiny leaves), 'Purpureus' (dark purple new leaves, retaining a purple tint), 'Rotundifolius' (spineless, slow growing), and 'Sasaba' (very spiny, to 4 feet, less cold tolerant). Zones 6 to 9.

❧ *Paeonia*

pay-OH-nee-uh. Peony family, Paeoniaceae.

Most gardeners are familiar with the clump-forming herbaceous perennials—from western North America, Europe, and Asia—that make up most of this genus. But it also includes several species (the number is under debate) of deciduous shrubs or subshrubs that have been interbred for many centuries. Highly prized for spring blossoms that range from immense doubles to more delicate singles and deeply incised leaves that provide fall color, the woody forms are almost always sold as cultivars or hybrids, rather than as species.

HOW TO GROW
Give tree peonies a bed of neutral to slightly acid soil, well amended both wide and deep with organic matter. High dappled shade is best, particularly during midday, as blooms will "melt out" quickly in full sun. Some growers strongly recommend fall planting, about six weeks before the last expected frost date. The bud union should be about ¾ inch underground. Mulch well, especially in fall if you live where hardiness may be borderline. After the first year or so, the deep root system makes these plants drought tolerant. Use them as specimens or in a herbaceous or shrub border. In spring, prune back to remove dead wood above swelling buds. Propagate by layering or by dividing mature plants.

Paeonia cultivars and hybrids   PP. 150, 151
Tree peony species are used primarily for breeding, rather than as ornamental garden plants, since they tend not to be cold hardy and have small flowers that are hidden in the foliage. *P. suffruticosa* has been the source of most large-flowered selections. *P. rockii*, which has maroon flares at the base of its white petals, is sometimes considered a separate species, some-

times a botanical variety of *P. suffruticosa,* and is often sold as 'Joseph Rock' or in double forms called "double rocks." Nurseries may specialize in either Chinese or Japanese hybrids (called moutan or sometimes mudan) and will argue strongly for their superiority over the other type. A good tree peony has strong stems that hold the flowers well above the foliage. These hybrids come in white, pink, red, and purple, and shapes can range from single through "thousand petal."

In recent years, European and American breeders have used *P. lutea* to add yellow to the color palette. Many of these have a lemon fragrance. 'Age of Gold', 'Golden Isles', 'Golden Era', and 'High Noon' are among the most popular. 'Gauguin' is sunset colored, its orange petals streaked with gold. Zones 4 to 8.

❦ *Paxistima*

pax-ISS-tih-muh. Bittersweet family, Celastraceae.

These two species of evergreen shrubs, native to North America and related to *Euonymous,* make a useful woody ground cover for shady gardens, where their glossy, leathery leaves can bring some much-needed sparkle.

HOW TO GROW

Growing naturally on limy, stony ground, these ground covers tolerate low fertility and high pH but need organic amendments to assure that soil is moisture retentive and well aerated. They thrive in part shade, although growth may be denser in full sun. Site at the edge of a woodland, use as a ground cover in dappled shade, or include in a rock garden. Propagates easily by division or by semiripe cuttings collected in summer.

P. canbyi   P. 151

p. KAN-bee-eye. Cliff-green. Native to mountains of Virginia and West Virginia, this ground cover, also called rat-stripper and mountain-lover, rarely reaches a foot tall. A single plant may spread up to 5 feet, as the stems root where they touch the ground. The narrow, serrated, evergreen leaves range from ¼ to 1 inch long on erect stems and may turn bronze in winter. Clusters of ¼-inch greenish white flowers bloom in summer. Zones 3 to 7.

P. myrtifolia (syn. *P. myrsinites*)

p. mer-tih-FOH-lee-uh. Oregon Boxwood. This western U.S. native is more upright and usually taller than *P. canbyi*, up to 3 feet, with finely serrated 1-inch leaves. It blooms in spring and summer. Zones 5 to 8.

❧ *Philadelphus*

fil-uh-DEL-fuss. Saxifrage family, Saxifragaceae.

The heady orange-blossom scent of these old garden favorites is second only to lilacs in evoking nostalgia. This genus comprises 60 species native to North America and from eastern Europe to East Asia. The origins of many hybrids and cultivars are somewhat unclear, but all offer gardeners an array of single and double white flowers, blooming in early summer with slightly varying scents.

HOW TO GROW

Mock orange blooms best in full sun but will grow in part shade. Although quite adaptable to varied pH and drought, like most shrubs it does best in organically enriched soil that both retains moisture and drains well. Because it can become ragged looking, it benefits from regular judicious pruning to shape and remove unproductive branches. Propagate from seeds or softwood cuttings, treated with hormones, in early to midsummer.

P. 'Buckley's Quill'. A compact selection to 6 feet tall and 4 feet wide. The unusual flowers have about 30 quill-like petals. Zones 4 to 7.

P. coronarius

p. kor-oh-NAR-ee-us. Sweet Mock Orange. From southeastern Europe and Asia Minor, this species grows stiffly upright to 10 or 12 feet high and wide and slightly rounded. The fragrant late-spring flowers have four petals and four sepals and bloom in racemes. For summer interest, look for yellow-foliaged 'Aureus' or 'Variegatus', which has leaves edged with white. Zones 4 to 8.

P. 'Galahad'. This relatively new selection is about 5 feet tall with a rounded habit. The fragrant single flowers have prominent yellow centers. Zones 5 to 8.

P × *lemoinei*

p. × lem-WON-ee-eye. These hybrids grow 4 to 5 feet tall and wide with arching branches. The 2-inch leaves are tapered and sparsely toothed. Single cup-shaped, 1-inch flowers bloom in groups of three to five in midsummer. Popular selections include 'Belle Etoile' (wide-spreading habit and single flowers more than 2 inches across with pale purple markings in the center), 'Innocence' (upright to 10 feet, leaves mottled yellow), and 'Silver Showers' (rounded form, profuse strawberry-scented flowers). Zones 5 to 8.

P. microphyllus P. 152

p. my-kro-PHIL-us. Littleleaf Mock Orange. Native to the southwest United States, this species is 4 feet tall with ½-inch-long leaves and 1-inch, sweetly scented flowers. Needs full sun. Zones 6 to 9.

P. 'Natchez'. A cultivar with especially profuse flowering. Zones 5 to 8.

P. 'Snowgoose'. A cold-hardy selection with profuse, fragrant flowers on arching branches. Zones 4 to 7.

P. × *virginalis* P. 152

p. × ver-jin-AL-iss. An old-fashioned favorite growing 10 feet high and wide with fragrant double flowers. Most of the named selections are smaller. They include 'Bouquet Blanc' (6 feet tall, with a name that reflects its mix of garden scents), 'Minnesota Snowflake' (double flowers in racemes of up to seven, hardy to Zone 4), and 'Virginal' (to 10 feet tall and 8 feet wide with double, very fragrant flowers). Zones 5 to 8.

❧ *Phlomis*

FLOW-miss. Mint family, Lamiaceae.

This is a genus of about 100 herbaceous perennials and evergreen shrubs and subshrubs from the Mediterranean and Asia. Several are grown in gardens for their whorls of tubular flowers, often hooded, and woolly gray-green leaves similar to those of sage.

HOW TO GROW

Phlomis tolerates relatively poor soil as long as the drainage is good. It may need supplemental watering in hot climates and requires full sun for flowering. Use these shrubs in masses or in mixed or shrub borders.

Smaller ones are suitable for rock gardens. Prune out old stems to keep plants dense and encourage rebloom. Propagate from softwood cuttings in summer.

P. fruticosa
P. 153

p. froo-tih-KOH-suh. Jerusalem Sage. A dense shrub to 4 feet tall with woolly lance-shaped leaves up to 3½ inches long. The midsummer flowers are golden yellow, blooming in ball-shaped clusters. Zones 7 to 10.

P. lanata

p. lan-AY-tuh. This dense shrub from Greece forms a mound about 20 inches tall and 30 inches wide and is a good choice for a rock garden. The 1-inch leaves have deep veins and a pebbly texture. Half-inch golden summer flowers are covered with brown hairs. Zones 8 to 10.

❦ Photinia

foe-TIN-ee-uh. Rose family, Rosaceae.

A genus of about 40 deciduous and evergreens shrubs and trees native to East Asia, grown widely throughout the South for colorful new foliage and berries. They are closely related to hawthorn and firethorn and have similar white midspring flower clusters. Some gardeners find the scent of the blossoms unpleasant and prune them off to stimulate new colorful leaves.

HOW TO GROW
Give photinia fertile, well-drained soil in full sun or part shade. *P. villosa* prefers acid soil. Photinia is often defoliated by leafspot in humid climates but is otherwise a tough plant, most commonly used as a hedge or screen. Prune off exuberant new growth that spoils its shape. Propagate with cold-stratified seeds or root semiripe cuttings in summer.

P. × fraseri
P. 153

p. × FRAY-zer-eye. An evergreen hybrid growing 15 feet tall and wide. New coppery growth lasts up to a month, followed by midspring clusters of white flowers to 6 inches across. Berries are rare. 'Birmingham' has especially red new growth; 'Indian Princess' grows more slowly and has smaller leaves. Once on the verge of overuse in the South, this species has declined in popularity because leafspot is almost inevitable. Zones 7 to 10.

P. glabra

p. GLAB-ruh. Japanese Photinia. Smallest of the evergreens, usually less than 12 feet tall, with smaller leaves that emerge red. The early-summer flower panicles, 4 inches across, are followed by red berries that turn black. Cultivars include 'Rubens' (especially red new leaves), 'Rosea Marginata' (leaves marbled with gray, white, and pink), and 'Variegata' (new leaves emerge pink, then turn green with white margins). Zones 8 to 9.

P. serrulata (syn. *P. serratifolia*)   P. 154

p. seh-roo-LAY-tuh. Chinese Photinia. Easily 25 feet tall and 16 feet wide and often larger, this species is too big for most home landscapes. The evergreen leaves, 4 to 8 inches long, remain bronzy purple as flowers unfold in midspring, then turn shiny dark green. They are highly resistant to leafspot. Bright red round fruits, ¼ inch across, can remain from late summer through spring. Zones 6 to 9.

P. villosa

p. vil-OH-suh. Oriental Photinia. A multistemmed deciduous shrub to 15 feet tall and about 10 feet wide that can be trimmed as a tree. Finely toothed leaves 1½ to 3 inches long emerge bronzy red, turn dark green, then color yellow to orange-red or scarlet in fall. Round red fall fruits are popular with birds. Prone to fireblight. Zones 4 to 7.

ᴡᴡ *Phygelius*

Fy-GEEL-yus. Snapdragon family, Scrophulariaceae.

Two evergreen species native to South Africa, usually grown as woody-based perennials for their fuchsia-shaped flowers. In warm climates they become woodier and are considered shrubs or subshrubs. They can spread widely by suckers.

HOW TO GROW

Give phygelius loose, well-draining soil amended to retain moisture, in full sun in the north of its range, part shade in hotter climates. May survive as a dieback subshrub in Zone 7. Elsewhere, prune to the base in spring. Propagate by seeds or layering.

P. aequalis   P. 154

p. eh-KWAL-iss. Grows to 3 feet tall with dark green oval leaves to 4½ inches long. From midsummer through fall, rosy mauve, curved tubular flowers are clustered at the ends of branches in upright clusters. 'Yellow Trumpet' has pale yellow flowers. Zones 8 to 10.

P. capensis

p. kuh-PEN-siss. Cape Phygelius. Growing 4 to 5 feet tall with 3½-inch oval leaves, this species bears clusters of orange-red flowers with yellow throats. Zones 8 to 10.

P. × rectus

Cultivars of this variable hybrid include 'African Queen' (pale red flowers) and 'Moonraker' (pale yellow). Zones 8 to 10.

❧ Physocarpus

fy-so-KAR-pus. Rose family, Rosaceae.

A genus of 10 species of deciduous shrubs from North America and East Asia, grown for ease of culture in difficult situations as well as seed capsules and bark that provide winter interest. The leaves look like a currant's while the flowers resemble the related spirea, or perhaps a scaled-down snowball viburnum.

HOW TO GROW

Ninebarks adapt to acid or alkaline soils, drought, and pollution, in full sun or part shade. Because they have a somewhat coarse habit, their best uses are for naturalizing and in informal hedges. Prune them to the ground in late winter or early spring. Propagate from seeds or untreated semiripe cuttings taken in summer.

P. opulifolius   P. 155

p. op-yew-lih-FOH-lee-us. Ninebark. Native to roughly the northeastern quadrant of the country and north into Quebec, ninebark grows 6 to 10 feet tall and wide. The leaves, which usually have three to five lobes, turn yellow or bronze in fall. Balls of small white flowers, with pink-tinged petals and stamens tipped with purple, bloom in late spring, followed in fall by reddish seed capsules (follicles). Its exfoliating bark is interesting in winter although often hidden. 'Dart's Gold' grows to about 5 feet with yellow foliage, 'Diablo' has reddish purple foliage, and 'Luteus' has yellow-green leaves and grows to 8 feet or more. Zones 2 to 7.

P. capitatus

p. kap-ih-TAY-tuss. Native to the mountainous northwest United States, this species grows to 8 feet tall with three-lobed leaves similar to a currant's and 2-inch rounded clusters of white flowers. Prefers moisture-retentive soil. Zones 5 to 7.

P. monogynus

p. mon-oh-JY-nus. Mountain Ninebark. This relatively diminutive species native from Texas to South Dakota averages 3 feet tall and wide with toothed, lobed leaves to 1½ inches long. Late-spring flower clusters, which have fewer blooms than other species, are followed by reddish seed capsules that are touched with green. Zones 5 to 7.

❧ Picea

PIE-see-uh. Pine family, Pinaceae.

Spruces, like other conifers, are primarily trees, but breeders have selected many dwarf and compact forms that can be used as shrubs in the landscape. There are some 30 to 40 species of these evergreens, native to cool regions of the Northern Hemisphere. The needles spiral around the branches; terminal female cones are at first upright, later hanging from the branch. Spruces are most appreciated for their dense, symmetrical shape.

HOW TO GROW

Give spruces moisture-retentive, fairly neutral soil that drains well, in full sun. Because of their shallow root system, you should amend a planting area that is wide but not especially deep. Mulch to improve moisture retention. They will tolerate clay soil, but not heat, drought, or pollution. Most can benefit from wind protection. Depending on habit, spruces are useful for specimens, foundations, rock gardens, borders, containers, or as background for flowering plants. Little pruning is required, although they will tolerate heavy pruning to encourage denser growth. Propagate with seeds or from cuttings.

P. abies   P. 155

p. AY-beez. Norway Spruce. The species is a fast-growing tree to 60 feet and half as wide from central Europe. Shrub-sized cultivars include 'Little Gem', a diminutive cushion-shaped cultivar to 2 feet high and 3½ feet wide with a depression in the middle. 'Nidiformis' (bird's-nest spruce) is a spreading plant slowly reaching 3 to 6 feet tall to twice as wide with a characteristic dip in the center. 'Repens' has the opposite characteristic, with a mounding in the middle. Zones 3 to 7.

P. glauca 'Conica'
p. GLAW-ka. Dwarf Alberta Spruce. A natural dwarf variety of the white spruce, growing slowly to 10 to 12 feet. Foliage is dense, soft, and light green. Prone to mites. Zones 2 to 6.

P. omorika   P. 156
p. oh-MOR-ih-kuh. Serbian Spruce. The species is native to Yugoslavia and often has dramatically drooping branches. 'Gnom' is conical to 5 feet tall, while 'Nana' can be slightly more rounded to 8 feet tall. Zones 4 to 7.

P. orientalis
p. or-ee-en-TAL-iss. Caucasian Spruce. This species has dark green needles on horizontal or drooping branches. Smaller forms include 'Gowdy', which forms a column about 8 feet tall; 'Nana', a 3-foot globe; and 'Pendula', sometimes called 'Weeping Dwarf'. Zones 4 to 7.

P. pungens   P. 156
p. PUN-genz. Colorado Spruce. This southwestern U.S. native has more than 45 cultivars, often with blue foliage but also golden, dwarf, and weeping forms. Two of the more widely available are 'Fat Albert', which has blue-gray foliage, and 'Montgomery', a silvery blue. Both form broad cones about 8 feet tall. Zones 3 to 7.

❦ Pieris
pee-AIR-iss. Heath family, Ericaceae.

These evergreen shrubs, five species native to North America and East Asia, provide year-round interest in gardens with colorful new foliage, urn-shaped flowers, and drooping tassels of beadlike buds that last from midsummer to the next spring's flowering. Fissured bark is attractive when exposed on older specimens.

HOW TO GROW
As with other members of the heath family, give pieris acid soil amended with peat or other organic matter for moisture retention and excellent drainage. Grows in full sun but benefits from part shade in the South.

Protect from strong winds. Use in masses, interplanted with rhododendrons and azaleas, or if compact, against a wall. Lace bugs can be a problem, especially on *P. japonica*. Pieris doesn't require pruning but can be trimmed lightly after flowering to remove seedpods. Older specimens are sometimes limbed up slightly to expose attractive bark. Seeds need light and mist to germinate; cuttings root readily.

P. 'Brouwer's Beauty'. A hybrid of *P. japonica* and *P. floribunda,* growing 6 feet tall and wide, with yellow-green new foliage and mahogany flower buds. Zones 5 to 8.

P. floribunda   P. 157

p. flor-ih-BUN-duh. Mountain Pieris. Native to the southeastern United States and sometimes called mountain fetterbush or mountain andromeda, this relatively compact species grows 2 to 6 feet tall and wide, bearing fragrant upright panicles of flowers in midspring. It resists the lace bug that often plagues Asian forms but doesn't like heat and humidity and will develop problems where drainage is poor. Zones 4 to 6.

P. 'Forest Flame'. A compact hybrid to 4 feet tall with especially bright red new shoots and heavy flower clusters. Does best in a mild climate. Zones 7 to 8.

P. japonica   P. 158

p. juh-PON-ih-kuh. Japanese Pieris. The species grows 9 to 12 feet tall, spreading 6 to 8 feet wide, with glossy oblong or lance-shaped leaves that emerge bronze to reddish. The white urn-shaped flowers are fragrant and borne in drooping panicles to 6 inches long in early to midspring. Cultivars allow gardeners to choose more spectacular new foliage, pink flowers, or more compact size. For pink flowers look for 'Christmas Cheer', 'Daisen', 'Dorothy Wycoff', 'Flamingo', or 'Valley Valentine'. Growing only 3 feet tall, 'Pygmaea' has tiny feathery leaves. The foliage of 'Bert Chandler' includes chartreuse, salmon, cream, and dark green. 'Mountain Fire' has bright red new growth unfolding earlier than others, so that it is sometimes damaged by late frosts. Zones 4 (south) to 7.

❧ *Pinus*

PY-nus. Pine family, Pinaceae.

A genus of 120 coniferous evergreen trees and shrubs from throughout the Northern Hemisphere. They are grown for their usually pyramid shape, interesting bark and branching, as well as better adaptability to adverse conditions than other conifers.

HOW TO GROW

Pines vary in their soil requirements but most tolerate any soil that is well drained. They prefer full sun but are not plants for regions that are hot and dry. Use shrub-sized cultivars as specimens, in rock gardens, along foundations, in containers, as the background for flower borders, or to give mixed borders winter interest. In late spring, remove half of new growth (candles) to make habit denser. Small pines are good subjects for bonsai. Cultivars are usually propagated by grafting.

P. densiflora

p. den-sih-FLOR-uh. Japanese Red Pine. The species is typified by brushy-looking needles to 6 inches long, held rather upright on the stems. 'Globosa' will grow slowly to 12 feet with a rounded head and needles less than 3 inches long. 'Oculus-Draconis' (dragon's-eye pine) grows 8 to 10 feet tall and has needles marked with yellow lines that form rings when the branches are viewed from above. Although single trunked, it branches low to the ground and can be pruned to assume an even more shrublike form. Zones 4 to 7.

P. mugo P. 158

p. MEW-goh. Swiss Mountain Pine. This variable species, which has blunt needles, is valued primarily for its dwarf cultivars. 'Gnom' forms a mound 15 inches tall and about twice as wide; 'Mops' is also a mound, about 3 feet tall and wide. Zones 3 to 7.

P. pumila

p. POO-mil-uh. Japanese Stone Pine. Another variable species, dwarf or prostrate from 1 to 10 feet tall, with blue-green needles and 1-inch cones. Zones 5 to 6.

P. strobus P. 159

p. STROH-bus. Eastern White Pine. Found from Canada south to Georgia and into the upper Midwest, white pine is known for its long soft needles that take well to shearing. Small cultivars include 'Compacta' (dense and rounded); 'Minima' (low and spreading), 'Nana' (dense, variable in habit but usually rounded), and 'Prostrata' (which will retain a weeping form if staked when young). Zones 3 to 7.

P. sylvestris
P. 159

p. sil-VES-tris. Scotch Pine. Native to Europe and Asia, the species develops a wide-spreading, open shape with blue-green needles and handsome scaly bark. 'Beuvronensis' grows to 3 feet tall and less than 5 feet wide with an irregular dome shape; 'Gold Coin' is 6 feet tall and wide with golden foliage; 'Watereri' grows slowly to about 10 feet. Zones 3 to 7.

❦ Pittosporum

pit-oh-SPOR-um. Pittosporum family, Pittosporaceae.

There are some 200 species in this genus from Australasia, south and East Asia, and Africa. They are mostly evergreen trees and shrubs grown for their glossy, leathery leaves and secondarily for fragrant flowers or showy fruit.

HOW TO GROW

The species listed here adapt to a range of soils and tend to make good seaside plantings, withstanding salt, drought, and wind, in full sun or shade. Use as windscreens, hedges, or in containers. Some species take to shearing. Head back *P. tobira* if you want to control its size or shape. Propagate from cuttings.

P. tobira
P. 160

p. toh-BY-ruh. Japanese Mock Orange. A dense shrub or small tree usually 6 to 15 feet tall with shiny, dark green leathery leaves. In early spring, creamy terminal flowers bloom in clusters and smell like orange blossoms. The round fruits turn brown and pop open to expose orange seeds. 'Variegata', with gray-green white-edged leaves, usually remains under 5 feet, and 'Wheeler's Dwarf' stops growing at 2 feet. Zones 9 to 10.

P. tenuifolium

p. ten-yew-ih-FOH-lee-um. Finely textured with dark green leaves and fragrant dark maroon spring flowers, this species can become a good-sized tree. Look for some of the many smaller cultivars, such as 'Irene Patterson', which grows slowly to about 8 feet tall and 4 feet wide. Zones 9 to 10.

❦ *Polygala*

pol-EE-gah-luh. Milkwort family, Polygonaceae.

A genus of more than 500 widely distributed species of annual and perennial herbs and shrubs. Just a handful of species have been cultivated for gardens, and they are valued for racemes of colorful, intricate pealike flowers with winged sepals and petals that form fringed "keels."

HOW TO GROW

Give polygala moisture-retentive but well-aerated acidic soil. It prefers full sun but will grow in light shade. Species vary in size and habit and, thus, in landscape use and pruning needs. Propagate from green or semiripe cuttings.

P. chamaebuxus

p. kam-ay-BUX-iss. A mat-forming evergreen, to 6 inches tall and 12 inches wide, often used in rock gardens. Its small leathery leaves resemble those of boxwood. The ½-inch white and yellow flowers, sometimes with a keel that turns purple-red, bloom in late spring. Those of *P. chamaebuxus* var. *grandiflora* have magenta wings and yellow lips. Zones 6 to 9.

P. × *dalmaisiana*   P. 160

p. × dal-mays-ee-AN-uh. An erect evergreen averaging 5 feet tall, round in youth then spreading, with sparse foliage at the base. Racemes of 1-inch magenta flowers with pale pink keels bloom midsummer to autumn. Best positioned at the back of a border to hide the bare lower branches. Zones 9 to 11.

❦ *Poncirus*

pon-CY-rus. Citrus family, Rutaceae.

This is a genus with a single thorny deciduous species, closely related to citrus, from Korea and China. It's a multiseason shrub, with fragrant white flowers and ornamental shoots and fruits that provide fall and winter interest.

HOW TO GROW

Give this species well-drained acidic soil in full sun, and if possible, some wind protection. Because its thorns are truly long and vicious, it is usually reserved for use as a security hedge, but can be pruned against a wall or included in a border. It blooms on the previous season's growth, so that it's difficult to prune hard at any one time without sacrificing flowers and/or fruit. It does not need pruning at all, but survives severe pruning and has even been shaped into bonsai. Propagate from stratified seeds or hormone-treated cuttings.

P. trifoliata
P. 161

p. try-foh-lee-AY-tuh. Trifoliate Orange. Grows 8 to 20 feet tall, about two-thirds that in width, slightly rounded and low branching. The three-part leaves are glossy green, yellowing in fall. New stems are bright green with long thorns. White midspring flowers are five-petaled, about 1 inch across, smelling faintly of orange blossoms. The round, yellow, 1½-inch fruits are especially prolific in the South in early autumn, tart flavored and used for marmalade. 'Flying Dragon' is a favorite of floral designers because of its twisted stems. Zones 6 to 9.

❦ Potentilla

poh-ten-TIL-uh. Rose family, Rosaceae.

This is a genus of primarily herbaceous plants from throughout the Northern Hemisphere, but it includes a few shrubs. The species described here (of which most other shrub forms of *Potentilla* are now considered varieties) includes dozens of cultivars, grown for bright-colored, usually single flowers borne from early spring to frost.

HOW TO GROW
Potentilla does best in fertile, moisture-retentive but well-drained soil that is neutral to slightly alkaline, but will adapt to some acidity. It tolerates drought and cold but does not perform well where nights are hot. It flowers best in sun, although part shade will keep orange or red forms from fading. Use as a low hedge, in a perennial border or the front of a shrub border, or along foundations. In late winter, remove one-third of old growth and reshape. Propagate from seeds or softwood cuttings.

P. fruticosa
P. 161

p. froo-tih-KOH-suh. Shrubby Cinquefoil. A variable deciduous shrub that can grow to 4 feet or more or remain closer to 1 foot and spread wide. The pinnate leaves, to 1½ inches long, have five to seven oblong leaflets. The species' saucer-shaped 1-inch flowers are bright yellow. A few popular cultivars include 'Abbottswood' (large white flowers with yellow centers, blue-green foliage), 'Coronation Triumph' (profuse yellow flowers, soft green leaves), 'Goldfinger' (large yellow flowers, dark green leaves), 'Katherine Dykes' (small with arching branches, paler yellow flowers), 'Klondike' (another dwarf, deep yellow flowers, bright green leaves), 'Primrose Beauty' (yellow flowers, gray-green leaves), 'Red Ace' (the best red, although performance varies), 'Sunset' (pale yellow flowers tinged with orange, shiny leaves), and 'Tangerine' (medium yellow flushed with copper, gray-green leaves). Zones 2 to 6.

❦ *Prostanthera*

pros-TAN-ther-uh. Mint family, Lamiaceae.

This genus of about 50 evergreen shrubs from Australia includes several species grown by warm-climate American gardeners for profuse, long-blooming small flowers of purple, blue, or white, as well as fragrant foliage.

HOW TO GROW

Mint bush prefers dappled shade and slightly acidic, well-drained soil. It will tolerate somewhat sandy soil and drought but needs protection from wind. A south wall is ideal for this tender plant. Grow it in masses, in a shrub border, or as a specimen. Prune after flowering to reshape, but avoid cutting into hard wood. Propagate from softwood cuttings.

P. rotundifolia   P. 162

p. roh-tun-dih-FOH-lee-uh. Round-leaved Mint Bush. This species grows to 8 feet tall and slightly narrower with ¼-inch glossy, strongly peppermint-scented leaves. Bell-shaped lavender flowers cover the branches for two months in spring. Zones 9 to 10.

❦ *Prunus*

PROO-nus. Rose family, Rosaceae.

This genus of more than 400 species of deciduous and evergreen shrubs and trees, native throughout the Northern Hemisphere, includes peaches, plums, cherries, and almonds. The shrub species are grown primarily for their white or pink spring flowers, but many also offer edible fruit or colorful fall foliage.

HOW TO GROW

The genus as a whole is adaptable to most soils as long as they are well drained, although organic amendments will ensure health and hasten growth. Useful for hedges or screens, in naturalized settings, or to attract wildlife. These shrubs withstand heavy pruning but either flowers or fruit may be sacrificed. Propagate from seeds sown in fall or cold treated, or softwood cuttings treated with hormone powder.

P. americana   P. 162

p. uh-mair-ih-KAY-nuh. Wild Plum. Native from New England to the southwestern United States, this deciduous shrub or small tree averages 15 to 20 feet tall, suckering to form colonies. Umbels of 1-inch sweet-scented white flowers bloom before the leaves emerge in early spring. Round red or yellow fruits with a tart flavor ripen in midsummer and can be used to make jams and jellies. Zones 3 to 8.

P. angustifolia

p. an-gus-tih-FOH-lee-uh. Chickasaw Plum. An evergreen, suckering shrub with thorny side branches, it is often the first woody plant to flower in its native range, from the Mid-Atlantic to Florida and west to Kansas and Texas. White ½-inch flowers appear before leaves in late winter to early spring, followed by small dark berries used for jelly. Zones 5 to 9.

P. besseyi   P. 163

p. BESS-ee-eye. Western Sand Cherry. Native to the central United States, this deciduous shrub suckers and spreads to about 5 feet high and wide with gray-green leaves. Midspring white flowers are followed in midsummer by sweet, blue-black ¾-inch berries used in jellies and desserts. Zones 3 to 6.

P. caroliniana

p. kar-oh-lin-ee-AY-nuh. Carolina Cherry. A southeastern native evergreen tree or shrub to 30 feet tall, about half as wide. Intensely fragrant flowers bloom in early spring, followed by shiny black berries that may last through winter if not eaten by birds. Stems are fragrant when crushed or pruned. Compact cultivars are available. Zones 7 to 10.

P. × cistena

p. × siss-TEEN-uh. Purple Sand Cherry. A hybrid to 10 feet tall and narrower with reddish purple foliage and fragrant pink flowers that appear with the leaves in midspring, followed by purple-black fruits. 'Minnesota Red' has a deeper color. Zones 4 to 7.

P. glandulosa

PP. 163, 164

p. glan-doo-LOH-suh. Dwarf Flowering Almond. A commonly available deciduous shrub from Asia, growing to 5 feet high and wide, with light green 4-inch leaves and white or pink flowers in midspring, rarely fruiting. 'Alba Plena' and 'Rosea Plena' ('Sinensis') have double white and pink flowers, respectively. Zones 4 to 8.

P. 'Hally Jolivette'.

Dwarf Flowering Cherry. A dense, rounded deciduous hybrid to 15 feet tall with 2-inch, oval, dark green leaves. For several weeks in midspring, pink buds open to double white flowers with pink centers. Zones 5 to 7.

P. laurocerasus 'Otto Luyken'

P. 164

p. lahr-oh-SER-uh-sus. Otto Luyken Cherry Laurel. This cultivar of an evergreen species from southeast Europe and Asia Minor grows to about 4 feet tall and twice as wide with 4-inch dark green leaves held at an acute angle to the stem. The white midspring flowers, borne in racemes, have numerous stamens and a strong fragrance. It tolerates heavy shade but must have good drainage. It may develop insect problems as a result of overhead watering or summer rain. Considered hardy to Zone 5 is 'Schipkaensis', which differs primarily in holding its leaves perpendicular to the stem. Zones 6 to 8.

P. lusitanica

p. loo-sih-TAN-ih-kuh. Portugese Cherry Laurel. A large evergreen shrub that may eventually reach 20 feet tall, it has slightly toothed glossy leaves to 5 inches long. The white fragrant flowers are in racemes 6 to 10 inches long in mid- to late spring, from both terminals and axils. The dark purple fruits are cone shaped. Zones 7 to 9.

P. maritima

p. mar-IT-ih-muh. Beach Plum. A dense suckering shrub to 6 feet tall with white flowers in midspring, followed in late summer by dull purple fruits that are used in jams and jellies. Native along the coast from Canada to Virginia, it flourishes in salt and sand. Zones 3 to 7.

P. tenella

p. teh-NEL-uh. Dwarf Russian Almond. A deciduous shrub with upright, suckering shoots 2 to 5 feet tall. Glossy leaves and deep pink flowers open together in midspring. 'Fire Hill' has bright red flowers on a plant that remains 2 feet tall. Zones 2 to 6.

❧ Punica

POO-nih-kuh. Pomegranate family, Punicaceae.

This genus includes only two species of deciduous shrubs or trees. The most commonly grown species is native to southwest Asia, southeast Europe, and the Himalayas and is cultivated for colorful funnel-shaped flowers and edible fruits.

HOW TO GROW

The pomegranate will do best in fertile, moisture-retentive soil, but adapts to both sandy and clay soils in a wide pH range as long as it has good drainage. It tolerates some shade but will flower and fruit best in full sun. Use in a shrub border, in a mass, or in a container. Where hardiness is borderline, grow it against a warm wall. Prune in spring to shape and to encourage summer flowers on new growth. Propagate from seeds or softwood cuttings.

P. granatum
P. 165

p. gran-AY-tum. Pomegranate. Upright, slightly rounded in habit, with most popular varieties about 10 feet tall and wide or slightly narrower. The glossy oblong leaves may be bronzed when new, chartreuse in autumn. The species has orange-red funnel-shaped flowers with five crinkled lobes, first appearing in mid- to late summer and continuing into fall. That's when the round, edible, yellow-brown fruits (sometimes shades of red) begin developing, up to 5 inches in diameter. *P. granatum* 'Nana' gets only 3 feet tall; 'Wonderful' has a fountainlike habit with red fruit. Zones 8 to 10.

❧ Pyracantha

py-ruh-KAN-thuh. Rose family, Rosaceae

A genus of seven spiny evergreens, mostly shrubs, native to East Asia and southeast Europe. From late spring to early summer they bear clusters of small white flowers, but the main attraction is the colorful persistent berries that follow.

HOW TO GROW

A good plant for hot, dry climates, firethorn prefers neutral to somewhat acid, well-drained soil. It needs full sun for best fruiting and doesn't transplant well once established. Grow as a specimen or in a shrub border. It's too thorny for an entire hedge, except as a security barrier. It is often espaliered since it tolerates hard pruning at any time and needs regular hard pruning to maintain an attractive shape. Propagate from cold-stratified seeds or semiripe cuttings.

P. coccinea   P. 166

p. kok-SIN-ee-uh. Scarlet Firethorn. An evergreen 6 to 18 feet tall and wide with stiff, sparse branches, long thorns, and glossy 2-inch dark green leaves. Clusters of ⅓-inch white flowers bloom along the previous season's stems in mid- to late spring. The orange-red pea-sized berries ripen in early fall and may last through winter. Lace bug can sometimes be a pest, but the biggest problems for pyracantha are scab and fireblight. Some resistant cultivars are 'Apache' (to 4 feet with red persistent fruits), 'Fiery Cascade' (upright, with orange berries turning red, cold tolerant), 'Goldrush' (densely branched, with yellow-orange fruits), 'Mohave' (upright with heavy flowering and fruiting), 'Navaho' (6 feet, dense branching), 'Pueblo' (wide spreading with profuse persistent fruit), 'Rutgers' (4 feet tall, wide spreading, cold tolerant), and 'Teton' (upright, yellow-orange fruits). 'Lalandei' is hardy to Zone 5 but susceptible to scab. Zones 6 to 9.

P. koidzumii   P. 166

p. koyd-ZOOM-ee-eye. Formosa Firethorn. Semievergreen to evergreen shrub with upright branching 8 to 12 feet high and wide. Racemes of ¼-inch white flowers bloom in midspring, followed by persistent red berries beginning in early fall. Disease-resistant cultivars include 'Santa Cruz' (horizontal form to 3 feet tall and 6 feet wide) and 'Victory' (upright and arching with dark red fruit). Zones 8 to 10.

P. 'Watereri'. This hybrid grows 8 feet tall and wide with fewer thorns and profuse, long-lasting dark red berries. Zones 7 to 10.

❧ *Rhaphiolepis*

raf-ee-oh-LEH-piss. Rose family, Rosaceae.

Up to 15 species of evergreen shrubs and small trees native to subtropical areas of East Asia, popular in mild-climate gardens for glossy, leathery leaves and midwinter to spring flowers in colors ranging from white through all shades of pink.

HOW TO GROW

These shrubs do best in neutral to slightly acid soils that are well drained yet moisture retentive, but will tolerate some drought and salt. Full sun will increase flowering and keep the habit compact. Good for a low hedge or walkway edging, they also adapt well to containers. Pinch or prune lightly after flowering to encourage compact growth, or thin interior branches for a more open shape. Propagate from seeds cleaned of pulp.

R. indica   P. 167

r. IN-dih-kuh. Indian Hawthorn. The species, to 5 feet tall with pink-tinged white flowers, is less well known than its hybrids or cultivars. The cultivars are listed separately below because of confusion about origins, many possibly stemming from a hybrid, *R. × delacourii.* Zones 8 to 10.

R. umbellata   P. 167

r. um-bel-AY-tuh. Yeddo Hawthorn. The most common forms are dense mounds to 6 feet tall and wide, with leaves at the ends of branches. The leaves are broad ovals, gray-green when new then turning dark blue-green, sometimes bronzy purple in winter. The five-petaled white flowers are slightly fragrant and borne in upright panicles to 3 inches across in midspring. Zones 8 to 10.

R. cultivars. 'Ballerina', less than 2 feet tall with deep rose-colored flowers; 'Enchantress', 3 feet tall and 5 feet wide with rosy pink flowers late winter through early summer; 'Indian Princess', 3 feet tall with pale pink flowers, 'Majestic Beauty', especially vigorous from 8 to 15 feet tall, often trained as a standard, with 4-inch leaves and fragrant, pale pink flowers in clusters up to 10 inches across; 'Snow White', dwarf with pure white flowers from early spring to early summer; and 'Springtime', 4 to 6 feet tall with pink flowers in late winter to early spring. Zones 8 to 10.

❦ Rhododendron

ro-doh-DEN-dron. Heath family, Ericaceae.

With the exception of roses, these have to be gardeners' favorite shrubs, including not only those commonly called "rhodies" but also azaleas. In all, the genus contains more than 900 species of deciduous and evergreen shrubs and trees native to North America, Asia, Europe, and Australasia. They are grown primarily for colorful flowers, often spotted inside, borne singly or in clusters called trusses. The list below, although a long one, barely skims the surface of available shrubs, as these plants have been widely hybridized by both bees and humans. Sizes range from tree-size ("rhododendron" is derived from Greek meaning "red tree") to prostrate forms with pinhead leaves; colors include yellows and dark reds as well as the more familiar pinks, purples, and white; fragrances can rival a daphne's; and bloom can occur not only in spring but also in midsummer and even fall. It is well worth looking for specialty nurseries that offer a wide range of these shrubs.

(So what is the difference between rhododendrons and azaleas? Even the experts may hem and haw. Rhododendrons *tend* to be evergreen and have flowers shaped liked bells, and azealeas *tend* to be deciduous with funnel-shaped flowers. But there are obviously exceptions. The best rule is to simply enjoy them.)

HOW TO GROW

All rhododendrons need excellent drainage and an acidic soil that is rich in organic matter. They will not tolerate hot, dry, or windy conditions, and a combination of these is lethal. High, dappled shade is best, but many will grow in full sun given moderate temperatures and adequate moisture. Make the planting hole shallow, as appropriate for their fine, surface-feeding roots, and mulch well with pine needles or leaf mold rather than cultivating near the base. Rhododendrons have endless uses in a semishady garden, from hedging and defining paths to brightening dark corners, as specimens, and mixed in borders with other acid-loving plants. Dwarf varieties are suitable for rock gardens. Pruning is rarely necessary except to renew neglected plants. Spent flowers should be pinched off to prevent seed formation. Propagate by planting the tiny seeds under plastic or misting daily, by layering, or by softwood or semihardwood cuttings treated with hormone powder.

R. alabamense

r. al-uh-bam-EN-see. Alabama Azalea. A fairly compact deciduous native of the southeast United States, growing to 8 feet tall and suckering to form colonies. The early to midspring flowers are usually white with a yellow blotch and prominent stamens and exude a lemony spice scent. Zones 6 to 8.

R. arborescens   P. 168

r. ar-bor-ES-ens. Sweet Azalea. This deciduous native of an area ranging from the Mid-Atlantic south to Georgia and Alabama grows anywhere from 10 to 20 feet tall, with foliage often turning red in fall. In midsummer, white flowers with pink stamens emit a heliotrope-like fragrance. Zones 5 to 8.

R. atlanticum   P. 168

r. at-LAN-tih-kum. Coastal Azalea. This suckering deciduous Mid-Atlantic species is also called dwarf azalea because it usually stays less than 3 feet tall. In early to midspring, white to pale pink, sweetly scented flowers with prominent stamens bloom as the leaves unfurl. Zones 6 to 8.

R. austrinum   P. 169

r. aws-TRY-num. Florida Flame Azalea. This deciduous species from the Deep South grows to about 10 feet tall with an open habit. The yellow-orange tubular blossoms that open from early to midspring have long stamens and a fruity sweet scent. Zones 7 to 9.

R. calendulaceum   P. 169

r. kal-en-doo-LAY-see-um. Flame Azalea. Ranging anywhere from 6 to more than 12 feet tall and equally wide, this deciduous species is native to mountainous areas from Pennsylvania to Georgia. The foliage may color yellow in fall. The unscented late-spring flowers are generally yellow-orange but may include pink tones. Zones 6 to 7.

R. canescens   P. 170

r. kan-ESS-ens. Piedmont Azalea. This is the Southeast's most common native azalea, deciduous and growing to 12 feet or taller, with sweet-scented light pink flowers from early to midspring. It can sucker to form colonies, so needs a firm hand with the pruners. Zones 6 to 8.

R. catawbiense   P. 170

r. kat-ah-bee-EN-see. Catawba rhododendron. This evergreen species gets its name from a river in the Carolinas, not from the wine-making grape, although its purple-pink color is that of a watered-down rosé. Native to mountainous areas from Alabama to West Virginia, it grows to around 10 feet tall and often as wide with oblong evergreen leaves 3 to 6 inches long. The rosy to pinkish purple flowers are streaked brown inside, in spectacular trusses up to 6 inches across in mid- to late spring. There are many cultivars and hybrids with flowers of purple, red, pink, white, and yellow, with some variation in cold hardiness. Zones 5 to 8.

R. Exbury, Knap Hill Hybrids

These hybrids of native East and West Coast and Asian species are deciduous, upright plants, with often fragrant flowers in sunset tones as well as white, pastels, and bitones. Of many cultivars, only a few are heat resistant. This group is also more prone than most to powdery mildew and lace bug. Zones 5 to 7.

R. flammeum   P. 171

r. FLAM-ee-um. Oconee Azalea. A deciduous southeastern U.S. native growing to about 8 feet tall with early to midspring tubular orange or red flowers in clusters of a dozen or more. Zones 6 to 8.

R. Kurume Group   P. 171

Compact and dense with small evergreen leaves and profuse small flowers, many with the double flower form called hose-in-hose. They vary in coldhardiness, most Zones 7 to 9.

R. maximum   P. 172

r. MAKS-ih-mum. Rosebay Rhododendron. This evergreen native from eastern North America earns its species name with elliptic leaves up to 8 inches long and its overall treelike proportions. It will grow up to 30 feet in the wild but usually half that in cultivation. It can make a dramatic hedge if you have space for it. In spring it produces 5-inch trusses of white flowers, sometimes blushing pink in the cooler parts of its range. Zones 5 to 8.

R. Northern Lights Group

Shrubs in this series, developed at the University of Minnesota, are exceedingly cold hardy. They grow about 10 feet tall and wide, and the fragrant flowers of white, pink, lavender, yellow, and orange bloom before the leaves emerge in late spring. Most of the cultivar names include the word "lights." Zones 4 to 7.

R. North Tisbury Group

A group of low-growing evergreen hybrids, primarily from the Japanese *R. nakahari*, bred as ground covers and rock garden plants. Most flowers are pink or brick red. Zones 6 to 8.

R. occidentale

r. oks-ih-den-TAL-ee. Western Azalea. Native to slopes in Oregon and California, this deciduous shrub grows to 10 feet tall and wide. It bears white to palest pink flowers, blotched with yellow inside, in trusses of 6 to 12. Zones 7 to 9.

R. periclymenoides   P. 172

r. pair-ih-kly-men-OY-dees. Pinxterbloom. Native to hills and piedmont from Maine to Georgia, this deciduous species was formerly called *R. nudiflorum* because its pink or white tubular flowers bloom on bare branches. (The shape of the flowers inspired another common name, wild honeysuckle.) Zones 4 to 8.

R. PJM Group

A cold-hardy group developed from crossing the native evergreen *R. carolinium* with an Asian deciduous species. The resulting plants are evergreens with a rounded habit to 6 feet tall and wide. Leaves may bronze in the fall. Bright lavender pink flowers appear reliably in midspring. Some selections offer flowers of white, darker pink, or magenta, as well as fragrance. Zones 4 to 8.

R. prinophyllum (syn. R. roseum)   P. 173

r. prin-oh-FIL-um. Roseshell Azalea. Native to the Mid-Atlantic and the northeastern United States, this deciduous species grows to 6 feet tall and wide with pure pink tubular flowers that have a distinctive clove scent. Zones 4 to 7.

R. prunifolium   P. 173

r. proo-nih-FOH-lee-um. Plumleaf Azalea. A southeastern U.S. native evergreen growing to about 10 feet tall, it blooms in mid- to late summer with brick red flowers that attract hummingbirds. Zones 6 to 8.

R. schlippenbachii   P. 174

r. schlip-en-BOCK-ee-eye. Royal Azalea. A deciduous native of Korea and Manchuria growing 6 to 8 feet tall. The leaves are red, orange, and yellow in autumn. Fragrant, delicate pale pink flowers expand in midspring with the leaves. Zones 4 to 6.

R. vaseyi
P. 175

r. VAY-zee-eye. Pinkshell Azalea. This deciduous native of North Carolina's Blue Ridge Mountains usually grows to about 6 feet tall, although it can reach more than twice that height. It tolerates moderately dry soil and is unusual in offering burgundy fall foliage. Rich pink flowers (occasionally white or paler pink) bloom in clusters of a half dozen before the leaves emerge in early to late spring. Zones 5 to 7.

R. viscosum

r. viss-KOH-sum. Swamp Azalea. A deciduous species native to wetlands from Maine into Georgia and Alabama, averaging about 5 feet tall with an open habit and shiny leaves. White spicy-scented flowers bloom in late spring. Zones 5 to 8.

R. yakushimanum
(syn. R. degronianum ssp. yakusimanum)
P. 175

r. yak-oo-shee-MAH-num. A Japanese evergreen species growing to 3 feet tall and wide with rosy pink buds opening to white flowers. Its many culti-vars include 'Yaku Princess', with flowers spotted pink and green, and 'Mist Maiden', with trusses of up to 17 flowers. Zones 5 to 8.

❦ Rhodotypos

roh-doh-TY-pohs. Rose family, Rosaceae.

There is only one species in this genus, a deciduous shrub native to woods and scrublands in Japan and China. It rewards gardeners not only with its four-petaled white flowers and the persistent shiny black fruits from which it gets its common name, but also an ability to shrug off the less than ideal circumstances of urban life.

HOW TO GROW

Jetbead is easy to grow in a wide range of soil types, in sun or shade, and tolerates pollution and other stressful situations. Useful in borders or massed in shade. Doesn't require much pruning, but one-third of old growth can be removed in early spring to promote new shoots. Propagate with softwood cuttings after the plant has leafed out.

R. scandens
P. 176

r. SKAN-dens. Jetbead. Sometimes called white kerria, this shrub grows rounded and slightly arching from 3 to 6 feet tall and up to 8 feet wide. Leaves up to 4 inches long are toothed and prominently veined and may be touched with yellow in autumn. The white flowers are 1¹/₂ inches across, borne in late spring at the ends of branches, and rebloom sporadically. The ¹/₂-inch fruits are hard and beadlike, unusual although not particularly showy. Zones 5 to 8.

❦ Rhus

RUS. Sumac family, Anacardiaceae.

It's often said that European gardeners appreciate America's native plants far more than we do, and our sumacs are a case in point. In spite of their dramatic fall color and berries, they have often been tarred with the unpleasant brush of their close relative, poison ivy. The genus includes a total of 200 deciduous or evergreen shrubs, trees, and vines from throughout much of North America as well as East Asia, South Africa, and parts of Australia. Gardeners in the know appreciate the species listed here for graceful dissected foliage that sets autumn ablaze and often interesting, persistent fruits.

HOW TO GROW

Most sumacs are tough, adaptable shrubs, needing only excellent drainage and a neutral to acid pH. They tolerate low fertility and pollution and will grow in shade but usually color best in full sun. Depending on size they can be massed or used for naturalizing, ground covers, or in a shrub border. They can be pruned hard: *R. glabra, R. × pulvinata,* and *R. typhina* are often cut to the ground in spring to stimulate new growth.

R. aromatica

r. air-oh-MAT-ih-kuh. Fragrant Sumac. Native to eastern North America from Ontario to Florida and Louisiana and west to Minnesota, this variable deciduous species can grow 2 to 6 feet tall and spread to 8 feet. The three-part oval leaves are toothed and turn orange-red or reddish purple in fall. The flower is a catkin, on male plants appearing late summer through winter. Females produce a hairy red fruit. Fall foliage is orange-red and purple. 'Gro-Low' is a spreading cultivar to 2 feet tall, useful as a ground cover. Zones 3 to 9.

R. chinensis
P. 176

r. chih-NEN-siss. Chinese Sumac. At 20 feet or taller and suckering aggressively, this deciduous shrub may be too large for most gardens. Valuable in open natural sites for late-summer cream-colored flower panicles that average 8 inches long and wide, often much larger, especially in the cultivar 'September Beauty'. These are followed by orange-red fruits and golden orange foliage. Zones 5 to 7.

R. copallina
P. 177

r. koh-pawl-EEN-uh. Flameleaf Sumac. Another deciduous species from eastern North America, sometimes called shining sumac, this one can grow 25 feet tall and wide but is useful for dry, rocky sites. It also tolerates salt and wind so is excellent in a coastal garden. It has picturesque branching and shiny, pinnate leaves that turn bright red and burgundy in fall. Zones 4 to 9.

R. glabra
P. 177

r. GLAB-ruh. Smooth Sumac. Found throughout the lower 48 states, this deciduous species grows 10 to 15 feet tall, suckering and forming colonies. The compound leaves turn yellow to reddish purple in autumn, and the female bears a conical cluster of persistent, hairy, bright red fruit. Zones 3 to 9.

R. integrifolia

r. in-teg-rih-FOH-lee-uh. Lemonade Berry. An evergreen species native to southern California, generally under 10 feet tall and wide. The leathery leaves are almost round. Clusters of pink or white flowers bloom in late winter, followed by soft red fruits used to give drinks a tart taste. Best in coastal conditions. Zones 9 to 10.

R. ovata

r. oh-VAHT-uh. Sugarbush. Another evergreen native to southern California, as well as Arizona, that grows up to 10 feet tall, often spreading, with pointed glossy leaves. White or pink flower clusters bloom for a long period in spring, followed by hairy, reddish fruits. Tolerates drought but not salt or wind. Zones 9 to 10.

R × pulvinata 'Red Autumn Lace' (syn. R. glabra 'Laciniata')

r. × pul-vin-AH-tuh. A female selection of a cross between R. glabra and R. typhina, with deeply cut, lobed leaves that give it a ferny appearance. The fall color is orange and reddish purple, and the hairy fruits are bright red. Zones 3 to 8.

R. trilobata

P. 178

r. try-loh-BAH-tuh. Skunkbush Sumac. Native to the western half of the United States, the species grows 3 to 6 feet tall and suckers to form a dense hedge. Good for alkaline soils. The common name comes from leaves that smell somewhat unpleasant when bruised. 'Autumn Amber' remains about 18 inches tall with yellow and red fall color but no fruit. Zones 4 to 6.

R. typhina

P. 178

r. ty-FEEN-uh. Staghorn Sumac. A deciduous shrub or small tree growing to 20 feet or more and suckering for an equal spread. It gets its common name from the reddish brown fuzz that covers its shoots, like the velvet on a deer's horns. The compound leaves have 13 to 27 leaflets up to 5 inches long that turn red, orange, and yellow in fall. Large panicles of yellow-green flowers are followed by a cone of red fruits that turn brown over winter. 'Dissecta' and 'Laciniata' have deeply divided leaves. Zones 4 to 8.

❦ Ribes

RY-beez, Saxifrage family, Saxifragaceae.

A genus of about 150 usually deciduous shrubs, sometimes spiny, found primarily in temperate areas. Several are cultivated for edible berries, while others are grown for colorful flowers. The leaves are usually lobed and toothed.

HOW TO GROW

Most currants and gooseberries are easy to grow in ordinary soil, preferably in sun but also in shade. *R. speciosum* is often grown against a wall and does best with some shade where the climate is dry. Good for massing in difficult sites. Many members of the genus are prone to rust and other problems and do best where air circulation is good and humidity low. To rejuvenate mature plants, cut back a portion of producing shoots after flowering or fruiting. *R. alpinum* can be sheared as a formal hedge.

R. alpinum

r. al-PY-num. Alpine Currant. A dense deciduous European species with upright branching, growing to about 5 feet tall and wide, popular as a hedge in cold climates. Inconspicuous yellow-green catkins bloom in early spring, followed by bright red berries that are quickly stripped by birds. 'Green Mound' remains under 3 feet tall. Zones 2 to 7.

R. aureum
P. 179

r. AR-ee-um. Golden Currant. A native of the Plains and Rocky Mountains, this deciduous species is upright, ranging from 3 to 9 feet tall. The clove-scented spring flowers are yellow tubes with a touch of red. Summer berries can be black, red, or yellow. Zones 2 to 7.

R. odoratum
P. 180

r. oh-dor-AH-tum. Clove Currant. Native to the central United States, this species has arching upright shoots about 7 feet tall, usually suckering. The blue-green leaves can turn a rich burgundy in fall. From early to midspring, yellow flowers smelling of cloves bloom in racemes. The edible ⅓-inch berries are black. 'Crandall' has yellow fruit. Zones 4 to 6.

R. sanguineum
P. 180

r. san-GWIN-ee-um. Winter Currant. Native to western North America, this deciduous shrub grows 4 to 12 feet tall with foliage that resembles small maple leaves. Dark pink to red flowers droop in racemes from early to late spring, followed by ⅓-inch berries. Zones 5 to 7.

R. speciosum
P. 181

r. spee-cee-OH-sum. Fuchsia-flowered Gooseberry. A California native with semievergreen foliage and spiny stems, growing 3 to 6 feet tall. Scentless, bright red fuchsialike flowers with protruding stamens are borne over a long period, from winter to spring. Cultivars offer pink and white flowers. 'Brocklebankii' has yellow foliage. Zones 8 to 10.

❦ Robinia

roh-BIN-ee-uh. Pea family, Fabaceae.

In this genus, eastern U.S. gardeners are most familiar with *R. pseudoacacia*, the native black locust tree that is rugged, weedy, and bears beautiful racemes of fragrant white flowers in spring. All of the 20 deciduous trees and shrubs are native to the United States. Their tough nature in challenging circumstances, coupled with the showy pealike flowers and divided leaves, can frequently make up for a rather coarse habit and tendency to spread.

Like many plants in the pea family, locusts need full sun but will grow in poor, dry soil because they fix their own nitrogen. The species listed here is often recommended for stabilizing sandy slopes. Locusts bleed if pruned in spring, so wait until late summer or fall. Propagate from suckers or root cuttings.

R. hispida

P. 181

r. HISS-pih-duh. Rose Acacia. Native to the upper American South, this suckering shrub grows loose and open to about 8 feet tall with pinnately compound leaves that have a lacy effect. It is sometimes called bristly locust for the stiff hairs on its stems. The clusters of flowers, which are rose pink or lavender, bloom in late spring, occasionally followed by some bristly seedpods. 'Arnot' is a cultivar often planted by the U.S. Soil Conservation Service for soil stabilization. Zones 5 to 8.

❧ Rosa

ROH-suh. Rose family, Rosaceae.

From about 150 species widely distributed in the Northern Hemisphere, breeders have developed thousands of cultivars that include climbers, cutting flowers, and miniatures. Below is a sample of species roses and hybrids with spreading habits that make them suitable for traditional shrub uses as hedges, specimens, and in shrub borders.

HOW TO GROW

Roses need full sun and an open site. Soil should be moderately rich, well drained, and generously amended with organic matter. The species and cultivars listed here are generally resistant to black spot and other fungal diseases to which some roses are prone. Good air circulation, full sun, and attentive garden hygiene will go a long way toward preventing problems. Companion planting with alliums (these include onions and garlics, but also many purely ornamental species) will also help deter some rose pests. Avoid giving roses too much nitrogen, which can make their growth succulent and delicious to pests.

Everblooming roses should be pruned in spring, removing one-third to half the length of flowered canes on mature plants. Prune once-blooming roses lightly after flowering, removing old unproductive stems on mature plants. Deadhead spent flowers except on shrubs grown for hips. Propagate from softwood cuttings in mid- to late summer.

R. Austin Roses   P. 182

Also called English roses, this group was bred for old-fashioned form and fragrance combined with disease resistance and repeat bloom. Popular choices in the 3- to 4-foot range include 'Graham Thomas' (fragrant golden yellow flowers), 'Gertrude Jekyll' (deep pink flowers), 'Heritage' (shell pink, intensely fragrant), 'Mary Rose' (cupped, rose pink), and 'Perdita' (fully double, fragrant, light apricot flowers). Zones 5 to 9.

R. Bonica   P. 183

This is the trademark name. The cultivar name is the impossible to remember 'Meidomonac'. It grows 4 to 5 feet tall and wide with glossy green leaves and fully double, 3-inch light pink flowers from spring to fall. Zones 4 to 10.

R. Carefree Beauty   P. 183

Another trademark, also called 'Beubi'. Grows 3 to 4 feet tall and wide with fragrant, semidouble pink flowers from early summer to frost, followed by orange hips. Carefree Delight grows in a low mound to 2½ feet tall and 4 feet wide with single, dark pink flowers; Carefree Wonder is upright to about 4 feet with semidouble deep pink flowers edged with white, opening midspring then reblooming sporadically along with hip formation. Despite the names, these selections are not problem-free in humid areas. Zones 4 to 9.

R. eglanteria (syn. R. rubiginosa)

r. egg-lan-TEER-ee-uh. Sweet Briar. The eglantine rose, native to China but grown in Western gardens for hundreds of years, is known for its apple-scented foliage. Growing 8 to 12 feet tall and wide with prickly stems, it bears single pink flowers in late spring, followed by red-orange hips. Shows potential to become invasive. Zones 4 to 9.

R. 'The Fairy'   P. 184

A "ground-cover" rose forming a mound to about 3 feet tall and wide. The 1-inch double, soft pink flowers (brighter in light shade) bloom in clusters along the arching canes. Blooming begins in early summer and can last until fall. Zones 5 to 10.

R. foetida   P. 184

r. FEET-ih-duh. Austrian Briar Rose. An Asian species, upright to 5 feet tall and wide with arching stems. Bears single, cupped, fragrant yellow flowers in late spring. 'Bicolor', the Austrian copper rose, has copper red petals backed with yellow. Zones 4 to 8.

R. gallica var. *officinalis* P. 185

r. GAL-ih-kuh var. oh-fiss-in-AL-iss. Apothecary's Rose. The best-known form of this European species, it grows to 3 feet tall. The leaves are rough and the flowers an intense rosy pink with gold stamens, semidouble in form and fragrant. They bloom in late spring, followed by orange-red hips. 'Versicolor' flowers have white, pink, and red stripes. Zones 4 to 8.

R. glauca (syn. *R. rubrifolia*) P. 185

r. GLAU-kuh. Redleaf Rose. A European native to about 6 feet tall, it stands out from other roses by having toothed gray-purple leaves. Single, flat, deep pink flowers with five widely spaced, pointed petals and paler pink centers bloom in late spring, followed by round orange-red hips. Zones 2 to 8.

R. × *harisonii* P. 186

r. × hair-ih-SOH-nee-eye. Harison's Yellow Rose. An old garden favorite growing upright to about 5 feet with small mid-green leaves and prickly brown stems, bearing semidouble or double bright yellow flowers in late spring. Zones 3 to 8.

R. hugonis

r. hew-GOH-niss. Father Hugo's Rose. A Chinese species growing to 6 to 8 feet and often wider with stout, arching, reddish canes and widely spaced prickles, bearing single, solitary pale lemon yellow flowers in late spring. Zones 5 to 8.

R. Meidiland Series P. 186

Developed by the same French breeders as Bonica, Carefree Delight, and Carefree Wonder, either low growing to about 2½ feet or upright to about 4 feet. Most have red fruits. They are trademarked under color names combined with the name Meidiland. Selections include Alba (low growing, double white), Fuchsia (low growing, double), Pearl (low growing, double, cream flushed pink), Pink (upright, single with white center), Red (low growing, single with white center), Scarlet (upright, double, with shiny leaves), and White (low growing, double, with shiny leaves). Zones 5 to 9.

R. rugosa PP. 187, 188

r. roo-GOH-suh. Species and cultivars are tolerant of difficult situations such as sandy soil, salt, and wind, and are often grown in seaside gardens.

Averaging about 6 feet tall and wide with disease-resistant, crinkled leaves, most have clove-scented flowers. 'Blanc Double de Coubert' is 5 feet tall with double, pure white, highly fragrant reblooming flowers. 'Fru Dagmar Hastrup' ('Frau Dagmar Hartopp') is 4 feet tall with pale pink flowers and dark red hips; 'Rosearie de l'Hay' grows to 8 feet tall with crimson purple flowers. 'Hansa' has reddish purple semidouble flowers but is grown primarily for its generous production of hips. Unfortunately, as with many nonnative plants recommended for erosion control, *R. rugosa* is beginning to appear on lists of invasive species. Zones 2 to 9.

R. virginiana

r. vir-gin-ee-AY-nuh. Virginia Rose. Native from Canada to the Mid-Atlantic and into the middle South, growing 4 to 6 feet tall with glossy dark green leaves that turn yellow, orange, and red in fall. Single, fragrant pink flowers in late spring are followed by shiny ½-inch red persistent fruits. Zones 3 to 7.

R. wichuraiana

r. wih-shur-ee-AY-nuh. Memorial Rose. A semievergreen Asian species some-times grown as a vine, or more naturally as a ground cover that roots from long canes with widely spaced prickles. Single white flowers with prominent yellow stamens bloom in midsummer, followed by ½-inch oval red fruits. Zones 5 to 8.

❦ Rosmarinus

rohs-ma-RINE-us. Mint family, Lamiaceae.

The ancient Greeks thought rosemary improved the memory, and mod-ern science says that consuming rosemary leaves may actually ward off senility. The genus contains just two species of evergreen shrubs from the Mediterranean (the name means "dew of the sea"), one of which is popu-lar in warm-climate gardens for the fragrant foliage we use as a season-ing, as well as for its tiny, usually bright lavender blue flowers.

Rosemary must have full sun, excellent drainage, and only moder-ately fertile soil. It is an excellent container plant and works well in a perennial border or herb garden, or as a low hedge. More prostrate vari-eties can be used on banks to control erosion or as ground covers. Pinch tips or prune lightly to keep shrubs compact. Root from semiripe cut-tings or by layering.

R. officinalis

P. 188

r. oh-fiss-in-AL-iss. Rosemary. The species grows 2 to 6 feet tall with leathery, needlelike leaves that are white underneath and smell of pine. The tubular, two-lipped blue flowers bloom in the leaf axils in late spring or early summer, often reblooming when weather cools in fall. Popular cultivars include 'Arp' (white flowers, hardy to at least Zone 7), 'Benenden Blue' (bright blue flowers), 'Golden Rain' (new leaves edged in gold), 'Majorca Pink' (pink flowers), 'Lockwood de Forest' (1 foot tall, 3 feet wide), and 'Tuscan Blue' (upright to 6 feet tall, deep blue flowers). There is also a weeping form, 'Prostratus'. Zones 8 to 10.

❦ Rubus

ROO-bus. Rose family, Rosaceae.

A genus of some 250 species of bristly or prickly deciduous or evergreen shrubs and climbers (and a few herbaceous perennials) native to a wide range of habitats throughout the world. Known primarily for bearing edible fruits, this group also includes plants grown for flowers or eye-catching shoots in winter.

HOW TO GROW

Give brambles ordinary, well-drained soil in full sun. Grow those with winter interest against a background of dark conifers or where they will catch early morning or late afternoon light. Prune in early spring. Propagate from suckers.

R. 'Benenden'

A deciduous, sterile hybrid shrub with thornless arching branches to 8 feet tall and peeling bark that provides winter interest. The dark green leaves are shallowly lobed while the solitary, five-petaled flowers — which look like single white roses with yellow centers — are 3 inches across and bloom in late spring and early summer. Zones 5 to 8.

R. cockburnianus

r. cok-burn-ee-AY-nus. Ghost Bramble. This deciduous shrub forms thickets of prickly arching canes to 8 feet tall. The leaves are pinnately compound, green above and fuzzy white underneath. Terminal racemes of ½-inch purple flowers in summer are followed by ½-inch inedible black fruits. The chief attraction is its silvery white shoots, which glow like "ghosts" in winter. Zones 5 to 8.

R. odoratus
P. 189

r. oh-doh-RAH-tus. Flowering Raspberry. Also called thimbleberry, this deciduous shrub is native to eastern North America as far west as Michigan and south to Georgia. It grows to 6 feet high with erect, suckering, thornless branches. Lobed, maple-shaped leaves are velvety, turning red in autumn in the northern part of its range. Fragrant mauve, five-petaled flowers bloom in 2-inch clusters in mid- to late summer. Zones 5 to 8.

R. spectabilis
P. 190

r. spec-TAH-bih-liss. Salmonberry. A deciduous, thicket-forming shrub of prickly shoots to about 6 feet tall. It has 6-inch palmate leaves with three glossy leaflets and fragrant purple-pink midspring flowers. Those of 'Olympic Double' are frilly and 2 inches across. Zones 5 to 8.

R. thibetanus

r. tih-bet-AY-nus. Erect prickly shoots form a thicket to 8 feet tall. The pinnately divided leaves have 7 to 13 gray fuzzy leaflets; ½-inch reddish purple summer flowers are followed by ½-inch black berries, lightly "frosted." The shoots are silver in winter. Zones 6 to 9.

R. tricolor

r. TRY-kuh-ler. A prostrate deciduous bramble with arching shoots to 2 feet tall, spreading to 10 feet and covered with red bristles. The 4-inch leaves have three to five lobes; 1-inch white flowers borne in summer are followed by edible red berries. Zones 6 to 9.

❦ Ruta

ROO-tuh. Citrus family, Rutaceae.

This genus embraces eight species of perennials and shrubs from the Mediterranean. The single species listed here, once thought to repel witches and safeguard eyesight, came to symbolize repentance. Known as the "herb of grace," it was used in the Roman Catholic Church to sprinkle holy water and, because of this history of symbolism, is often found in herb gardens today. It has a place in the ornamental garden because of its feathery, bluish foliage and airy cymes of summer flowers.

HOW TO GROW

Give rue average, well-drained, neutral to slightly alkaline soil in full sun. Handle the plants with caution, as they can cause an allergic reaction in some people. In spring, prune back flowered shoots just above last year's growth. Plant in herb or perennial beds for contrast in foliage color and texture, or use as low hedging. Seedpods are used in arrangements. Propagate from seeds, cuttings, or division.

R. graveolens   P. 190

r. grav-ee-OH-lens. Rue. This subshrub grows 2 to 3 feet tall with pungent, blue-green leaves coated with white, much divided and ferny. The tiny greenish yellow leaves bloom in flat clusters for a long period beginning in midsummer. 'Jackman's Blue' is compact with bluer foliage. Zones 4 to 9.

❦ Salix

SAY-licks. Willow family, Salicaceae.

In landscapes, the most familiar willows are the huge weeping forms that so often hang over ponds and streams. Herbalists know that the white willow *(S. alba)* and several other species contain the active ingredient in aspirin (salicin). The little pussy willow is regarded as a harbinger of spring, but is probably seen in arrangements more often than in gardens. There are many more choices among this genus's approximately 300 deciduous trees and shrubs, primarily dioecious and native to the temperate Northern Hemisphere. The shrub species are showy for their graceful habit and foliage, furry spring catkins, and colorful winter shoots.

HOW TO GROW

Most willows tolerate damp conditions better than other shrubs. Give them full sun in moderately fertile clay or loam. Use for hedges, screens, specimens, shrub borders, or cutting for arrangements. They are handsome in pondside plantings, but their aggressive roots can tear rubber liners. Keep them away from water mains and septic systems. They are also prone to developing cankers and fungal diseases. Willows grown for colorful winter shoots need old branches removed regularly. They propagate easily from cuttings.

S. caprea

s. KAP-ree-uh. French Pussy Willow. The Latin-derived species name refers to goats, since it was once used for fodder, and another common name is goat willow. Upright and often treelike at 25 feet tall and 15 feet wide, with pink-gray woolly catkins in early spring. 'Pendula' (Kilmarnock willow) and 'Weeping Sally' are weeping forms that require staking when young. Zones 4 to 8.

S. chaenomyloides

P. 191

s. ky-noh-my-LOY-deez. Japanese Pussy Willow. This species grows quickly into a large shrub 12 to 15 feet tall with stunning catkins more than 2 inches long. Emerging from red buds they are tinged with deep pink and are set off by yellow-orange anthers. Zones 6 to 8.

S. exigua

s. eks-IG-ew-uh. Coyote Willow. A western U.S. native shrub growing 10 to 12 feet tall, suckering and spreading to 15 feet. The narrow silvery leaves are 4 inches long and hairy when new. Spring catkins about 2 inches long appear with the leaves. It does well in sandy soil. Zones 4 to 6.

S. fargesii.

s. far-GEE-see-eye. A Chinese species to 8 feet tall with shiny reddish brown shoots and bright red buds. The 6-inch leaves are glossy with prominent veins. Green spring catkins averaging 6 inches long appear with the leaves. Zones 6 to 8.

S. gracilistyla

s. gras-il-IS-til-uh. Rose-gold Pussy Willow. Upright shrub to 6 to 10 feet with gray-green leaves. The common name comes from gold and rose stamens on the gray 1½-inch early-spring catkins. S. 'Melanostachys' (black pussy willow), sometimes listed as a botanical variety or separate species, has purple-black stems and black catkins with red anthers that turn yellow. Zones 5 to 7.

S. hastata 'Wehrhahnii'

P. 191

s. has-TAH-tuh. Upright to 4 feet tall and wide with dark purple-brown shoots, bright green oval leaves, and silvery catkins in spring before the leaves. Zones 5 to 8.

S. lanata

s. lan-AH-tuh. Woolly Willow. A low-growing native of Europe and Asia to 4 feet tall and a bit wider, with silvery, hairy, oval leaves 1 to 2 inches long. The 2- to 4-inch-long catkins are yellow with some gray and bloom with the leaves in spring. Zones 2 to 4.

S. sachalinensis 'Sekka' (syn. *S. udensis* 'Sekka')

s. sak-uh-lih-NEN-siss. Japanese Fantail Willow. A male cultivar with contorted branches, sometimes curled and flattened. A broad and graceful shrub that grows 10 to 15 feet tall and wide, with 4-inch leaves that are dark green and shiny on top, silver beneath. Gray ½-inch catkins appear in March. Zones 4 to 7.

❦ *Sambucus*

sam-BEW-kus. Honeysuckle family, Caprifoliaceae.

Elders may be better known for their folk uses—elderberry wine, pancakes, and an herbal pain reliever—than they are in the ornamental landscape. They represent a genus of about 25 herbaceous perennials and deciduous shrubs and trees widely distributed throughout temperate and subtropical areas. Some are a bit shaggy for a formal garden, but they work well for naturalizing and attracting birds. Some cultivars have striking divided foliage.

HOW TO GROW

Elders do best in moisture-retentive, well-drained soil but adapt to some drought and a wide range of pH. The yellow-foliaged types need dappled shade to prevent fading. European species are not heat tolerant. Use species for naturalizing or for windbreaks, cultivars in a shrub border. They tolerate hard pruning and require it to keep from becoming unkempt. Propagate from seeds or cuttings, or by dividing suckers.

S. canadensis   P. 192

s. kan-uh-DEN-siss. American Elder. A variable shrub from 5 to 12 feet high and wide with pinnately compound leaves and in midsummer, profuse flat-topped clusters of white flowers with prominent yellow stamens. Late-summer berries are purple-black, eaten by birds but also used for jelly, pies, and juice. 'Aurea' has yellow foliage and red fruit. Zones 3 to 9.

S. mexicana (syn. *S. caerulea*)

s. mex-ih-KAN-uh. Blue Elderberry. Native from British Columbia into southern California and east to the Rockies, this species ranges from a large shrub to a tree 30 feet or taller. Five to nine leaflets form leaves up to 8 inches long. The flat-topped clusters of creamy white flowers bloom late spring to midsummer, followed by blue-black ¼-inch berries. Zones 5 to 7.

S. nigra
s. NY-gruh. European Elder. The species grows 10 to 20 feet tall with early-summer clusters of white flowers, smaller than those of the American species. There are almost 30 cultivars offering foliage that is golden ('Aurea'), variegated ('Marginata'), finely cut ('Laciniata') or even purple ('Guincho Purple'). Zones 5 to 7.

S. racemosa 'Plumosa Aurea'   P. 192
s. rass-eh-MOH-suh. European Red Elder cultivar. A multistemmed shrub 8 to 12 feet tall and wide with finely cut, compound, toothed leaflets of bright yellow or chartreuse. Tiny yellow flowers bloom in round-topped clusters in midspring, followed by bright red, ¼-inch berries. Zones 5 to 7.

❦ Santolina
san-toh-LEE-nuh. Aster family, Asteraceae.

Like a lot of other subshrubs with aromatic foliage, santolinas are a favorite in the herb garden — not for medicine or cooking, but for making a neat edge around the other herbs. They have button flowers and spiky foliage that may have some insect-repelling properties. The genus includes 18 evergreen shrub species from the Mediterranean.

HOW TO GROW
These small evergreen shrubs need full sun, excellent drainage, and soil that isn't too rich, otherwise adapting to sand or clay and a wide range of pH. Use them in rock gardens, as low hedges, or for edging herb beds. Prune them back hard in spring to keep them from looking tattered, and prune lightly after flowering. They may die to the ground in the northern part of their range but recover in spring. Propagate from seed or cuttings.

S. chamaecyparissus   P. 193
s. kam-ee-sip-ar-ISS-us. Lavender Cotton. This popular species, whose name means dwarf cypress, forms a mound 2 feet high and 3 feet wide with fine, pale gray leaves that look like cypress needles and smell like camphor. Gold button flowers (rayless disk flowers) bloom early to midsummer on stems above the foliage. Zones 6 to 9.

S. rosmarinifolia   P. 193
s. rohs-mar-een-ih-FOH-lee-uh. Green Santolina. Almost identical to lavender cotton except that the resinous foliage is bright green. Zones 7 to 10.

❦ *Sarcococca*

sar-koh-KOKE-uh. Boxwood family, Buxaceae.

This is a genus of 14 evergreen Asian shrubs, surprisingly underused in gardens given the plants' many attributes: fragrant, petalless winter flowers; glossy lance-shaped or elliptical leaves; tolerance of shade and shearing; and generally trouble-free nature.

HOW TO GROW

Give sweetbox soil that is organically amended, slightly acid, and moisture retentive but well aerated. It will not tolerate both full sun and dry soil. Grow as a low hedge, tall ground cover, edging for a path, in a foundation, or to face down shrubs of contrasting texture in a shrub border.

S. confusa

s. con-FEW-suh. A dense, rounded shrub to 6 feet tall and 3 feet wide with elliptical, glossy leaves and clusters of fragrant spring flowers borne in the leaf axils. The ¼-inch fruits are round and glossy black. Zones 6 to 10.

S. hookeriana var. *humilis*   P. 194

s. hook-ur-ee-AY-nuh var. HEW-mil-us. Sweetbox variety. This is the most commonly available variety, slightly more regular in form and more cold hardy than the species. Averaging 18 inches tall, it suckers to form a nonaggressive, mounded colony. The 3-inch dark green leaves usually hide the ½-inch flowers, white and sweetly aromatic, that bloom late winter to early spring. The fruits are glossy and blue-black. Zones 5 to 10.

S. ruscifolia

s. rus-kih-FOH-lee-uh. Fragrant Sarcococca. This species grows slowly to form a mound about 5 feet high, varying in width from 3 to 7 feet. Arching shoots bear lance-shaped, pointed, glossy leaves. The fragrant white early-spring flowers are followed by ¼-inch dark red fruits. Zones 7 to 10.

❦ *Shepherdia*

shep-HER-dee-uh. Oleaster family, Elaeagnaceae.

A species of three evergreen or deciduous shrubs and trees native to North America, grown for silvery foliage and tolerance of difficult conditions. Gardeners who are discovering their regional natives appreciate these rugged species, which have adapted to the rigors of the Plains.

HOW TO GROW

Shepherdia thrives in full sun on dry, alkaline soils and tolerates the cold wind and salt of coastal situations. You need to have both male and female plants to produce berries. Use for naturalizing, attracting birds, or as a hedge in a harsh climate. Does not need pruning. Propagate from cold-stratified seeds or root cuttings.

S. argentea

s. ar-JEN-tee-uh. Silver Buffalo Berry. Native from Canada south to Kansas and west to Nevada. Thorny, erect branches usually grow 6 to 10 feet tall and spread by suckering. The 1-inch deciduous leaves are silvery and scaly. Inconspicuous yellow springtime flowers are followed on female shrubs by tart red oval berries appreciated by birds and used for jellies. Zones 3 to 6.

S. canadensis   P. 194

s. kan-uh-DEN-siss. Russet Buffalo Berry. Native to the contiguous northern states and Alaska. Usually 8 feet tall or less with more gray-green foliage and yellower fruits than *S. argentea*. Zones 2 to 6.

❦ Skimmia

SKIM-ee-uh. Citrus family, Rutaceae.

A genus of four evergreen shrubs and trees from Asia, grown for aromatic foliage, often fragrant flower clusters, and, on some species, ornamental fruits. A good choice for small shady gardens.

HOW TO GROW

Give skimmia organically rich acidic soil that retains moisture and drains well, in either part or full shade. It will discolor in full sun and does not tolerate heat well. Use in woodland gardens, along foundations, or in borders with other shade-loving evergreen shrubs. Does not need pruning. Propagate from cleaned seeds or cuttings taken in fall.

S. japonica   P. 195

s. juh-PON-ih-kuh. Japanese Skimmia. A dense rounded shrub to about 4 feet tall with glossy elliptic leaves, slightly fragrant when bruised, and held in whorls near the ends of branches. Males are somewhat smaller and denser than females and have smaller leaves. Red buds open to small white fragrant flowers in 3-inch upright panicles in early to midspring. If both male and female plants are present, females produce ⅓-inch bright red berries held at the ends of branches from midautumn to spring; both flowers and fruit are sometimes present at the same time. Zones 7 to 8.

S. reevesiana

s. reev-see-AY-nuh. Reeves Skimmia. A compact form to about 2 feet tall with both male and female flowers on a single plant. Zones 6 to 7.

❦ *Sorbus*

SORE-bus. Rose family, Rosaceae.

Despite their common name, these plants, a genus of about 100 decidu-ous trees and shrubs from throughout northern temperate climates, aren't even in the same family as ash trees (*Fraxinus* species), but have similar pinnately compound leaves. The following species is small enough for cramped urban gardens and worth growing for its flowers, fruits, and especially its outstanding fall foliage.

HOW TO GROW

Mountain ash likes slightly acid, relatively fertile loam with good drainage in either sun or high shade. Use it for a low hedge or in a shrub border where you need fall color. Does not require pruning. Propagate from root cuttings.

S. reducta   P. 196

s. reh-DUK-tuh. Dwarf Mountain Ash. This diminutive Chinese native forms a thicket of upright shoots about 3 feet tall. The dark green leaves are composed of 9 to 15 leaflets that in fall turn bronze, orange-red, and pur-ple-red. The late-spring flowers, in terminal clusters, are white, and the ¼-inch berries are pink. Zones 5 to 8.

❦ *Spartium*

SPAR-tee-um. Pea family, Fabaceae

A single-species genus of deciduous shrub native to the Mediterranean and related to *Cytisus* species, which are also commonly called brooms. It is grown primarily for fragrant, pealike flowers that bloom for several months.

HOW TO GROW

Spanish broom needs full sun and tolerates poor, dry, rocky or sandy soil. Because it spreads by underground stems it can be used to stabilize banks, but also can become invasive. It is crowding out native species in the foothills of the California chapparal and has also escaped into the wild in Oregon. Gardeners in those states should avoid it. Elsewhere, remove shoots to keep it under control in the garden, and prune hard to keep it from becoming leggy.

S. junceum   P. 196

s. YUN-kee-um. Spanish Broom. An almost leafless shrub of erect green stems 6 to 10 feet tall. The bright yellow 1-inch flowers, borne at the end of branches from early summer to early autumn, have a citrusy scent that adds to their charm as cut flowers. They are followed by hairy brown seedpods up to 3 inches long. Zones 8 to 10.

❦ Spiraea

spy-REE-uh. Rose family, Rosaceae.

A genus of about 80 generally deciduous shrubs found in a diversity of habitats throughout North America, Asia, and Europe. Some cultivars are old garden favorites for their profuse clusters of small spring or summer flowers, or in a few cases, colorful foliage, and breeders continue to develop new variations on these themes. Two of the species, particularly *S. japonica* but also *S. prunifolia,* are invading natural habitats.

HOW TO GROW

Given full sun, spireas are easy to grow in any soil as long as it isn't waterlogged. They can be used as hedges or in a mixed shrub border. Some gardeners use the smallest cultivars in rock gardens or massed as a tall ground cover. Prune back summer-flowering varieties *(S. × bumalda* and *S. japonica)* in early spring; selectively remove shoots of spring-flowering spireas when their bloom is finished. They propagate easily by softwood cuttings in summer.

S. × arguta 'Compacta'

s. × ar-GEW-tuh. Dwarf Garland Spirea. The species grows 6 to 8 feet tall, but this cultivar stops at about 3 feet. White flowers are clustered along the graceful arching shoots in midspring. The bright green leaves are serrated. Zones 5 to 8.

S. × bumalda
P. 197

s. × bew-MAWL-duh. Bumald Spirea. A flat-topped twiggy shrub, slightly mounded, growing 3 to 4 feet tall and 5 to 6 feet wide. 'Anthony Waterer' has reddish new foliage that turns blue-green, then reddish purple in fall. Some of its leaves have yellow or white markings. The flat-topped rosy pink flowers bloom for several weeks in summer. 'Froebelii' is slightly taller, more upright, and cold tolerant. Popular 'Goldflame' has bronze new growth that turns yellow, then green (more so in hot climates), and reddish again in autumn. 'Limemound' stays about a foot smaller, with chartreuse leaves. Zones 4 to 8.

S. cinerea 'Grefsheim'

s. sin-eh-REE-uh. Grefsheim Spirea. A 5-foot shrub with arching shoots, narrow soft green leaves that turn yellow in fall, and spikes of fragrant white flowers that smother the branches before leaves unfurl in mid-spring. Zones 4 to 8.

S. japonica

s. juh-PON-ih-kuh. Japanese Spirea. Some consider this the same as S. × bumalda, while others describe it as more upright (to 4 or 5 feet) with leaves that are more serrated. Flat-topped summer flowers are usually pink. 'Gold Mound' averages 3 feet tall with golden yellow leaves. 'Shirobana', also known as 'Shibori', has blooms of pink and white, sometimes on the same flower cluster, and reblooms. Dwarf cultivars are 'Alpina' (sometimes called daphne spirea, 1 to 2 feet) and 'Little Princess' (to about 2½ feet). Zones 3 to 8.

S. nipponica 'Snowmound'
P. 198

s. nip-PON-ih-kuh. Snowmound Nippon Spirea. Dense with a rounded mature habit, to 3 to 5 feet tall and wide, it has blue-green leaves and is heavily clothed in white flowers in late spring. Zones 4 to 8.

S. prunifolia
P. 198

s. proo-nih-FOH-lee-uh. Bridalwreath Spirea. This old favorite has an open habit from 6 to 9 feet tall. The dark green leaves are toothed and somewhat shiny and turn bronzy yellow or red in fall. Double white ⅓-inch flowers bloom on old wood in midspring before the plant leafs out. Zones 4 to 8.

S. thunbergii P. 199

s. thun-BERG-ee-eye. Thunberg Spirea. This is a dense shrub to 5 feet tall and 6 feet wide, given a delicate appearance by arching branches and willowlike, light green leaves. They turn bronzy orange in fall. Round 2-inch clusters of white flowers march down the branches in early to midspring. Zones 4 to 8.

S. tomentosa

s. toh-men-TOH-suh. Hardhack. This species, native from Nova Scotia to the mountains of Georgia, is similar to *S. japonica,* except that the rosy purple or deep pink summer flowers appear in a more rounded plume. Growing 3 to 4 feet tall, it looks best in a sunny wildflower border. It tolerates considerable moisture, but not drought or shade. Zones 4 to 8.

S. × vanhouttei

s. × van-HOO-tee-eye. Vanhoutte Spirea. A ubiquitous shrub, fountainlike to 6 or 8 feet tall and 10 to 12 feet wide, with blue-green three-lobed leaves. After the leaves emerge, clusters of cup-shaped white flowers bloom on old wood in midspring to early summer. Zones 4 to 8.

❧ Stachyurus

stah-kee-YU-rus. Stachyurus family, Stachyuraceae.

Need a winter garden conversation piece? This Asian genus boasts a half dozen species of deciduous or semievergreen shrubs or small trees, but you're likely to find only this one, grown for unusual beadlike clusters of flowers.

HOW TO GROW

This shrub needs acid soil, high in organic matter, that holds moisture and drains well. Situate it in partial or high shade, sheltered from heavy frost. Use in an informal, shady shrub border, or as a specimen against a dark background. Does not require pruning, but a proportion of flowered branches can be pruned to the ground for rejuvenation. Propagate by sowing fresh seeds or by layering.

S. praecox P. 199

s. PRAY-cox. Early Spiketail. An upright shrub growing 6 to 10 feet tall. The bright green toothed leaves grow 3 to 7 inches long with a sharp tip and turn yellow or pinkish red in autumn. In late winter to early spring, 3- to 4-inch racemes of buds hang from the branches, opening to bell-shaped, pale yellow-green flowers. A berrylike fruit follows in late summer. Zones 6 to 8.

᭵ *Staphylea*

staf-ih-LEE-uh. Bladdernut family, Staphyleaceae.

A genus of 11 deciduous shrubs and small trees found in woods of northern temperate climates. Cultivated varieties are grown for both their bell-shaped flowers and unusual bladderlike fruit capsules.

HOW TO GROW

Bladdernuts need moisture-retentive but well-drained soil in either sun or part shade. Use for naturalizing, in the shrub border, or at the edge of a woodland. Needs minimal pruning but shoots can be selectively trimmed back to promote new growth and suckers removed to restrict size. Seeds have double dormancy; propagation is easier from cuttings.

S. colchica   P. 200

s. KAHL-keh-kuh. Colchis Bladdernut. A species from the Caucasus growing to 10 feet tall, suckering and spreading wider. The compound leaves have three or five leaflets. In mid- to late spring, it bears fragrant white bell-shaped flowers in upright panicles up to 5 inches long, followed by light green 4-inch fruit capsules. Zones 6 to 7.

S. trifolia

s. try-FOH-lee-uh. American Bladdernut. Native from Ontario to Georgia, west to Minnesota and Missouri, this upright, brushy, suckering shrub grows 10 to 15 feet tall and usually about half as wide. The bark is smooth with white stripes. Pinnate leaves with three sharply pointed leaflets are dark green, then dull yellow in autumn. Bell-shaped greenish white flowers are produced in abundant 2-inch panicles in midspring. Pale green fruit capsules, to 1½ inches long and often used in dried arrangements, form in early fall. Zones 3 to 8.

❦ *Stephanandra*

stef-uh-NAN-druh. Rose family, Rosaceae.

A genus of four species of deciduous shrubs from eastern Asia, closely related to spirea. The following cultivar is probably the most widely available representative of the group, admired for its graceful habit, finely textured leaves, and fall color.

HOW TO GROW

Give stephanandra acidic soil, well amended with organic matter to retain moisture and improve drainage, in full sun or part shade. It makes a good low hedge, or it can be massed for a tall, low-maintenance ground cover or for erosion control. Pruning stimulates new growth and is sometimes required when tips are winterburned in exposed areas. Propagate from suckers or cuttings.

S. incisa   P. 200

s. in-SY-zuh. This dense shrub grows from 4 to 7 feet tall with arching shoots that root along their length. The bright green triangular leaves are deeply cut and serrated, touched with bronzy red when new and turning reddish orange in fall. Small greenish white flowers appear in 3-inch panicles in late spring. 'Crispa' grows to only 1½ to 3 feet tall. Zones 5 to 8.

❦ *Styrax*

STY-rax. Storax family, Styraceae.

This is a genus of about 100 species of woody plants, most of them tree-like, native to warm areas of the Northern Hemisphere. The following shrub species are cultivated for bell-like white flowers that waft a welcome light fragrance in spring.

HOW TO GROW

Found naturally along streamsides, our native snowbell is one of the few shrubs that will tolerate water around its roots. The Asian species listed here needs good drainage, like most shrubs. Amend the soil heavily with peat moss to assure acidity and moisture retention, and mulch well to keep roots cool, in part shade. Styrax doesn't compete well with other shrubs, so plant it as a specimen or give it a spot of its own at the edge of a moist woodland. Does not require pruning. Propagate from fresh seeds or softwood cuttings in midsummer.

S. americanus
P. 201

s. uh-mair-ih-KAY-nus. American Snowbell. Native from Virginia to Florida and west to Missouri, this snowbell is rounded to about 10 feet with slender stems and elliptic bright green leaves 3 inches long. The white bell flowers, which have petals that curve sharply backward and a sweet fragrance, are borne in the leaf axils in late spring. Gray oval fruits appear in early fall. Zones 6 to 8.

S. obassia
P. 201

s. oh-BAYS-ee-uh. Fragrant Snowbell. This Asian species walks a fine line between shrub and tree at 20 feet and taller, but provides multiseason interest with 8-inch arched racemes of fragrant white flowers, ¾-inch fruits, occasional yellow fall foliage, and sinuous gray bark. Zones 5 to 8.

❦ *Symphoricarpos*

sim-for-ih-KAR-pos. Honeysuckle family, Caprifoliaceae.

A genus of 17 species of deciduous shrubs native to North America, Mexico, and China. Although they have been in and out of style over the years, their showy fruits consistently make them a hot item for collectors.

HOW TO GROW

These shrubs are tolerant of almost any soil, in sun as well as relatively heavy shade. They are most useful for erosion control or naturalizing difficult areas. They don't need pruning except for shaping, and they propagate easily from cuttings.

S. albus
P. 202

s. AL-bus. Common Snowberry. Native to most of Canada south to Minnesota and Virginia, this bushy, rounded 3- to 6-foot shrub has numerous upright arching shoots and 2-inch dark green leaves, occasionally lobed. Relatively inconspicuous spikes of small pink flowers bloom in late spring, followed by ½-inch white berries that can last to late fall. *S. albus* var. *laevigatus* is more vigorous with larger leaves. Zones 3 to 7.

S. × chenaultii 'Hancock'

s. × shen-OH-ee-eye. Chenault Coralberry cultivar. A low- and wide-growing selection to 2 feet tall and 12 feet wide with small blue-green leaves. Gardeners grow it for its graceful arching habit rather than the dark pink flowers or small greenish white fruits. Zones 4 to 7.

S. × doorenbosii

s. × dor-en-BOH-see-eye. These hybrids bloom in early summer with greenish white flowers sometimes tinged with pink, but are grown for the dense fruit clusters, which range from rosy lilac to off-white blushed with pink. Zones 4 to 7.

S. orbiculatus

s. or-bih-kew-LAY-tus. Indian Currant Coralberry. Native from the central United States to New Jersey and Georgia, this shrub has arching branches and grows 2 to 6 feet tall. Early to midsummer flowers are off-white touched with rose, borne in axils and at the ends of branches. Persistent reddish purple fruits develop in midautumn. Zones 2 to 7.

꩜ Symplocos

sim-PLOH-kos. Sweetleaf family, Symplocaceae.

This is a genus of some 250 species of widely distributed evergreen and deciduous trees and shrubs. Only one species, known for showy berries and easy care, is commonly grown in gardens.

HOW TO GROW
Give sapphireberry soil that is fertile, moist but well aerated, and acid to neutral, in full sun or light shade. It can be grown as a specimen, but more than one plant will ensure better fruiting. Try it as an informal hedge or screen. It should not require pruning. Propagate from softwood cuttings.

S. paniculata   P. 202

s. pan-ih-kew-LAY-tuh. Sapphireberry. From China, Japan, and the Himalayas, this deciduous species forms a large spreading shrub or small tree at 10 to 20 feet. The upright branches are covered with gray furrowed bark and finely toothed, somewhat hairy 3-inch leaves. Fragrant white star-shaped flowers, each with 30 prominent yellow stamens, are borne profusely in late spring to early summer. The bright turquoise berries ripen in early fall and last several weeks before being stripped by birds. Zones 4 to 8.

🌿 *Syringa*

sigh-RING-guh. Olive family, Oleaceae.

Approximately 20 species of deciduous shrubs native to Europe and Asia have been hybridized and selected to produce an estimated 1,600 named varieties of lilacs, grown for their strongly fragrant tubular spring flowers, borne in cone- or pyramid-shaped clusters.

HOW TO GROW

Lilacs do best in neutral to alkaline soil that is moist but well drained, in open areas where they will have full sun and good air circulation. In cool, dry climates where mildew doesn't mar foliage in summer, all lilacs make good specimen shrubs. They are also often used in masses, against buildings, or in shrub borders.

In humid regions, all lilacs (although some more than others) are prone to develop powdery mildew, which coats the leaves with an unsightly white powder but won't kill the plant. More serious are blights, which first appear as brown blotches on foliage. They can be prevented by pruning to provide good air circulation and keeping tools sterile, and they can be treated with a spray of Bordeaux mix. Scale and lilac borers, which look like wasps, are the most common insect pests.

Lilac stems should be pruned out in winter so they don't rub each other. Remove spent blooms to prevent seed formation. Propagate from stratified seeds, cuttings treated with hormone powder, or from suckers.

S. × chinensis   P. 203

s. × chin-EN-siss. Chinese Lilac. An old hybrid 8 to 15 feet tall and wide with arching branches and fragrant lilac-colored flowers. More delicate looking and less mildew-prone than common lilac *(S. vulgaris)*. 'Lilac Sunday' from the Arnold Arboretum forms a fountain of pale purple panicles at both the branch tips and along the willowy stems. Zones 3 to 7.

S. × hyacinthiflora   P. 203

s. × hy-uh-sin-thih-FLOR-uh. Hybrid of Chinese *S. oblata* and *S. vulgaris* growing to 10 or even 12 feet tall and wide with bronze new growth and purple foliage in fall. Blooms one to two weeks sooner than common lilac with slightly more open panicles. There are many cultivars, offering single or double flowers in white, lavender, pink, and magenta. 'Blanche Sweet' has blue buds opening to palest lavender pink with an almost sugary scent. Zones 3 to 7.

S. × *josiflexa*

s. × joh-sih-FLEX-uh. Vigorous, upright shrub to 20 feet but usually maintained at about half that. Blooms somewhat later than other lilacs. 'Bellicent' is pink, while 'Royalty' is a popular lavender selection. Zones 4 to 7.

S. × *laciniata*

s. × lah-cin-ee-AY-tah. Cutleaf Lilac. Growing 6 to 8 feet tall and up to 10 feet wide with slender arching stems and leaves with up to nine lobes, cutleaf lilac is resistant to mildew. Pale lilac flowers bloom in mid- to late spring. Zones 4 to 8.

S. meyeri   P. 204

s. MY-er-eye. Meyer Lilac. Uniform, dense, rounded shrub 4 to 8 feet tall and spreading wider with small rounded leaves. It flowers when quite young, covering the plant with violet panicles up to 4 inches long in midspring. 'Palibin' is especially compact with reddish purple buds opening to pink tinged with white or lavender-pink. Zones 4 to 7.

S. microphylla (syn. *S. pubescens* var. *microphylla*)

s. my-kroh-FIL-uh. Littleleaf Lilac. A dense shrub growing to 6 feet or taller and twice as wide. Lilac pink flowers open in mid- to late spring with some rebloom in early fall. 'Superba' has lighter pink flowers and a longer bloom period. Zones 4 to 7.

S. patula 'Miss Kim'   P. 204

s. PAT-yew-luh. Manchurian Lilac cultivar. Upright and vigorous to about 8 feet and not as wide with leaves up to 5 inches long. Pale lilac blue flowers are in upright panicles in mid- to late spring. Zones 4 to 7.

S. × *pekinensis*

s. × pee-kin-EN-siss. Pekin Lilac. Upright to 15 or 20 feet with many slender stems. Blooms in late spring with cream-colored 3- to 6-inch panicles. Reddish brown bark can be cherrylike with horizontal lines, or exfoliating. Zones 4 to 7.

S. × *persica*   P. 205

s. × PER-sih-kuh. Persian Lilac. Relatively small shrub at 4 to 8 feet and slightly wider, with fragrant pale lilac flowers in midspring. Zones 3 to 7.

S. reticulata
P. 205

s. reh-tih-kew-LAY-tuh. Japanese Tree Lilac. A huge shrub or broad tree up to 30 feet tall and 25 feet wide with cherrylike bark. Creamy white flowers bloom in fragrant panicles up to 12 inches long and 10 inches wide in late spring to early summer. Good disease and pest resistance. Zones 4 to 7.

S. vulgaris

s. vul-GAIR-iss. Common Lilac. An upright, suckering shrub, native to southeastern Europe, with an irregular habit. It loses its lower branches with maturity, exposing often picturesque rough bark. May be defoliated by mildew in hot, humid climates. There are virtually hundreds of cultivars, all with intensely fragrant midspring flowers of lavender, purple, pink, white, or bicolors. Zones 3 to 7.

🌾 Tamarix

TAM-ar-ix. Tamarix family, Tamaricaceae.

A genus of about 50 species of deciduous shrubs and trees from Europe, Asia, and North Africa. A half dozen or so are cultivated for delicate foliage and flowers and resistance to difficult situations, including drought, salt, and wind. Aggressive roots can outcompete other species. The species below has outspread its welcome and wiped out native wetland species in the American West; its cultivation is discouraged in areas where it can become a problem. There are some reports of invasiveness in the East, as well.

HOW TO GROW
Give tamarix full sun in almost any type of soil. Prune after flowering, since the blooms appear on the previous season's growth. May need heavy pruning to prevent its becoming top-heavy. Tamarix is sometimes pruned to the ground for increased foliage effect in mixed borders and masses or as specimens. Propagate from seeds or cuttings.

T. ramosissima (syn. T. pentandra)
P. 206

t. ram-oh-SISS-ih-muh. Salt Cedar. A native of Europe and Asia, usually growing to about 15 feet tall and wide with a loose, open habit and long slender reddish brown shoots. They are clothed with ⅛-inch leaves and, in midspring or early summer, in airy racemes of rose pink flowers. Zones 3 to 8.

❧ *Taxus*

TAX-us. Yew family, Taxaceae.

This is a genus of 5 to 10 evergreen conifers found from northern temperate zones south to Central America, grown for handsome, problem-free foliage and, on some types, attractive red fruits.

HOW TO GROW

Yews can handle any kind of soil as long as the drainage is excellent, in full sun to dense shade. They tolerate pollution and drought, although most need some protection from harsh winds and extreme heat. Yews can take heavy pruning, but the cultivars listed here should not need it except to remove browned or broken stems. Propagate by cuttings collected in winter. All parts of the yew are toxic except the seed covering, but this doesn't deter deer, who find them irresistible.

T. baccata   P. 206

t. buk-AH-tuh. English Yew. The species, native to Europe, Africa, and Asia, can grow 60 feet tall and 25 feet wide with dark, spirally arranged needles. Low-growing cultivars include 'Fowle' (sometimes called 'Adpressa Fowle'), the midget boxleaf English yew, compact and dense, growing slowly to 7 feet tall and 16 feet wide; and 'Repandens', a low-growing female 2 to 4 feet tall and spreading 12 to 15 feet wide with sickle-shaped leaves and drooping branch tips. Zones 5 to 7.

T. cuspidata 'Nana'   P. 207

t. kus-pih-DAH-tuh. Dwarf Japanese Yew. Very slow growing to 10 or 20 feet high and twice as wide, this cultivar is a reliable producer of bright red fruits. Zones 4 to 7.

T. × *media*

t. × MEE-dee-uh. These hybrids of *T. cuspidata* and *T. baccata* have produced numerous shrub-sized cultivars useful for smaller gardens and low to medium hedges. They include 'Brownii', with a rounded form 9 to 12 feet tall; 'Densiformis', a 4-foot ball; 'Green Wave', low and mounding to 4 feet tall and 8 feet wide with graceful arching branches; and 'Hatfieldii', forming a column or pyramid about 10 feet tall and wide. 'Tauntonii' is a 3-foot-high spreader that tolerates both cold and heat. Zones 4 to 7.

Tecoma

teh-KOH-muh. Bignonia family, Bignoniaceae.

This genus includes a dozen species of evergreen vines, shrubs, and trees from the southern United States, south to Argentina, grown for colorful funnel-shaped flowers produced over many months.

HOW TO GROW

Give this shrub full sun and deeply worked, fertile soil that retains moisture but drains well. Unlike some subtropical plants, it likes moisture in summer as well as winter and also requires regular fertilizing. Use it in a shrub border or for screening. Remove spent flowers and prune at the same time if you need to reshape it. It may die back in cooler areas but regrows quickly. Propagate from seeds or semiripe summer cuttings.

T. stans P. 208

t. STANZ. Yellow bells. Also called trumpet bush for the shape of its flowers, this shrub can become a small tree, open and bushy to 20 feet tall and about 15 feet wide, often with multiple trunks. The pinnate leaves have up to 13 lance-shaped leaflets. Clusters of bright yellow flaring flowers can bloom from early summer to winter in mild areas. Zone 10.

Ternstroemia

tern-STROH-mee-uh. Tea family, Theaceae.

A genus of about 85 evergreen shrubs and trees, most of them tropical. This hardy species is grown primarily for its handsome foliage, summer and fall.

HOW TO GROW

Site this camellia relative in part shade and give it acidic soil that has been generously amended with organic matter to retain moisture and enhance drainage. It's appropriate for a specimen as well as a hedge or screen. Trim lightly after flowering. Propagate from fresh seeds planted in fall or from cuttings collected in late summer or early autumn.

T. gymnanthera P. 208

t. jim-NAN-ther-uh. Often incorrectly sold as *Cleyera japonica*, this densely branched shrub has an oval habit and grows slowly to 8 feet, more often about half that. The evergreen leaves are lustrous and leathery to 4 inches long, bronzy when new and turning reddish purple in fall. Cream-colored ½-inch flowers, borne in late spring to early summer, are fragrant but not showy. There are variegated and gold-leaved cultivars. Zones 7 to 10.

❦ Tetrapanax

tet-ruh-PAN-aks. Aralia family, Araliaceae.

This is one of those plants that landscape designers call "architectural." An evergreen native to China and Taiwan and the only species in its genus, rice-paper plant is bold in both habit and leaf and produces unusual flowers as well.

HOW TO GROW

This shrub grows in any average soil with good drainage, in full sun. Its best use is in a shrub border. It may die to the ground in the north of its range and can be pruned to the ground to stimulate larger new foliage. Propagate from suckers.

T. papyrifer   P. 209

t. pap-ih-RIH-fer. Rice-paper Plant. The thick, nearly unbranched shoots sucker and form thickets to 15 feet tall and wide. The leaves, which have 5 to 11 lobes, can be almost 2 feet across, scaly on top and white and felted underneath, held at the ends of the shoots. Small creamy white flowers in panicles up to 20 inches long bloom in fall, followed by ⅛-inch yellow or red-orange berries that split to reveal glossy black seeds. Fuzz on new stems and leaves can irritate skin. Zones 7 to 10.

❦ Teucrium

TOO-kree-um. Mint family, Lamiaceae.

A genus of about 300 species of herbaceous perennials and deciduous and evergreen shrubs, mainly from the Mediterranean. Their greatest garden attribute is their aromatic foliage.

HOW TO GROW

Germander will grow in relatively poor, sandy soil, preferably neutral to alkaline, in full sun. Shelter from wind is beneficial. Use it to edge a path, border, or knot garden, as a low hedge, in containers, or as topiary. Plants may die to the ground in the northern part of their range and can be pruned low to the ground for rejuvenation. Propagate from softwood cuttings in early summer.

T. chamaedrys   P. 209

t. kam-EE-drus. Wall Germander. This subshrub was once so popular in knot gardens it was called "poor man's box," since it could substitute for more expensive boxwood. As an herb in its own right, it was recommended for curing gout. Germander grows about 18 inches tall with glossy, aromatic dark green leaves that are evergreen to about Zone 7. From midsummer to fall it bears racemes of rose pink or magenta flowers. Zones 5 to 10.

T. fruticans   P. 210

t. FREW-tih-kanz. Shrubby Germander. A bushy evergreen to 3 feet tall and 1 foot wide with fuzzy white shoots. The aromatic gray-green oval to lance-shaped leaves are shiny on top, white and felted underneath. Terminal whorls of pale blue flowers bloom for several weeks in summer. Zones 8 to 10.

☙ Thuja

THOO-yuh. Cypress family, Cupressaceae.

This genus includes a half dozen species of columnar to conical evergreen conifers native to North America and East Asia, cultivated for their tidy, geometric shape.

HOW TO GROW

Give arborvitae full sun to very light shade in fertile, moist, well-aerated soil. Popular for hedges, screens, windbreaks, and accents. Prune lightly before growth starts in spring; heavy pruning spoils the conifer's natural grace. Propagate from stratified seeds or cuttings taken from late summer through early winter.

T. occidentalis   PP. 210, 211

t. ox-ih-den-TAL-iss. American Arborvitae. The scalelike leaves on this eastern U.S. native have prominent glands and are fragrant when bruised; branches turn up at the tips. The species grows to 20 or 30 feet in cultivation but there are many cultivars offering dwarf size, globe shape, or golden foliage, often combined with resistance to heat or winter discoloration. This group does best where air is moist. Cultivars include 'Smaragd' (trademarked Emerald), a narrow pyramid 10 to 15 feet tall and about 4 feet wide, wind and heat tolerant; 'Hetz Midget', globe shaped to 4 feet tall; 'Rheingold', oval or conical to 4 feet tall and wide with dark gold foliage; and 'Techny', which grows slowly to a pyramid about 12 feet tall, half as wide. 'Smaragd' and 'Techny' are good choices for gardeners in the Midwest, where other arborvitae brown in winter. Zones 3 to 7.

T. plicata
t. plih-KAH-tuh. Western Red Cedar. Native from the West Coast inland to Montana, it has darker green, less scaly leaves than the eastern species, and slender drooping branches. A giant in the wild with many small cultivars. They include 'Hileri', with irregular heavy leaves, blue-green foliage, growing to 10 feet, and 'Stoneham Gold', which forms a broad cone to 10 feet tall with bright gold new growth. Zones 5 to 8.

☙ *Thujopsis*
thoo-YOP-siss. Cypress family, Cupressaceae.

A single evergreen conifer species native to Japan, appreciated by conifer collectors for handsome foliage that usually keeps its color in winter.

HOW TO GROW
Grow in acidic soil rich in organic matter to retain moisture. It likes humidity but not wind or heat and will need some shade in the south of its range. Use this dwarf in a rock garden, as a low hedge, in a border, or as a specimen. Don't ruin the graceful foliage with pruning. Propagates easily from cuttings.

T. dolobrata 'Nana'   P. 212
t. doh-loh-BRAH-tuh. Hiba Arborvitae cultivar. This selection grows 3 feet tall and wide with a mounded habit. The foliage is scalelike with hatchet-shaped side leaves and distinctive silver-white markings underneath. The cones are tipped with a "horn." Zones 5 to 7.

❦ *Tibouchina*

ty-boo-CHEE-nuh. Melastome family, Melastomataceae.

A genus of about 350 herbaceous perennials, shrubs, and subshrubs from tropical America. The species listed here is grown for its striking purple flowers that bloom over a long period.

HOW TO GROW

Give glory bush full sun in fertile, acid, moisture-retentive soil, out of strong wind. In frost-free areas it makes a colorful addition to shrub borders and elsewhere can be grown in containers to move to a protected area in winter. It can be pruned heavily in spring to control size and reduce legginess. Deadhead by pinching or pruning lightly after each bloom cycle. Propagate from seeds or cuttings.

T. urvilleana   P. 212

t. ur-vil-lee-AY-nuh. Glory Bush. An upright evergreen to 15 feet or taller, roughly half as wide, with reddish hairs on both buds and new growth. Velvety oval leaves are 3 to 6 inches across, sometimes with blotches of yellow, orange, or red. From summer through fall, it produces satiny, deep purple flowers with dark curved stamens that have inspired the name "Brazilian spider flower." Zone 10.

❦ *Tsuga*

SOO-guh. Pine family, Pinaceae.

A genus of 10 coniferous evergreens native to North America and Asia. The species are all considered trees, but numerous cultivars of the Canadian hemlock lend themselves to traditional shrub uses.

HOW TO GROW

Canadian hemlock needs moisture-retentive, well-drained soil, preferring acid but tolerating alkaline, rocky, and sandy situations. It needs some summer humidity, part shade, and protection from wind. Woolly adelgid is a lethal insect pest in the Northeast; avoid heavy feeding with nitrogen fertilizers, which may make plants more susceptible. It can be pruned heavily for formal hedges. Small cultivars can be used in rock gardens, as ground covers, as accents, or in shrub borders. Pruning new shoots early in the growing season will control size yet maintain the natural shape. Propagate by layering, stratified seeds, or cuttings treated with hormones.

T. canadensis

PP. 213, 214

t. kan-uh-DEN-siss. Canadian Hemlock. This species, native to mountain slopes of eastern North America, grows into a pyramid 40 to 80 feet tall and about half that in spread with furrowed bark, sometimes showing purple streaks. Linear leaves grow in twos, white banded underneath. Among more than 50 cultivars are 'Jeddeloh', hemispherical with a central depression, about 4 feet tall and 6 feet wide; 'Jervis', twiggy, dense, and irregular to about 2 feet; and 'Pendula' (Sargent's weeping hemlock), broadly spreading and about 12 feet tall. Zones 3 to 7.

❦ Vaccinium

vax-SIN-ee-um. Heath family, Ericaceae.

A genus of 450 deciduous and evergreen shrubs and trees primarily from the Northern Hemisphere, usually cultivated for their edible fruits. Breeders are just beginning to develop plants with greater ornamental potential, stressing their usually white urn-shaped flowers and colorful fall foliage.

HOW TO GROW

These shrubs must have acid soil (pH 4.5 to 5.5) that retains moisture but drains well; a peat/sand mix is excellent. Growing in sun or part shade, they make a handsome hedge and mix well in a border with other acid-lovers. Plant more than one cultivar for best pollination. Prune lightly after fruiting. Propagate from cuttings.

V. ashei

v. ASH-ee-eye. Rabbiteye Blueberry. A deciduous southeastern U.S. native growing upright 8 to 10 feet tall, similar to the better-known highbush blueberry but better suited to southern gardens. Zones 8 to 9.

V. corymbosum

PP. 214, 215

v. kor-im-BOH-sum. Highbush Blueberry. Upright and many branched, 6 to 12 feet high and as wide, with lustrous often blue-green leaves turning bronze, orange, reddish, and purple in fall. Racemes of pink-tinged white urn-shaped flowers bloom in midspring, followed by the blue-black edible fruits. Zones 3 to 7.

❦ *Viburnum*

vy-BURN-um. Honeysuckle family, Caprifoliaceae.

A genus of 150 species of deciduous to evergreen shrubs and trees from northern temperate zones, with a few from Southeast Asia and South America. Many are garden worthy for either fragrant flower clusters, ornamental fruits, colorful fall foliage, or, often, a combination of these. The species listed here are deciduous unless otherwise noted.

HOW TO GROW

Most viburnums are easy to grow given slightly acid, moisture-retentive but well-drained soil in sun to part shade. They are generally not wind tolerant. Depending on size and habit they are excellent for naturalizing, hedges, massing, shrub borders, or as specimens. Prune only to restrict size or remove suckers. Propagate from semiripe cuttings in summer.

V. acerifolium   P. 215

v. ay-ser-ih-FOH-lee-um. Mapleleaf Viburnum. An eastern U.S. native growing to 6 feet tall and 4 feet wide, suckering to form thickets, it gets its common name from its three-lobed 4-inch leaves that turn reddish purple in autumn. Creamy flowers bloom in flat-topped terminal clusters in late spring, followed by black elliptical, persistent fruits. Tolerates shade and drought. Zones 4 to 8.

V. alnifolium   P. 216

v. al-nih-FOH-lee-um. Hobblebush. Native from Maine down through the mountains of Georgia, this species grows to 6, rarely 12, feet tall, with drooping outer branches that may take root. Toothed leaves to 8 inches long turn wine red in fall. Lacy white flower clusters in mid- to late spring are followed by red berries that turn purple-black. Zones 4 to 7.

V. × burkwoodii 'Mohawk'   P. 216

v. × burk-WOOD-ee-eye. Burkwood Viburnum cultivar. An upright compact shrub to 7 feet high and wide with rough leaves that turn orange-red to reddish purple in autumn. In early to midspring, dark pink flower buds open to domed clusters of tubular white, intensely clove-scented flowers. Semievergreen in the South. A recipient of the Pennsylvania Horticultural Society Gold Medal. Zones 5 to 8.

V. carlesii
P. 217

v. kar-LEE-see-eye. Korean Spice Viburnum. A compact shrub growing slowly to about 6 feet tall and wide with leaves that may turn red in fall. In midspring, pink buds open to ½-inch white, intensely fragrant flowers in domed clusters, followed by red fruits that turn black. Zones 5 to 8.

V. cassinoides
P. 217

v. kass-in-OY-deez. Witherod Viburnum. Native to moist habitats from Canada to Minnesota and south into Florida, this dense rounded shrub can exceed 10 feet but usually grows about 6 feet tall and wide. New leaves emerge bronze and in fall may be dark red, orange-red, or purple. Midsummer flowers are white in flat clusters to 5 inches across, followed by fruits that turn green, then pink, red, blue, and black, often with several colors in the same cluster. Zones 3 to 8.

V. 'Cayuga'
P. 218

A deciduous shrub to 5 feet or taller, with pink buds that open midspring to waxy white, beginning from one side of a rounded cluster. Slightly fragrant. Zones 5 to 8.

V. 'Conoy'

An evergreen growing 4 to 5 feet tall and 7 feet wide, with small, shiny, leathery leaves sometimes bronzing. Red buds open to white clusters of up to 70 flowers in midspring, followed in late summer by red fruits that turn black and remain for many weeks. A 1997 winner of the Pennsylvania Horticultural Society Gold Medal, it will survive as a deciduous shrub in Zone 6. Zones 7 to 8

V. dentatum
P. 218

v. den-TAY-tum. Arrowwood Viburnum. A suckering, spreading shrub native to much of the eastern United States, with toothed dark green leaves that turn yellow, red, or purple-red in autumn. The late-spring flowers are white with prominent yellow stamens in flat-topped clusters, followed by blue-black fruits that attract birds. The species can grow more than 10 feet wide and tall, but compact selections are being introduced. Zones 3 to 8.

V. dilatatum
P. 219

v. dil-ih-TAY-tum. Linden Viburnum. East Asian species growing to about 9 feet tall and 6 feet wide, with toothed leaves that turn dark red or bronze in fall. Cream-colored flowers bloom profusely in 4-inch flat clusters in mid- to late spring. Bright red fruits last from early to late fall. Cultivars include 'Erie', a Pennsylvania Horticultural Society award winner, with yellow, orange, and red fall foliage and red berries persisting as coral; and 'Iroquois', with thick leaves, heavy flowering, and large fruits. Zones 5 to 7.

V. 'Eskimo'. P. 220

Dense, semievergreen to 5 feet tall and wide with shiny dark green leaves. White "snowballs" of more than 100 cream-colored florets tinged with pink open in midspring, followed in late summer by elliptical dark red fruits that turn black. Another Pennsylvania Horticultural Society award winner. Zones 6 to 8.

V. × juddii

v. × JUD-ee-eye. Spice Viburnum. This hybrid grows 6 to 8 feet tall. In midspring, white snowball flowers tinged with pink invite gardeners out to sample their fragrance, or snip some samples to bring indoors. Zones 5 to 8.

V. lantana 'Mohican' P. 220

v. lan-TAN-uh. Wayfaring Tree cultivar. Deciduous shrub to 7 feet tall and 9 feet wide with thick, oval 4-inch leaves. Cream-colored flowers bloom in flat-topped clusters as leaves emerge in midspring, followed in late summer by yellow berries that turn red then black, with all colors in a single cluster. Tolerates some drought and alkalinity. Zones 4 to 7.

V. lentago

v. len-TAH-goh. Nannyberry. Native from the Northeast into Georgia and Mississippi, nannyberry is a large shrub or small tree becoming open and arching to 15 feet or taller and about 10 feet wide, with finely toothed glossy green leaves, sometimes coloring red in fall. Creamy white flowers in flat clusters bloom midspring, followed by ½-inch fruits that are deep pink or somewhat yellow before turning blue-black. Good for attracting birds. Zones 3 to 7.

V. macrocephalum

v. mak-roh-en-SEF-al-um. Chinese Snowball Viburnum. A rounded shrub ranging from deciduous to evergreen and from 8 feet to more than 15 feet tall. In mid- to late spring it bears white flowers in balls up to 8 inches across. Zones 6 to 10.

V. nudum 'Winterthur'

v. NOO-dum. Smooth Witherod cultivar. Compact to about 10 feet with shiny leaves that turn red to purple in autumn. Off-white flowers are in flat clusters in midsummer, followed by pink berries that turn blue. Tolerates wind better than most viburnums. Another Pennsylvania Horticultural Society award winner. Zones 5 to 9.

V. opulus
P. 221

v. op-YEW-lus. Cranberrybush Viburnum. This native of Europe, northern Asia, and Africa grows 8 to 12 feet high and wide. The coarse, somewhat shiny, rounded 3-inch leaves have three lobes and may color red in fall. Flowers bloom in lacecap clusters, followed by ¼-inch fruit that turns from yellow to red. It tolerates wet soil but is prone to aphids. V. opulus 'Roseum' is a sterile form with large balls of white flowers, also known as snowball bush. Zones 3 to 8.

V. plicatum var. tomentosum
P. 222

v. plih-KAH-tum var. toh-men-TOH-sum. Doublefile Viburnum. Strong horizontal branching to 6 feet tall and twice as wide. Leaves are toothed and prominently veined, turning reddish purple in fall. In midspring, double rows of white 4- to 6-inch flower clusters resembling those of lacecap hydrangea march down the branches. Oval fruits are bright red turning black. 'Shasta' won a Pennsylvania Horticultural Society award in 1991. 'Shoshoni' is somewhat smaller in all respects. Zones 5 to 8.

V. × pragense

v. × prag-EN-see. Prague Viburnum. A hardy, fast-growing evergreen hybrid with shiny elliptic leaves to 4 inches long and lightly fragrant flat-topped clusters of white flowers that open from pink buds in midspring. Zones 5 to 8.

V. prunifolium

v. proo-nih-FOL-ee-um. Blackhaw Viburnum. Native throughout the eastern United States, this shrub grows to more than 12 feet tall and almost as wide with leaves that turn purple-red in fall. Cream-colored flowers are borne in flat-topped clusters in midspring, followed by edible fruits that turn from dark pink to blue-black. Don't plant near ponds or similar sites, since the fallen leaves can develop an unpleasant aroma when wet. Zones 3 to 9.

V. × rhytidophylloides 'Alleghany'

v. × ry-tih-doh-fy-LOY-deez. Upright, coarse shrub with leathery leaves that are gray and fuzzy underneath. White or off-white flowers bloom in flat-topped clusters in midspring, followed by red fruits that turn black. Zones 5 to 8.

V. rhytidophyllum

v. ry-tih-doh-FY-lum. Leatherleaf Viburnum. A vigorous evergreen up to 15 feet tall and about 12 feet wide with narrow, wrinkled leaves up to 7 inches long. A prominent knot of rusty flower buds is borne through winter. In late spring they open as domed umbels of small creamy flowers with prominent stamens. Oval red fruits ripen to black. This shrub loses its leaves and may even be killed to the roots in Zone 5. Zones 5 to 9.

V. sargentii 'Onondaga'

v. sar-GEN-tee-eye. Sargent Viburnum cultivar. Compact selection growing about half the size of the 12-foot Asian species. Three-lobed, maplelike leaves retain a maroon tinge and may turn red in fall. Red buds open to white flowers in lacecap clusters, followed by ½-inch red fruits. Zones 4 to 7.

V. trilobum   P. 223

v. try-LOH-bum. American Cranberrybush Viburnum. Native to Canada and the northern United States, this deciduous species grows 8 to 12 feet tall and wide with broad, three-lobed leaves that turn yellow to reddish purple in fall. The white midspring lacecap flowers are followed by ⅓-inch bright red fruits that last from early fall into late winter. Zones 2 to 7.

❧ Vitex

VY-tecks. Verbena family, Verbenaceae.

This is a genus of 250 primarily tropical evergreen and deciduous trees and shrubs. The two deciduous species listed here are cultivated in gardens for their mid- to late-summer purple flower spikes and aromatic silvery foliage. There are some white-flowering cultivars. The shrubs get their common name of chasteberry or chaste tree from the days when monks would season their food with the peppery seeds in the belief that they inhibited carnal desire. Modern herbalists use them to treat problems related to menstruation.

HOW TO GROW

Chaste trees need full sun in any well-drained soil. They can be pruned hard, to within a few inches of the ground, to reshape or rejuvenate, or trained to a single trunk. Grow as a specimen, in a shrub border, or as a flowering hedge. Propagate from seeds or from softwood cuttings. May self-sow.

V. agnus-castus   P. 223

v. AG-nus-KAS-tus. Chaste Tree. A native of western Asia and southern Europe, this open species will form a shrub about 10 feet tall and wide but can be pruned as a tree up to 20 feet tall. The compound palmate leaves are gray-green, silvery underneath, and aromatic. Lavender flowers are borne in spiky panicles from mid- to late summer. Zones 7 to 10.

V. negundo

v. neh-GUN-doh. Chaste Tree. Native from East Asia to southeast Africa, this shrub is openly branched and grows 10 to 15 feet tall and wide. The grayish green compound palmate leaves have three to seven leaflets, often serrated. The blue to lavender flowers bloom in spikes from mid- to late summer. Zones 6 to 10.

❦ *Weigela*

wy-GEE-luh. Honeysuckle family, Caprifoliaceae.

From a genus of a dozen deciduous Asian shrubs, one species has been plumbed exhaustively by breeders to develop variations on the funnel-shaped, late-spring to summer flowers.

HOW TO GROW

As long as it has full sun and good drainage, weigela is happy in any soil and tolerates pollution well. Mix with other shrubs in the border, since it is not particularly interesting when out of bloom. Prune after flowering to reshape young branches, removing a portion of old growth to the ground. Propagate from seeds or softwood cuttings.

W. florida   P. 224

w. FLOR-ih-duh. A spreading shrub 6 to 9 feet tall and about 10 feet wide with coarse branches that arch to the ground. In late spring to early summer it is smothered in the funnel-shaped flowers, lavender pink in the species while usually various shades of pink or red in the cultivars. It reblooms lightly through fall. Cultivars include 'Canary' (yellow flowers, sometimes mixed with pink), 'Eva Rathke' (red flowers, good reblooming), 'Evita' (3 feet tall with red flowers), and 'Variegata' (light pink flowers, leaves with cream edge). Rated hardy to Zone 4 are 'Red Prince' (rich red flowers, upright, long blooming) and 'Alexandra' (trademarked as Wine and Roses, with disease-resistant dark burgundy-purple leaves). The latter is a Pennsylvania Horticultural Society award winner. Zones 5 to 8.

✿ *Wisteria*

Wis-TEER-ee-uh. Pea family, Fabaceae.

There are 10 species of these deciduous plants, which grow naturally as woody vines, to 30 feet or higher, but are often trained to a shrubby form. The large leaves are pinnately compound. Racemes of purple, sweetpea flowers bloom in spring, followed by long pods. Asian forms, particularly *W. floribunda*, have become highly invasive, and their weight and shade is able to topple trees. Don't plant them near parks or wild lands, and prune them heavily to prevent seed formation or rooting from shoots. There are two native species that are less problematic.

HOW TO GROW

Give wisteria full sun. It grows in a wide range of soils, as long as they are of moderate fertility (as a legume, wisteria makes its own nitrogen) and pH isn't extreme. Oriental wisterias are more invasive in areas with abundant rainfall and trees that they can climb. Use one as a specimen shrub or grow against a wall. Native wisterias are best viewed from the side or above. Because they leaf out later in the year than Asian species they are less prone to frost damage. They also differ in developing terminal flowers on new growth. To develop shrublike forms, prune off vigorous upward-growing shoots to promote a strong woody framework at the desired height. They may root where branches touch the ground or spread by root sprouts or seeds. To prevent escape, remove spent racemes and any seedpods. Prune the most vigorous new shoots back to two or three leaves in spring, and in late summer, prune off new shoot growth not conforming to the shape of your shrub. Mow or clip any root sprouts.

W. floribunda

w. flor-ih-BUN-duh. Japanese Wisteria. Blooms in midspring on old wood, after leaves appear, but can be damaged by late frosts. Twines clockwise.

The species has violet, slightly fragrant flowers in racemes 8 to 20 inches long. There are many cultivars selected for pink or white flowers, longer racemes, or stronger fragrance. Zones 5 to 9.

W. frustescens

w. froo-TESS-ens. American Wisteria. This eastern U.S. native bears blue-violet flowers in abundant racemes of 30 to 65 in late spring. 'Amethyst Falls' begins blooming when young and may rebloom later in the season. There is also a white-flowered form. Zones 5 to 9.

W. macrostachys

P. 225

w. mak-roh-STAK-eez. Kentucky Wisteria. In late spring or early summer this native produces lightly scented soft violet flowers in racemes of 70 to 80. It is more cold hardy and tolerant of wet soil than *W. frustescens*. Cultivars include white-flowered, heavy-blooming 'Clara Mack', cold-hardy and vigorous 'Aunt Dee', and cold-hardy, reblooming 'Blue Moon'. Zones 4 to 8.

W. sinensis

w. sin-EN-siss. Chinese Wisteria. Similar to the Japanese species, but blooming a couple of weeks later with blue-violet flowers. Racemes are shorter with less fragrance, and it twines counterclockwise. Cultivars offer deeper purple, dark pink, double, or bicolored flowers. Zones 5 to 8.

❦ Xanthorhiza

zan-thoh-RIZE-uh. Buttercup family, Ranunculaceae.

This species is represented by a single low-growing deciduous shrub native to streambanks and moist woods in the eastern United States, cultivated for attractive foliage that colors well in fall. Native Americans once used its sap as a dye, hence the common name yellowroot.

HOW TO GROW

Yellowroot likes moist but not soggy soil in sun or part shade. It tolerates heavy clay. If planted in sun, mulching may be beneficial to keep roots cool. Use as a ground cover for large areas such as moist, shady banks. It doesn't require pruning, but can be pruned selectively to reshape or remove suckers. Propagate by dividing suckers.

X. simplicissima   P. 225

x. sim-PLISS-ih-muh. Yellowroot. A suckering shrub forming a thicket 2 to 3 feet tall and spreading twice as wide. Erect stems bear compound leaves, usually with five toothed leaflets, often compared to those of celery. Bronzy purple when new, they turn yellow, bronze, and purple in autumn. Racemes of inconspicuous purple-brown star-shaped flowers appear in spring before the leaves. Zones 3 to 9.

❦ *Yucca*

YUK-uh. Agave family, Agavaceae.

A genus of 40 species of perennials, evergreen shrubs, and trees native primarily to North and Central America. They are grown in gardens for their dramatic spear-shaped leaves, usually in a rosette, and tall upright panicles of white flowers.

HOW TO GROW

Yuccas grow in any well-drained soil in full sun. They are often grouped in desert gardens with other members of the agave family or succulents. They are also valuable as vertical accents and lend themselves to container culture. Keep sharp-leaved species away from high-traffic areas. Prune off flowering stems after bloom. Propagate from suckers or root cuttings.

Y. aloifolia   P. 226

y. al-loh-ih-FOH-lee-uh. Dagger Plant. This southeastern U.S. native, sometimes misleadingly called Spanish bayonet, is capable of growing to more than 20 feet but in cultivation usually remains at about half that with either one or multiple trunks. The dense leaves are 2 feet long and 2 inches wide with a sharp point. White 4-inch flowers bloom in 18-inch panicles in summer. Zones 7 to 10.

Y. filamentosa   P. 226

y. fil-uh-men-TOH-suh. Adam's Needle. This commonly grown species, native from the Mid-Atlantic to Florida, forms an almost stemless clump of rosettes, 2½ feet tall and twice as wide. The 1- to 2½-foot leaves are edged with curly threads. In early to midsummer, 2-inch off-white flowers bloom in erect panicles up to 6 feet tall. 'Bright Edge' has yellow margins. Zones 4 to 9.

Y. flaccida

y. FLAS-ih-duh. Weakleaf Yucca. This Southeast native is similar to *Y. fila-mentosa* but the leaves are shorter, narrower, bent near the middle, and the marginal threads are straight. Zones 4 to 9.

Y. gloriosa

y. glor-ee-OH-suh. Spanish Bayonet. A Southeast native developing multiple branches to 10 feet tall, with 2-foot, soft-pointed leaves in whorls at the branch ends. Panicles of white flowers to 8 feet long bloom in late summer. Leaves of 'Variegata' have white edges. Zones 7 to 9.

Y. recurvifolia

y. ree-ker-vih-FOH-lee-uh. A native of the south-central United States that tends to be single-trunked, 6 to 10 feet tall. Pliable blue-green leaves up to 3 feet long curve downward. The white 3-inch flowers bloom in upright panicles from mid- to late summer. Zones 7 to 9.

❧ *Zenobia*

zen-OH-bee-uh. Heath family, Ericaceae.

This genus is a lone deciduous or semievergreen shrub species native to streambanks and other damp environs from North Carolina to Florida, grown by gardeners for its fragrant bell-shaped white flowers and, on cultivars, blue-green foliage.

HOW TO GROW

Give zenobia acidic, moist soil in sun or part shade. Excellent for natural pondsides or low-lying moist areas. Prune in early spring to control height and stimulate new growth. Propagate from seeds collected while light brown and dried in a paper bag, then sown on top of peat. Semihard cuttings collected in midsummer will root in a well-drained medium.

Z. pulverulenta   P. 227

z. pul-ver-YEW-len-tuh. Dusty Zenobia. Irregular, with stems upright then arching, from 2 to 6 feet tall and 6 feet wide. Gray-green or blue-green leaves are covered with a waxy bloom (hence the common name) and in fall turn yellow-orange or burgundy. May lose its leaves north of Zone 8. The white ½-inch flowers dangle from the shoot tips in long racemes in midsummer. 'Woodlander's Blue' is a blue-foliaged form growing to 4 feet. Zones 6 to 9.

❧ Photo Credits

KEN DRUSE: 48 top, 73 bottom, 222 bottom

DEREK FELL: 15, 43 bottom, 44 top, 45 top, 50 bottom, 52 top, 52 bottom, 54 top, 55 top, 55 bottom, 60 right, 64 bottom, 66 top, 67 bottom, 69 bottom, 70 top, 75 bottom, 76 bottom, 77 bottom, 87 bottom, 89 bottom, 90 bottom, 95 bottom, 98 top, 101 bottom, 102 top, 105 bottom, 106 bottom, 108 bottom, 112 bottom, 116 bottom, 117 bottom, 118 bottom, 122 bottom, 124 top, 127 bottom, 136 bottom, 138 bottom, 141 top, 144 top, 146 top, 146 bottom, 148 top, 151 bottom, 158 bottom, 161 bottom, 162 bottom, 163 top, 163 bottom, 164 top, 166 top, 168 top, 169 bottom, 176 top, 179 bottom, 189 top, 189 bottom, 203 top, 206 top, 207 top, 212 bottom, 214 top, 223 bottom, 226 top

JESSIE M. HARRIS: 47 bottom, 51 top, 53 top, 54 bottom, 66 bottom, 70 bottom, 145 top, 202 bottom, 204 top, 215 bottom, 216 bottom, 217 bottom, 219 top, 220 top, 225 bottom

JERRY PAVIA PHOTOGRAPHY, INC.: 41 top, 42 top, 42 bottom, 44 bottom, 47 top, 50 top, 56 top, 56 bottom, 57 top, 57 bottom, 58 top, 58 bottom, 62 top, 62 bottom, 64 top, 65 top, 67 top, 68 top, 68 bottom, 69 top, 71 top, 74 top, 74 bottom, 76 top, 78 top, 78 bottom, 81 top, 81 bottom, 82 top, 83 top, 84 top, 84 bottom, 85 bottom, 86 top, 87 top, 88 bottom, 89 top, 90 top, 91 bottom, 92 top, 93 top, 97 top, 97 bottom, 107 top, 100 top, 103 top, 105 top, 107 bottom, 109 top, 110 top, 110 bottom, 111 bottom, 112 top, 114 top, 115 bottom, 118 top, 119 top, 121 top, 121 bottom, 122 top, 124 bottom, 125 bottom, 128 bottom, 131 top, 131 bottom, 132 top, 134 top, 135 bottom, 139 top, 140 bottom, 144 bottom, 147 top, 147 bottom, 148 bottom, 150 top, 152 top, 153 top, 154 top, 154 bottom, 155 top, 155 bottom, 156 top, 156 bottom, 157 top, 157 bottom, 159 bottom, 160 top, 161 top, 164 bottom, 165 top, 167 top, 167 bottom, 168 bottom, 170 bottom, 171 top, 171 bottom, 172 bottom, 173 bottom, 174 top, 175 top, 176 bottom, 179 top, 180 top, 182 bottom, 183 bottom, 185 top, 185 bottom, 187 bottom, 190 bottom, 193 bottom, 194 bottom, 195 top, 196 top, 196 bottom, 197 top, 198 top, 198 bottom, 201 top, 202 top, 203 bottom, 205 bottom, 207 bottom, 208 bottom, 209 top, 209 bottom, 210 top, 210 bottom, 211 bottom, 213 top, 216 top, 217 top, 218 top, 218 bottom, 219 bottom, 221 top, 223 top, 224 top, 225 top, 226 bottom

MICHAEL S. THOMPSON: ii-iii, vi-1, 11, 14, 22, 36, 41 bottom, 43 top, 45 bottom, 48 bottom, 51 bottom, 53 bottom, 59 top, 59 bottom, 60 left, 61 top, 63 top, 71 bottom, 72 top, 72 bottom, 73 top, 75 top, 79 top, 79 bottom, 80 bottom, 82 bottom, 83 bottom, 88 top, 91 top, 93 bottom, 94 bottom, 95 top, 96 top, 96 bottom, 98 bottom, 99 top, 100 bottom, 101 top, 102 bottom, 103 bottom, 104 top, 104 bottom, 106 top, 111 top, 113 top, 116 top, 117 top, 119 bottom, 123 top, 123 bottom, 125 top, 126 top, 126 bottom, 127 top, 129 bottom, 130 top, 130 bottom, 132 bottom, 135 top, 136 top, 137 top, 137 bottom, 138 top, 139 bottom,

141 bottom, 142 top, 142 bottom, 143 bottom, 145 bottom, 149 top, 149 bottom, 150 bottom, 151 top, 153 bottom, 159 top, 160 bottom, 162 top, 166 bottom, 169 top, 170 top, 173 top, 174 bottom, 175 bottom, 178 top, 178 bottom, 181 top, 181 bottom, 182 top, 183 top, 184 bottom, 186 top, 188 top, 191 top, 191 bottom, 192 bottom, 194 top, 195 bottom, 197 bottom, 199 top, 199 bottom, 200 top, 200 bottom, 201 bottom, 204 bottom, 206 bottom, 208 top, 211 top, 212 top, 213 bottom, 214 bottom, 215 top, 220 bottom, 221 bottom, 224 bottom, 227 top, 228, 229

MARK TURNER: 39, 40 top, 40 bottom, 46 top, 46 bottom, 49 top, 49 bottom, 61 bottom, 63 bottom, 65 bottom, 77 top, 80 top, 85 top, 86 bottom, 92 bottom, 94 top, 99 bottom, 108 top, 109 bottom, 113 bottom, 114 bottom, 115 top, 120 top, 120 bottom, 128 top, 129 top, 133 top, 133 bottom, 134 bottom, 140 top, 143 top, 152 bottom, 158 top, 165 bottom, 172 top, 177 top, 177 bottom, 180 bottom, 184 top, 186 bottom, 187 top, 188 bottom, 190 top, 192 top, 193 top, 205 top, 222 top

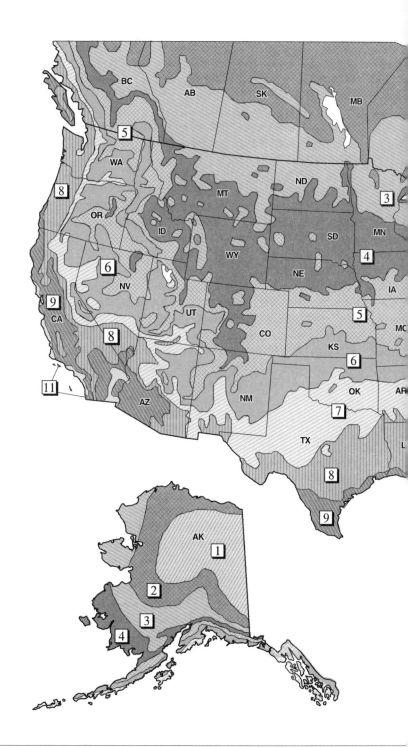

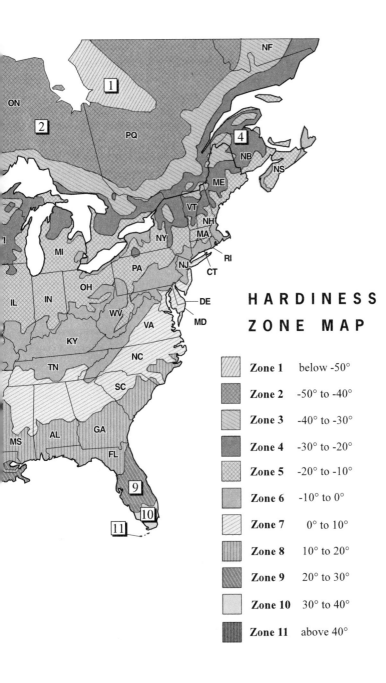

HARDINESS ZONE MAP

	Zone 1	below -50°
	Zone 2	-50° to -40°
	Zone 3	-40° to -30°
	Zone 4	-30° to -20°
	Zone 5	-20° to -10°
	Zone 6	-10° to 0°
	Zone 7	0° to 10°
	Zone 8	10° to 20°
	Zone 9	20° to 30°
	Zone 10	30° to 40°
	Zone 11	above 40°

❧Index

Page numbers in italics refer to illustrations.

Mahonia, 341–43
  aquifolium, 342
  aquifolium 'Smaragd' (Emerald),
    143
  bealei, 144, 342
  fortunei, 342
  japonica, 342
  nervosa, 342
  repens, 144, 343
  × wagneri 'King's Ransom', 343
Mallow, tree, 134, 328
Manchurian lilac cultivar, 204, 401
Many-flowered cotoneaster, 282
Manzanita, 49, 242–43
Maple, 2, 5, 34, 43, 236–37
Mapleleaf viburnum, 215, 410
Marigold, 25
Marlberry, 50, 244
Memorial rose, 383
Mentor barberry, 249
Metaseiulus occidentalis, 26
Mexican orange blossom, 75, 270
Meyer lilac, 204, 401
Michelia figo, 145, 343
Microbiota decussata, 145, 344
Mint bush, round-leaved, 162, 365
Mirror plant, 79, 275
Mock orange, 2, 14, 36, 152, 160,
    353–54, 362
Mophead hydrangea, 36
Morrow's honeysuckle, 8
Mountain ash, dwarf, 196, 392
Mountain laurel, 12, 129, 130, 324
Mountain ninebark, 358
Mountain pieris, 157, 360
Multiflora rose, 8
Myrica, 344–46
  californica, 345
  cerifera, 345
  gale, 345
  pensylvanica, 5, 146, 345–46
Myrtle, 131, 135, 147, 326, 330, 346
Myrtus communis, 147, 346

Nandina domestica, 8, 147, 346–47
Nannyberry, 412
Natal plum, 66, 259
Natchez mock orange, 152
Nerium oleander, 347–48
  'Tangier', 148
Neviusia alabamensis, 148, 348
New Jersey tea, 68, 262
New Zealand tea tree, 135, 136, 331
Night jessamine, 70, 266
Nikko deutzia, 95
Ninebark, 155, 357–58
Northern bayberry, 5
Norway spruce, 155, 358–59

Oakleaf hydrangea, 122, 314
Ocean spray, 119, 312
Oconee azalea, 171, 373
Ocotillo, 107, 108, 300
Oemleria cerasiformis, 149, 349
Oleander, 38, 148, 348
Oregon boxwood, 353
Oregon grape-holly, 143, 342
Oriental photinia, 356
Osmanthus, 349–51
  americanus, 350
  delavayi, 149, 350
  × fortunei, 350
  fragrans, 350
  heterophyllus, 350–51
  heterophyllus 'Variegatus', 150
Oso berry, 149, 349
Otto Luyken cherry laurel, 164, 367
Oyama magnolia, 142, 341

Paeonia
  'Gauguin', 150
  'Joseph Rock', 151, 352
  rockii, 351–52
  suffruticosa, 351
  suffruticosa var. rockii, 151
  cultivars and hybrids, 351–52
Pagoda dogwood, 81, 82, 276